UNDERSTANDING
CHINA

Also by John Bryan Starr

Ideology and Culture

Continuing the Revolution: The Political Thought of Mao

UNDERSTANDING
CHINA

A Guide to China's Economy, History, and Political Structure

(Revised and Updated Edition)

JOHN BRYAN STARR

Hill and Wang
A division of Farrar, Straus and Giroux
New York

Hill and Wang
A division of Farrar, Straus and Giroux
19 Union Square West, New York 10003

Copyright © 1997, 2001 by John Bryan Starr
Maps copyright © 2001 by Virginia Norey
All rights reserved
Distributed in Canada by Douglas & McIntyre Ltd.
Printed in the United States of America
First edition published in 1997 by Hill and Wang
First revised paperback edition, 2001

Grateful acknowledgment is made to Virginia Norey
for the maps in this new edition.

Library of Congress Cataloging-in-Publication Data
Starr, John Bryan.
    Understanding China : a guide to China's economy, history, and political
structure = [Liao jie Zhongguo] / John Bryan Starr. — Rev. and updated
ed., 1st pbk. ed.
        p.   cm.
    Parallel title in Chinese characters.
    Includes bibliographical references and index.
    ISBN-13: 978-0-8090-9489-9
    ISBN-10: 0-8090-9489-4 (paperback)
    1. China—Politics and government—1976–2002.   2. China—Economic
conditions—1976–2000.   3. China.   I. Title.
DS779.26.S737   2001
951.05—dc21   00-63429

Designed by Thomas Frank

www.fsgbooks.com

9   11   13   15   16   14   12   10

For Lynne and Kate

CONTENTS

TABLES

MAPS

UNDERSTANDING
CHINA

INTRODUCTION

TO THE LIMITED EXTENT that Westerners pay attention to what is going on beyond their shores, China commands a disproportionate share of that attention. Moreover, those of us who have some knowledge of what is going on in China tend to have strong feelings about the country, acting as cheerleaders for its successes and as harsh critics of its failings. We find it difficult to be indifferent.

There has been a great deal of good news coming out of China in recent years. China has one of the world's fastest growing economies. Indeed, there are those who predict that at its current rate of growth, China's will be the world's largest economy by 2040, surpassing Japan's and the United States'. Economic growth has substantially improved the standard of living for most if not all Chinese people. In nominal terms, per capita income is fifteen times what it was in 1978, the beginning of the current period of economic reform, though income in the cities is more than double that in the countryside. Economic liberalization has been accompanied by some relaxation of the Chinese government's tight control over its population. Most Chinese people are enjoying substantially more freedom from government interference in their lives than they did before reform began.

There is also bad news. American enthusiasm for an opening and reforming China in the 1980s had the unintended effect of filtering out much of the bad news, but that filter ceased to function when, on the night of 3 June 1989, tanks clattered through Beijing, clearing the streets of demonstrators and killing many hundreds of them in the process. Since then we have been attentive to the repressive measures taken against its own people by a government deeply concerned about the consequences of political instability.

Our attentiveness to China's shortcomings in governance was amplified with the collapse of the Soviet Union in 1991. The demise of what Ronald Reagan had called "the evil empire" and the emergence of a new democratic state from its ashes made the resilience of authoritarianism in China all the more repugnant. To those of us with a Manichaean streak who like identifying a principal adversary, the shoes just shed by the Soviet Union seemed to fit China perfectly.

Economic success has made the Chinese government—and perhaps also the Chinese people—much less malleable and easy to deal with than it once was. China has run up a trade surplus with the United States second only to Japan's. It demands full membership in the world economy but balks at playing by the rules. Recently it has taken actions outside its borders that may be evidence of a dangerous new military expansionism on the part of Asia's largest power.

Complicating any attempt to resolve the contradictions that China presents is the fact that, with the death of Deng Xiaoping, the country passed a milestone in its recent history and is experiencing all the uncertainties that accompany major change. China may prove an exception to the rule that no socialist system has yet made a smooth transition following the death of its principal leader. There was a rocky changing of the guard when Mao Zedong, leader of the Chinese Communist Party for forty years and of the People's Republic of China since its founding, died in 1976. Having maneuvered his way through those rocky shoals, Deng tried twice to put in place a group of capable leaders whom he could trust to carry on his political program. By avoiding the top positions and by retiring early from the positions he did hold, he hoped to make himself thoroughly dispensable and thus easily and smoothly replaced. He failed on all counts. His trusted successors proved insufficient to the task. He had to abandon his efforts to retire to the distant role of éminence grise when student demonstrators called into question his authority and his legacy.

On his third attempt, Deng selected Jiang Zemin, the current head of the state, of the Party, and of the People's Liberation Army. Jiang is eager to prove that his claim to be a worthy successor is more than merely transitory, but he is of a very different caliber from his predecessors. Deng's death in 1997 marked the end of a unique political generation, the generation of the leaders of the Chinese Communist revolution and the founders of the contemporary Chinese political system. Rapid change has been a permanent feature of China for the last half century. As a result, members of each political generation after Deng's have had very different lives, careers, and experiences. The people who make up those generations differ in training, perceptions, connections, and aspirations.

Although Deng was not wholly characteristic of his generation, most of his revolutionary cohorts were born in China's hinterlands, ill-educated in a formal sense, and limited in their knowledge of and experience in the world outside China. The next generation, born too late to have been active in the revolution and civil war, grew up in a China heavily dependent on the Soviet Union. They were educated in schools modeled after Soviet schools, they learned the Russian language, and many of them spent time studying or working in the Soviet Union. They are technologically adept, ideologically cautious, and instinctively bureaucratic. At the time Mao died and reforms began, they were late-middle-aged dogs who found the new tricks difficult to master.

The third generation had their lives and careers shaped by their participation in the chaos of the Cultural Revolution launched by Mao in the 1960s. This experience rendered many of them at best skeptical, at worst highly cynical. As such, although they are significantly better educated and their opportunities to interact with the outside world are infinitely greater than those available to their elders, the new ideas they have encountered have not engendered great optimism in them. Having lost their idealism at an early age, they now find the materialism of contemporary China a comfortable fit.

The youngest generation has come to maturity since the post-Mao reform period began. It is made up of bright, brash, hardworking, and cosmopolitan people, but they are more self-interested than public-minded. Their goal is personal wealth, and that is best pursued in the rapidly expanding private sector. Devoting their energies to solving major problems in the public realm is out of the question.

Jiang and his colleagues in the highest echelons of power have one foot in the second and one foot in the third of these generations. Although Russian educated and trained, they have developed a degree of cosmopolitanism through their extensive contact with Japan, Europe, and the United States. They possess a grasp, sometimes imperfect, of what China was and what it can become and are proving reasonably successful in bridging the gaps that separate the generations. But they lack the compelling stature and vision of their predecessors.

Given the diversity of these generations, the transition period will surely be protracted, complicated by the fact that the youngest of them does not appear to contain a group of capable, intelligent, honest, forward-looking, and enthusiastic political leaders. But then, China is not the only country about which one can say that.

The purpose of this book is to look beyond the immediate situation and to explore three questions: What are the principal problems confronting China today? What is the capacity of the Chinese political system to deal with these problems successfully? And, given the answers to these two questions, how might the political situation play itself out in the near term?

My answers to these three questions, which I will elaborate on in the chapters that follow, are, first, that the extraordinarily serious problems that China confronts would tax the capability of the strongest and most able of governments. But, second, the capacity of the Chinese government is severely diminished and its capability is weak. Hence, third, China's near-term future looks rather dark.

At least a dozen critical problems face China's leaders. Each of them threatens the nation's ability to continue on its current trajectory of economic development. Some of them threaten the viability of the state itself. Four of them affect primarily the 30 percent of the population that lives in cities. Three of them affect primarily the remaining 70 percent of the population that lives in the towns and villages of the countryside. Four are problems that affect Chinese society as a whole, and the others concern China's relations with the outside world.

The first, and thorniest, urban problem is that most state-owned enterprises are in serious financial straits. More than two-thirds of the sixty thousand industrial enterprises owned by the government are losing money, some at a staggering rate. They are kept alive by government loans and subsidies that in 1999 totaled more than $540 billion (equivalent to nearly half of China's annual gross domestic product). The government has avoided the obvious solution—allowing money-losing enterprises to go out of business—because it would put so many people out of work. It is a solution the government also avoids for ideological reasons. China claims to be a socialist system "with Chinese characteristics." Whatever its characteristics, a socialist system that closes down its state-owned sector risks becoming an oxymoron.

A second problem originating in China's urban centers but affecting the country as a whole is closely related to the first. In attempting to save failing state-owned enterprises, China's banking system has put itself in a parlous state. Conservative estimates suggest that some 20 percent of loans made by the four large state banks are nonperforming. This amounts to some $200 billion in bad debt, resulting in a negative net worth for these four banks. Shoring up China's banking system is thus a problem of the first magnitude.

Employment-related issues are the third problem the Chinese

state faces in the urban economy. The official unemployment rate stands at 3.1 percent and is not in itself a cause of concern, but concealed unemployment is. Because of financial problems, state-owned enterprises have put a portion of their workforce on reduced hours or temporary furlough. And the underemployment of those who remain on the job is a related problem. One reason for China's financial crisis in the state sector is that its workforce is excessively large. Estimates vary, but they suggest that up to one-third of the state-sector workforce is superfluous to production processes. Enterprises are attempting to downsize; about twenty million workers have lost their jobs since 1995. While the private and collective sectors are growing rapidly, they cannot absorb all those who are jobless or underemployed.

Another serious employment-related problem facing municipal authorities concerns the more than 100 million workers who have come from the countryside into China's cities in search of more lucrative work. These floating workers are hired on a short-term basis, most frequently as day laborers in construction. Because they are not official residents of the cities they are living in, they are not entitled to housing or social services and tend to camp out wherever they can find shelter—often in exurban shantytowns.

As a large group outside the organizational web that controls the population, the floating workers are a novel anomaly in China. Municipal officials look on them as a dangerous necessity. On the one hand, they are needed to do the unskilled labor that even the unemployed among urban residents spurn as too hard and too ill-paid. On the other hand, they are blamed for an increase in violent crime in China's cities, and it is assumed that they will be a dangerous source of political unrest if they can no longer find regular work.

There are serious problems in the countryside as well. First among them is the growing gap in the standard of living between urban and rural China. Average income in the cities has always exceeded that in the countryside, but during the early years of reform the gap began to close. Beginning in the mid-1980s, the gap widened once again. While the ratio of urban to rural incomes has remained relatively steady at 2.5:1 over the last twenty years, the gap in monetary terms today is sixteen times what it was in 1978. The gap is even wider if average rural per capita income is compared with per capita income in China's most prosperous cities. The difference between rural and urban incomes used to matter very little, since country people were only dimly aware of living conditions in the cities, and even if they knew that life was better there, they were prevented by the government from moving. Neither of these conditions prevails today.

A second source of dissatisfaction in the countryside is excessive taxation. Although taxes are nominally restricted to 5 percent of household income, the local governments' need for additional revenue leads them to impose every imaginable kind of fee, fine, toll, and levy so that peasant households are regularly paying between 15 and 50 percent of their income to the local authorities. This would be unsatisfactory to most citizens under any circumstances, but it is especially galling here because a significant portion of that revenue ends up being used by local officials in ostentatious personal expenditures.

To add insult to injury, local governments frequently experience cash-flow problems that interfere with their ability to pay farmers for the commodities they have contracted to sell to the state. Farmers bring their harvested crops to state purchasing depots, where, instead of cash, they are given chits, or "green slips," redeemable for cash when the cash flow improves; meanwhile the money that would have gone to pay the farmers for their grain is often invested by entrepreneurial officials in speculative ventures that promise a large return. These unredeemed green slips are a major source of dissatisfaction in the rural communities and have led on many recent occasions to demonstrations—occasionally violent ones.

Then there are issues that are not particular to the city or the countryside. The first is the fraught relationship between ethnic groups in China's border regions. More than nine-tenths of the population consider themselves of the same Han ethnicity, but the remaining tenth is divided among fifty-seven distinct ethnic groups. In many instances, these groups occupy territory that spans the borders with China's neighbors to the north and west. Most of them inhabit what the Chinese government calls "autonomous regions," but in fact they enjoy little if any autonomy. Increasingly in recent years, they have come to demand genuine autonomy, often engaging in acts of violence to underscore their point and, in some instances, eliciting international support for their cause.

The second and third issues are interrelated: How will it be possible to feed a growing population on a rapidly shrinking amount of arable land? The government is dealing with a fraction, the numerator of which is agricultural production, the denominator of which is population. Its task is to increase the numerator and keep the denominator as small as possible.

The government's population-control program, or "one-child policy," addresses the denominator. And though the government credits the policy with reducing the rate at which the population is growing, the average family in China still has 1.84 children; the one-child policy has been fully effective only when draconian measures have been used to enforce it, measures that further alienate a population already highly dissatisfied with its government. At its current rate of growth, the Chinese population will reach 1.5 billion by 2015, having trebled in less than a hundred years.

As for the numerator, grain production currently stands at 490 million tons per year. That is a substantial increase over what was being produced in the 1950s, but the growth rate in production has begun to slow. Per-acre yields are already impressively high, and many observers are skeptical that they can be raised much higher. Meanwhile, arable land, already a scarce commodity in China, is being taken out of cultivation with alarming speed. China feeds 20 percent of the world's population on less than 7 percent of the world's arable land; recent economic development has resulted in substantial quantities of this land being taken out of cultivation and used for factories, roads, and houses. Finally, like that of all developing societies, the Chinese diet is evolving. As the living standard improves, consumption of meat and eggs is increasing, raising the demand for grain to feed the animals. Taking all these factors into account, pessimists some years ago forecast a grain deficit in 2030 so large that it will be impossible for world grain exporters to fill it.

Another grave issue that affects not only the Chinese population but the rest of the world as well is that of environmental degradation. Two-thirds of all factories in China are polluting the air and water in violation of the state's environmental regulations, which are hardly as strong as in Western countries. Nine-tenths of Chinese cities do not meet Chinese clean-air standards. Eighty percent of China's bodies of freshwater are polluted, and 90 percent of the water flowing through cities is impotable. At its current rate of economic growth, by 2025 China will produce three times the amount of greenhouse gases currently produced in the United States.

As though this domestic agenda were not a sufficient challenge, China has problems in its interactions with the rest of what has come to be called Greater China—Hong Kong, Macao, and Taiwan—and with the world beyond Greater China. Administering the special administrative region of Hong Kong in such a way as not to disturb the delicate equilibrium on which the remarkable success of that territory rests is of particular importance. Between the time the Sino-British agreement on Hong Kong was signed in 1984 and the actual transfer of sovereignty in 1997, considerable rancor developed on both sides; reactions in Hong Kong to the Tiananmen Square massacre in 1989 fundamentally altered China's view of that city and Hong Kong citizens' view of their future. These changes are expressed in some of the specific provisions that filled in the vague outline of Hong Kong as a special administrative region contained in the Joint Declaration of 1984. Hong Kong thrived under British administration, many argue, because of its government's light hand on the tiller of the economy. Even after three years of having Hong Kong under its control, it remains an open question whether the Chinese government will prove willing and able to maintain an equally light hand. It is normally heavy-handed in its own domestic affairs; even if it were willing, will it be *able* to lighten its touch in dealing with Hong Kong?

The relationship between Taiwan and the mainland is closely related. Hong Kong is intended to be a model of the Chinese government's ability to keep the promise of "one country, two systems" that it has extended to Taiwan as well. Success in administering Hong Kong, so the argument goes, will arouse confidence on Taiwan that under Beijing's rule after reunification, its political, economic, and social systems will remain unchanged.

In 1987, the Taiwan government began a process of opening up contact with the mainland. That process has eventuated in a sizable amount of trade and investment closely linking the two economies. Informal talks between the two sides aimed at facilitating their relations began in 1993, but the process of coming together was interrupted in 1995 by a strong reaction on the Chinese side to what the Taiwan government calls its "flexible diplomacy": what the Taiwan authorities depict as efforts at securing informal recognition of Taiwan's standing in the world as a political and economic power, the Beijing authorities construe as moves in the direction of a declaration of independence, which is absolutely unacceptable to them, and they have pledged to use force to ensure that it does not come about. Taiwan's president Lee Teng-hui's statement, in the summer of 1999, that relations across the Taiwan Strait could only be conducted on a "state-to-state" basis and the subsequent election, as his successor, of Chen Shui-bian, the candidate of a party that had earlier advocated Taiwan's independence, have both served to heighten the tension.

All too closely intertwined with relations across the Taiwan Strait is China's relationship with the United States. With the Shanghai Communiqué in 1972, the United States attempted to recuse itself from this entire issue, but in the ensuing years, politicians in Beijing, Washington, and Taipei have worked to prevent that from happening. Chinese leaders have sought U.S. assistance in bringing Taiwan to accept their terms for reunification. Taiwan authorities have sought U.S. endorsement of their claim to being other than merely a province of China. And some Americans, mindful of the special relationship between the United States and the Republic of China, argue for a revival of American guarantees for Taiwan's interests.

The Taiwan question is but one of a series of conflicts between Beijing and Washington that, as the century drew to a close, brought Sino-American relations to a low point reminiscent of the near rupture of ties following the Tiananmen massacre in 1989. Americans are repulsed by the Chinese government's violation of the human rights of its citizens and alarmed by the mounting deficit in U.S. trade with China. Chinese see the United States as reviving a Cold War policy of containing China and thwarting its taking a deserved place as a nascent world power.

In addition to negotiating its relationship with Washington, Beijing must attend to its immediate neighbors—Japan, the Koreas, Southeast Asia, Pakistan, India, and Russia. What is now a complementary economic relationship with Japan is very likely to become a competitive one as China's economy expands. China's armed forces are growing and flexing their muscles, and Japan feels pressure to respond in kind. Its doing so will confirm long-standing Chinese concerns about a revival of the Japanese militarism of which China was the victim in the first half of the twentieth century. In short, the two nations must come to a new strategic and economic understanding that takes into account the altered circumstances in which they both find themselves in the new millennium.

There are territorial disputes with China's neighbors in Southeast Asia that arise from Beijing's claim to sovereignty over much of the South China Sea, its island chains, and the oil that may or may not lie beneath its waters. China's relations with Pakistan, once close, have become strained, as Islamic fundamentalism has become a force within China's own Muslim population. That Pakistan and India have developed and tested nuclear weapons has complicated Beijing's approach to the South Asian peninsula.

As the United States has claimed the position of sole superpower in recent years and has acted on several occasions in ways that China regards as arbitrary and hegemonic, Beijing has begun to look toward Russia and India as potential partners in an alliance that might serve as a makeweight against unilateral actions by the United States. Russia has for some years been a source of military hardware for China. More recently, China has initiated conversations on global strategy with both Russia and India.

It is hard to imagine a government that would have the vision, the political capital, and the tenacity to address successfully this daunting agenda. The Chinese government at present is far from that ideal. It has suffered a serious loss of credibility in the eyes of its own people. It is deeply enmeshed in corruption and seems incapable of disentangling itself. It is weakened by rigidity in the face of change and by its absolute refusal to countenance organized opposition of any kind. It is vying for authority, often unsuccessfully, with insubordinate cities and provinces. Finally, it is beholden to its army to the point that it is unable to countermand military initiatives, many of which exacerbate rather than help to solve the problems the government confronts.

The Chinese Communist Party (CCP) has as little political credibility today as it has ever had since its founding in 1921. It came to power in 1949 with a tremendous reservoir of popular support. It added to that reservoir with reforms it undertook in the early 1950s, then soon lost credibility with a series of misguided movements undertaken at Mao's insistence that had disastrous consequences for the Chinese people. The Cultural Revolution had a devastating effect on the Party's reputation. So complete was the loss of popular confidence that even a reversal of the Party's policy line and a partial repudiation of its past mistakes were not enough to repair the damage.

Most Chinese people are quick to acknowledge that the reform policies put in place by Deng Xiaoping in 1978 have put modern China in a position to realize its great potential for the first time and have substantially improved their standard of living. Paradoxically, however, these successes have done little to bolster the Party's reputation, probably because most people inseparably associate the Party with the Marxist-Leninist rhetoric that they find so irrelevant to their lives. And Deng's own reputation suffered a serious blow when it became clear that it was he who had instructed that martial law be declared in Beijing, he who ordered distant but loyal troops into the capital, and he who determined that Tiananmen Square must be cleared of protesters at any cost.

The collapse of the Communist Party in the Soviet Union appears to have given the CCP's credibility an unanticipated boost. One might have expected the CCP, an illegitimate party with an illegitimate elder leader, like virtually every other Communist party in the socialist bloc, to collapse of its own weight. Unlike those other parties, however, the CCP had been remarkably effective in ensuring that no other organization in the country could take its place. There was no Solidarity, no Protestant Church, no nationally elected parliament. Because no other institution stood between the Chinese people and a disorder such as that which they witnessed in Eastern Europe and Russia, they accorded the Party a limited vote of confidence: living under the CCP was preferable to living in anarchy.

China's burgeoning economy has multiplied the already numerous opportunities for corrupt behavior on the part of government and Party officials, and few have failed to take advantage of them. From village councils to the Party's politburo, officials have been profiting from their positions. Campaigns are launched to stamp out the pervasive corruption, but the officials put in charge of the campaigns are themselves deeply involved in corrupt behavior; the campaigns stagnate, and even the Party newspaper opines that "a certain amount of corruption is inevitable." With their eyes firmly fixed on personal gain, not the public weal, officials are hardly in a position to tackle the complex problems facing them.

The capability of China's political system is further diminished by an advanced case of arteriosclerosis. Conscious that its status is precarious, the Party-state has become more and more rigid, less and less tolerant of disagreement and dissent, more and more prone to act, often unpredictably and counterproductively, on its habits of repression. At a time of rapid economic and social change, the Party has grown less flexible, less open to political reform. Always a society ruled by men and not by law, China finds itself with a group of late-middle-aged leaders who give lip service to the principle of subordinating themselves and their actions to a fully developed code of law but who, when push comes to shove, ignore the law in favor of arbitrary and often self-serving action.

Meanwhile, political power and authority have shifted noticeably from the center of the Party-state to its periphery. Central government and Party organs have relinquished power, and provincial and local governments have gained it. The economy's market reform has been accompanied by an appropriate loosening of central control. Problems arise, however, because this loosening has occurred without a clear-cut or uniform allocation of authority between center and regions. Each region has negotiated its own arrangements, and none is prepared to give back what it has obtained. At the same time, regional interests have begun to diverge from those of the center and, adding to the complications, among themselves. There is a real possibility that, were any one or a combination of these political problems to reach crisis stage, the center might not hold.

The glue that the Party-state has come to rely on since 1989 to hold China's political system together is the People's Liberation Army (PLA). It is the only organization with national scope that is capable of supporting a collapsing Party-state or of taking its place. Given that fact, the Party-state finds itself beholden to it in a way that is unparalleled since the violent phase of the Cultural Revolution threatened to spin out of control in early 1967. China's military budget is growing, and it is acquiring substantial, new, and sophisticated equipment. To help support its growth, the Army has become a major player in the Chinese domestic economy and has extensive connections in the global economy. At the same time, actions it has taken in Burma, in the South China Sea, in the Taiwan Strait, and elsewhere raise the question whether China's foreign policy is being made in the Foreign Ministry or by uniformed officers.

The PLA paid dearly for its decision to respond to Deng's orders in 1989 at Tiananmen Square. Its public image suffered, and it found all its carefully cultivated contacts with foreign military establishments suddenly severed, leaving it without the technology, training, or intelligence it had come to depend on. In exchange, it has received substantial budget increases each year, but only now is it beginning to rebuild its credibility and contacts, and it would be very reluctant to repeat this unhappy scenario. On the other hand, military officers are patriots—indeed many are xenophobes—and unlikely to sit on the sidelines were China to come apart at the seams or sink into anarchy. Whether or not their intervention into the political sphere would be successful is another question.

I begin this book with an exploration of China's geography, illustrating some of the natural constraints on the country's growth and pointing up the unevenness of the endowments of its regions. Then I describe the political system as a power grid, with central agencies constituting the vertical elements and regional agencies the horizontal elements. When center and region are at odds with each other, as is often the case, the grid thwarts rather than facilitates the implementation of central directives. Next, the description of China's economy in transition focuses on three questions: Who owns what? Who works where? And who is making the economic decisions? The final chapter in this initial section is devoted to China's armed forces—their strategic capability, role in the economy, and political potential.

Subsequent chapters take up the problems I have briefly outlined in this introduction: problems in the countryside, urban concerns, and the problems that affect the country as a whole, such as regional fragmentation, ethnic separatism, environmental pollution, and population growth. Three chapters are devoted to the status of rights and freedoms in China: human rights and the rule of law, intellectual and artistic freedom.

In the closing section of the book, I consider China's interaction with the outside world. Separate chapters on Hong Kong and Macao and on Taiwan are followed by a final chapter on China's strategic, economic, and political relations with its neighbors and with the United States. The conclusion takes a cautious stroke or two through the dangerous waters of predicting China's future.

This book originated as a seminar on issues in contemporary Chinese politics that I offered at Yale University for seventeen years beginning in 1978. I am grateful to my Yale students for what I learned with and from them.

I

GEOGRAPHICAL INEQUALITIES

AS A FIRST STEP toward understanding China, one can hardly do better than to spend some time with a good atlas. It is vital to understand China's diversity, and a key element in that diversity is its geography.

Superimposing an outline of the United States on an outline of China shows us two important geographical similarities between the two countries. China, covering some 3.7 million square miles, is nearly identical in size to the United States, which covers just over 3.6 million square miles. The two countries are located at more or less the same latitude; New York and Beijing are at roughly the same latitude, as are New Orleans and Shanghai.

A topographical map, on the other hand, shows us important geographical differences between China and the United States. Only about a third of the United States is taken up with mountains and desert, and the remainder is reasonably flat and easily habitable, but in China, these proportions are reversed. The difference in the amount of land available for cultivation in the two countries is even more striking: 40 percent in the United States versus only 10 percent in China.

In any country, rivers serve as arteries for transportation and sources of both irrigation and energy. Silting improves the fertility of river-basin fields, but flooding destroys crops and homes and often claims lives. The major river systems on the North American conti-

CHINA AND THE UNITED STATES:
COMPARISON OF SIZE AND LATITUDE

nent run from north to south, while China's three major river systems all flow from west to east. The northernmost is the Huang He (Yellow River), which runs for more than three thousand miles from the western territory of Tibet to its mouth in Shandong Province. The river takes its name from the color of the extraordinary amount of silt it carries, deposits of which continuously raise its level; it now flows well above the level of the North China plain and is contained between high dikes.

The second major river system, the Yangzi or Changjiang (Long River), also originates in Tibet. It is somewhat longer than the Yellow and has ten times the discharge. It is navigable by oceangoing ships from its mouth near Shanghai as far upstream as the city of Wuhan. About three hundred miles upstream from Wuhan, ground was broken in 1993 for the very large and controversial Three Gorges Dam, among the purposes of which is to extend the navigability of the river to the city of Chongqing, to produce hydroelectric power, and to regulate the flow of the river to control downstream flooding.

The Xi Jiang (West River) in Guangdong Province, the third of China's major river systems, is the shortest of the three, flowing 1,650 miles before merging with the Zhu Jiang (Pearl River) in the delta, at the mouth of which are located Guangzhou (more familiarly known to Westerners as Canton) and Hong Kong.

China's most fertile agricultural regions are in the deltas of the Yellow, Yangzi, and West Rivers. A fourth area of high fertility is along the upper reaches of the Yangzi River in the Sichuan basin, just south of the center of the Chinese landmass.

A striking difference between the North American and the Chinese landmasses is found in the nature of their western borders. In the United States, of course, it is an ocean coast, while in China it is marked with mountains, plateaus, and deserts. This difference accounts for major dissimilarities in the prevailing climates of the two landmasses. America's weather is governed by the movement of the jet stream carrying moisture-laden Pacific storms across the conti-

TOPOGRAPHY OF CHINA

HEIGHT ABOVE SEA LEVEL
(in meters)

0–350
350–1,350
1,350–1,850
1,850–2,500
2,500–5,000
OVER 5,000

Yellow River

Yangzi River

West River

nent. China's weather is determined by monsoon winds that between December and March blow northwest to southeast; coming from the Siberian landmass, the air crossing the northwestern provinces is very dry and provides little rainfall. Then, during the summer months from April to November, the monsoon winds reverse themselves, and, now moving across the South China Sea, they are heavily laden with moisture, which descends as rainfall on China's southeastern coast; the winds are relatively dry by the time they reach the northwestern provinces. Annual rainfall on the southern coast exceeds seventy-five inches, but along the Mongolian border, it is no more than five inches.

Temperatures along the southeastern coast of China are moderate enough even in the winter that there is a year-round growing season, and as many as three crops of rice can be harvested. North of the Great Wall, by contrast, the growing season is only 140 days, and farmers consider themselves fortunate to harvest a single crop of spring wheat.

Coal accounts for just over 70 percent of all energy consumed in China. Oil is currently about 20 percent and electric power about 7 percent of the country's energy resources, percentages about the same as in the United States. The important difference is that about half the energy supplied by coal in China is supplied by natural gas in the United States; in China, natural gas accounts for only 2 percent of energy consumption.

Energy resources and raw materials are somewhat more equally distributed across China than is its scant supply of agricultural land, for coal is found in substantial quantities across the eastern half of the country as well as in Xinjiang, while principal onshore oil fields are located in Gansu, Xinjiang, Shanxi, Sichuan, and Heilongjiang. Annual coal production is running at a rate of just under 1.4 billion tons. The vast majority of China's coal is bituminous, or soft, the burning of which contributes heavily to air pollution. Weaning China of its heavy dependence on soft coal is a necessary first step toward solving its serious environmental problems.

CHINA'S ANNUAL PRECIPITATION

MEASURED RAINFALL
(in centimeters)

20–25
25–50
50–100
100–150
150–200
200–300

Before the beginning of exploration in the Tarim Basin in Xinjiang in 1993, the Chinese estimated their onshore oil reserves at 75 billion barrels. Early estimates of the Tarim Basin reserves were as high as 180 billion barrels—which would have more than tripled their reserves—but most recent estimates are as low as 4 to 5 billion barrels. Meanwhile, offshore oil exploration undertaken with foreign assistance has been under way for more than twenty years. Assessing China's offshore reserves is complicated by a lack of reliable survey data and by issues of territorial rights; estimates have varied from a low of 37 billion barrels to a high of more than 200 billion barrels. Combining onshore and offshore reserves, then, China may have as little as 116 billion barrels or as much as 455 billion barrels. (To put these figures into perspective: the onshore and offshore oil reserves of the United States are about 156 billion barrels, those of Saudi Arabia about 260 billion barrels.)

In the late 1970s, when China began to interact with the world economy, Chinese planners estimated that oil would double its share of China's total energy consumption and reach about 40 percent by the early 1990s and that revenues from oil exports would be sufficient to fund imports of Western and Japanese technology. But the ensuing development of the economy increased domestic demand for petroleum at a rate that exceeded the rate of increase in oil production: whereas total economic growth has averaged in excess of 10 percent per year, oil production is increasing at about 3 percent. Thus oil occupies about the same position in China's energy pool that it did twenty years ago, and, as of 1994, China became a net importer of oil.

Electric power is China's third source of energy, providing about 6.5 percent of the total. The existing electric-power grid serves the eastern third of the country quite effectively, the western two-thirds less so. Total electric-power generation in 1997 was 1.1 trillion kilowatt hours, but 80 percent of that power was thermal-generated, using soft coal. Electric-power generation is increasing annually at a rate of about 10 percent, but the ratio of hydroelectric power to coal-burning thermal-generated electricity has decreased steadily over the last fifteen years. Only about 1 percent of China's electric power is nuclear-generated.

The Three Gorges Dam project is expected to produce some 100 billion kilowatt hours of hydroelectric power when it is fully operative in 2015. In theory, that could help reduce the use of coal by sixty million tons per year. But in fact, at that point the annual electrical energy needs of eastern China alone are projected to be between 900 billion and 1 trillion kilowatt hours, so it is most likely that power from the new dam will simply augment the supply of thermal-generated electricity, not supplant it.

The distribution of China's population accords closely with the location of fertile soil and adequate growing seasons. Approximately 75 percent of the population lives on 15 percent of the landmass, being most heavily concentrated in the fertile river basins, where densities in excess of two thousand people per square mile are not uncommon.[1] (This compares with a population density of fewer than four hundred people per square mile in the northeastern United States, the most highly populated area.) Compared with the river basins, western China is sparsely populated, but even these wide-open spaces have a fair number of people. The autonomous region of Xinjiang, China's largest province, is also the country's least densely populated, with some twenty-six people per square mile. (By comparison, Wyoming and Alaska have five and one per square mile, respectively.)

Some 390 million people—30 percent of the Chinese population—reside in China's 570 cities, and the density of the network of these cities generally conforms to the pattern of population density shown in the map. This is a more even distribution than is the case with many other countries at a comparable level of economic development, and for three distinct reasons.

As the territory over which China's sovereignty extended began to expand as early as the third century B.C., the central government established administrative seats from which its officials exerted control over the populace. At the beginning of the nineteenth century, a net-

POPULATION OF CHINA

DENSITY PER SQUARE KILOMETER

| 0 | 50–200 |
| 0–50 | OVER 200 |

work of some two thousand cities and towns covered all of what we now think of as Chinese territory, with, at the center of each, a walled compound housing the local representative of imperial authority. Each administrative seat was part of a hierarchy organized according to the respective ranks and positions of the imperial officials. Beijing, the imperial capital, stood at the apex of this hierarchy, provincial capitals formed its mid-levels, and county seats formed its base.

A second reason for the rise of urban aggregations in China was commercial. The exchange of agricultural goods and handicraft products and, subsequently, the exchange of both of these for manufactured items led to the rise of itinerant merchants, moving periodically from village to village, and then to a whole stratum of society devoted entirely to commerce. While some villages were centers of commercial activity only occasionally, others, by virtue of their location, proved more durably convenient for marketing purposes. Market days in these villages became more frequent; eventually the markets became permanent. Thus was created a hierarchy of commercial centers that was integrated with, but at the same time distinguishable from, the hierarchy of administrative centers.

Whereas the administrative centers were laid out from the top down in a reasonably orderly fashion so as to exert imperial control as uniformly as possible over China's hinterlands, the network of market towns grew naturally from the bottom up. The former were called *cheng*, a word that also means "wall" and that conjures up an image of a formally laid-out and enclosed urban space; market towns were called *zhen*, which connotes an outpost or garrison without a formal layout or walls. Administrative centers were large—the smallest had a population of between three and ten thousand—while the market towns were much smaller, the lowest ranking among them being mere hamlets of as few as five hundred people, half or more of whom were full-time farmers.

The third force that gave rise to urban agglomeration in China came much later in the country's history and resulted from the government's unsuccessful effort to prevent or at least limit foreigners' commercial and cultural contact with China. One result of the series of defeats that the Chinese endured in the modern period at the hands of Westerners superior in modern armaments and the tactics to employ them was that for the first time in its history China was forced open to the influence and influx of non-Chinese. Because Western nations were themselves in rivalry with one another for slices of what came to be called the "Chinese melon," the Chinese used this rivalry to their advantage in order to restrict the points of Sino-Western contact to a few locations called treaty ports. Unlike administrative and market towns, treaty ports were part of neither a hierarchy nor an effective network. To the extent that the Chinese government was able to control their designation, they were located where contact between Chinese people and nefarious foreigners

Table 1

CHINA'S FIFTEEN LARGEST CITIES

	Nonagricultural population (in millions)	U.S. cities population (in millions)
Shanghai	9.5	
Beijing	7.3	New York 7.3
Chongqing	6.1	
Tianjin	5.2	
Shenyang	4.2	
Wuhan	4.2	
Harbin	4.2	
Guangzhou	4.1	
Chengdu	3.2	Los Angeles 3.5
Changchun	2.7	Chicago 2.8
Nanjing	2.7	
Xi'an	2.7	
Dalian	2.6	
Qingdao	2.5	
Jinan	2.2	
		Houston 1.7

(Sources: *China Statistical Yearbook 1999* and *World Almanac 2000*)

would be minimal and easily controlled. To the extent that Western powers succeeded in imposing their preferences, the treaty ports sprang up where Western entrepreneurs found maximal ease of access to what they sought in China: cheap labor, cheap raw materials, cheap maritime transport, and abundant consumers.

Today, even the smallest of China's 570 cities seem very large to Americans; at the other end of the scale, 15 cities in China have more than two million people.

China is by modern standards inadequately interconnected, with less than 800,000 miles of highways and roads, about 85 percent of which are paved—roughly one-fifth of the highway network in the United States. Moreover, the roads are unequally distributed: dense in China's eastern provinces and sparse in the west. About 13 percent of the country's freight traffic and just under half of its passenger traffic are carried on these roads and highways, and highway construction is a high priority in the country's economic development program. Between 15,000 and 20,000 miles of new highway are being added annually, much of it at the expense of China's limited supply of arable land.

The rail network covers about thirty-five thousand miles, only a quarter of which is double tracked. (The United States currently has a rail network four times that size.) This rail system carries about 35 percent of the country's freight and passenger traffic (coal accounting for nearly half the freight). As China's economy expands, its railways are operating at or close to capacity and are meeting less than 60 percent of the demand for rail transport. Major construction is under way to add six thousand miles of track to the system. The largest of these projects, a second north-south rail corridor connecting Beijing and Guangzhou and paralleling the existing line to the east, was opened to traffic in 1996. Projections suggest that the railroad system's share of passenger and freight traffic will decline to about 30 percent each over the next fifteen years, with highways and airlines attracting away passengers and trucking absorbing the difference in freight traffic.

China's system of navigable inland waterways, both rivers and canals, is twice as long as its rail network. More freight is carried on inland and coastal waterways than on either road or rail.

The thousand-plus domestic commercial air routes in China (a number that shows an increase by a factor of five in the twenty years since the economic reforms began) now cover almost the same distance as that covered by highways, though the volume of air transport remains small. Until the mid-1980s, air transport was handled by a single state-owned corporation, the Civil Air Administration of China (CAAC); between 1985 and 1995, CAAC was broken up into more than a dozen local companies, which have taken over domestic and some international routes; CAAC is now an exclusively international airline. A shortage of equipment and trained personnel has hampered the expansion of air transportation, which in any case has a dauntingly bad safety record. Currently, only about 7 percent of China's passenger travel and less than 1 percent of its freight movement are completed by air.

As with the network of roads and highways, so with waterways, railways, and air routes: eastern China is well linked; western China is much less accessible.

Mountains and deserts rendered interaction with China's neighbors to the north and west problematic throughout the nation's history, and for most of that time, the ocean on the east was also a barrier to, rather than an avenue for, interaction. Capable of an autarkic existence, China cut itself off from contact with the outside world for much of its long history. Exceptions to this habit of isolation are seen with the expansion of maritime trade during the Tang and Song dynasties, in the tenth and eleventh centuries, and with the opening of the overland Silk Road, connecting China to central Asia and the Middle East, during the Yuan dynasty in the thirteenth century.

In the nineteenth century, the European nations, Japan, and the United States began to push on China's closed door. They initially came to buy tea and silk; later they began to think of China as a potential market for Western manufactures and a source of inexpensive labor to produce those goods. Almost all the intercourse into which

China was reluctantly forced took place at ports on the eastern littoral, a pattern that was revived when China rejoined the world economy in the late 1970s. The vast preponderance of China's now
extensive interaction with the outside world occurs in the major
coastal cities that were once treaty ports—Tianjin, Dalian, Shanghai,
Fuzhou, Xiamen, and Guangzhou. To be sure, there is cross-border
economic interaction with Russia and the former Soviet Central
Asian republics to the north and west and with Burma and Vietnam
in the south. But this economic activity pales by comparison with the
volume of transactions initiated in the coastal provinces.

In ethnic terms, the Chinese population is unusually uniform. Despite great cultural differences among various groups, more than
nine-tenths of the population consider themselves of the same Han
ethnicity. The remaining population is divided among fifty-seven distinct minority nationalities, each with its own language. This small
fraction of the total population, however, inhabits nearly two-thirds of
the Chinese landmass, including northern, western, and southern
China.

Beneath the ethnic uniformity of the Han Chinese population lies
a strong sense of local loyalty that is reinforced by language, cuisine,
and a remarkably persistent regional stereotyping. The Chinese term
difang guannian, best translated as "sense of place," has great importance in the individual Chinese psyche, despite the homogenizing
tendencies of a rapidly modernizing society. Ask an American where
he or she is from, and you are likely to get some variation of a current
zip code as an answer. Ask that same question of a Chinese, and you
are likely to receive an answer that will call into question your command of the first lessons of elementary Chinese.

"Where are you from?" I have asked a new acquaintance. "I am
from Shanghai" comes the answer. "Shanghai is changing very
rapidly," I respond. "When is the last time you visited there?" "I've
never been to Shanghai," he replies, and I wonder where my simple
conversation went astray. As it turns out, my Chinese is not at fault.
My friend has, in fact, never been to Shanghai, nor has his father. It

was his *grandfather* who was born in Shanghai and who left at the age of twenty never to return; yet at some important level, my friend continues to consider himself a Shanghainese and to identify with the fortunes of his "native" place.

Local dialects are an important ingredient of this persistent sense of place. All of the Han population share the same written language, and about three-quarters of them speak a more or less mutually intelligible version of the language that we Westerners often refer to as Mandarin. The remainder, who live in the southeastern quadrant of the country, speak mutually unintelligible dialects that adhere to seven major dialect groups and countless local subgroupings. The northern dialect, or Mandarin, forms the basis of what the Chinese call *putong hua* (the common language), which is taught in schools throughout China, is used as the medium of spoken communication in official life, and until quite recently was the only language spoken in radio and television broadcasting.

Diet and cuisine vary by region in China, as they do in many countries, and constitute an important part of this strong regional self-identification. The most significant distinction is found between the northern provinces, where wheat is the principal grain, and the south, where rice predominates. Northern cuisine is best known for its flavorful sauces; southern cuisine features fresh ingredients with light, often sweet sauces that enhance the fresh flavors. South-central Chinese cuisine makes copious use of the red pepper. Fish and seafood figure prominently in the coastal provinces; pork and chicken predominate inland. In areas inhabited by Muslim minorities, lamb is the preferred meat. Throughout China, grain and vegetables are still the principal sources of protein, though with growing affluence a preference for meat is increasing—a trend viewed with concern by those worried about feeding a growing population on a limited supply of arable land.

The enduring regional identities have created, over the centuries, regional stereotypes that Chinese people never abandon. As is the case in other parts of the Northern Hemisphere, northerners in China are often thought of as reserved, formal, and aloof; southerners, by contrast, are seen as more outgoing, volatile, and spontaneous. Residents of Beijing, like those who live inside our Washington Beltway, have a reputation for being highly political and power seeking; like New Yorkers, people from Shanghai consider themselves, and are considered by others, sophisticated, cosmopolitan, and managerially capable. Residents of Guangzhou are often characterized as having a highly developed commercial sense; natives of the south-central provinces of Sichuan and Hunan, perhaps because of their peppery cuisine, are called hot tempered and impetuous.

The People's Republic of China is divided administratively into twenty-two provinces and five so-called autonomous regions, where the majority of the population is non-Han. In addition, there are four "directly administered cities"—Beijing, Tianjin, Chongqing, and Shanghai—which with their surrounding counties are treated, for administrative purposes, as equivalent to provinces. Finally, there are the Hong Kong and Macao special administrative regions. The provinces are divided into counties, of which there are just over two thousand nationwide, and cities. Under the supervision of the county governments, rural political and economic administration is conducted at the level of the township or town. Each county has, on average, some two dozen townships and towns, with a national total of twenty-six thousand townships and twenty thousand town governments. There are just under 800,000 village governments, the lowest level of rural administration, or about two dozen per township. The average village population is a little over one thousand—though the villages vary significantly depending on whether they are located in densely or sparsely populated regions.

Translating China's geographical inequalities into economic terms, one begins to sense the significance of regionalism in China today. Consider the data in Table 2 on economic output in coastal, central, and western China. It shows that the significant advantages enjoyed by the coastal region are long-lived. The table also confirms that the coastal region, with a significantly higher growth rate than the center

POLITICAL MAP OF CHINA

or the west and a very substantial lead in foreign investment, is set to widen the gap in the years ahead. The distinction between coastal China and the rest of the country is obvious, but the lead of the center over the west is less clear-cut. Per capita gross domestic product in central China is measurably higher than in the west, but the average growth rates in the two regions are barely distinguishable.

The more detailed version of Table 2 that appears in the Appendix includes data on individual provinces. There, one can see that some provinces and cities altered their relative positions significantly between 1952 and 1998. The southern coastal provinces of Guangdong and Fujian, for example, stand out as late bloomers, while provinces in China's northeastern "rust belt" have slipped significantly.

The information in Table 2 substantiates the hypothesis that the policies of the economic-reform period have caused the influence of China's geographical inequalities to reemerge. Before, development policy in China operated according to a different logic. Mao Zedong's first principle of economic development was egalitarianism. Mindful of the regional differences and geographical inequalities, he argued that resources should be preferentially allocated to the poorest regions, allowing them to develop to the level already achieved by the richest; only then would the richest regions be encouraged to move forward, and the pace of their development would be kept to a rate that could be matched by China as a whole. Comparing the data for 1952 and for 1979 in Table 2 illustrates the effects of the policies Mao based on this developmental philosophy.

The inauguration of reform policies in the late 1970s shifted away from Maoist egalitarianism. Deng and his like-minded colleagues believed that egalitarian development for China was inevitably development at an unacceptably slow pace. Arguing that the Chinese people could not be persuaded to "delay gratification" any longer, the reformers adopted a policy of "building on the best." Resources once devoted to developing China's poorest regions were reallocated to its most promising regions—that is, the coastal provinces.

Moreover, the reform policies themselves, substituting market forces for central planning in the national economy, gave a signifi-

Table 2

COMPARATIVE OUTPUT, GROWTH, AND INVESTMENT BY REGION, 1952–1998

	Index of 1952 per capita output[4] (national average=100)	Rank	Index of 1979 per capita output[4] (national average=100)	Rank	Index of 1998 per capita GDP (national average=100)	Rank	Growth 1997–1998 (%)	Rank	1998 Foreign direct investment per province (billion $)	Rank
Coastal China[1]	215	1	137	1	156	1	9.78	1	3.01	1
Central China[2]	77	3	55	2	68	2	9.07	2	0.50	2
Western China[3]	87	2	52	3	58	3	8.82	3	0.18	3

(Sources: *China Statistical Yearbook* 1985 and 1999).

[1] Coastal China includes Beijing, Fujian, Guangdong, Hainan, Hebei, Heilongjiang, Jiangsu, Jilin, Liaoning, Shandong, Shanghai, Tianjin, and Zhejiang.

[2] Central China includes Anhui, Chongqing, Henan, Hubei, Hunan, Jiangxi, Shaanxi, Shanxi, and Sichuan.

[3] Western China includes Gansu, Guangxi, Guizhou, Inner Mongolia, Ningxia, Qinghai, Tibet, Xinjiang, and Yunnan.

[4] Figures for 1952 and 1979 show industrial and agricultural output. Figures for 1998 show gross domestic product, which, in addition to industrial and agricultural output, includes output of the commercial and service sectors.

cant advantage to the well-endowed coastal regions, since they favored areas that could generate capital through agricultural surpluses, or had surplus labor with skill levels appropriate to new
industrial processes, or had access to domestic and foreign markets in
which new products could be sold, or, finally, could develop global
connections to potential sources of investment capital. The coastal
provinces possessed all of these characteristics, the provinces in central China some of them, and the poorest provinces in western China
few if any. So the coastal provinces, perfectly positioned to take full
advantage of the policies of market reform and opening to the world
economy, benefited accordingly. As we shall see, the central
provinces are just beginning to be able to take advantage of the reform policies, and the western provinces are still unable to do so.

While it is useful to think of coastal China as a single, well-
endowed economic region, it is important to understand that its
provinces are rivals for scarce resources, particularly as regards their
foreign economic relations. As is clear from Table 2, foreign investment is concentrated almost exclusively on the coast, and many of
the coastal provinces have been disproportionately successful in cultivating economic ties with a specific foreign nation: as a result, after
two decades of growth one sees a pattern that looks like the "spheres
of influence" into which foreign powers carved China a century ago.

Hong Kong is the principal source of outside investment in
China, contributing about two-fifths of the $45 billion placed in
China by external investors in 1998. These Hong Kong investments
are heavily concentrated in Guangdong Province, where in 1998 a
very substantial proportion of the $12 billion in outside investment
came from Hong Kong. Taiwan is contributing just over 6 percent,
according to 1998 figures, much of it in Fujian Province. Shandong
Province has been especially successful in attracting South Korean
investors, while foreign investment in the northeast—in Heilongjiang, Jilin, and Liaoning Provinces—is dominated by Japan.

But these linkages differ in important ways from the spheres of influence in nineteenth-century China. First, the nations most active
in "carving the Chinese melon" a century ago—Britain, Germany,

and France—neither are the most important investors in the Chinese economy today nor have they concentrated in particular areas. Second, the spheres of influence were created by means of decisions made by foreign governments and firms, whereas in the current situation, Chinese economic actors are as involved in soliciting investment as the investors are involved in selecting the areas of China where they will invest.

This brief geographical foray gives us a background for trying to understand the major issues with which China's political and economic systems must contend in the near term. One of them involves that critical fraction that will determine China's ability to realize its economic potential: the numerator being food supply and the denominator, population. A second set of issues concerns energy resources—how they will be developed and the effect of that development on the environment of China and that of the world. A final issue is whether or not the geographical inequalities among regions of China and the infrastructure put in place thus far will make for divisiveness.

II

PATTERNS FROM THE PAST

THE CHINESE PHRASE *henduo yiqian* means "a long time ago." A literal translation reads "a long way in front of me," which suggests a very different sense of the direction one faces to look at the past from the one we are accustomed to. It calls to mind the image of a Chinese historian seated beside the stream of events looking toward its source, while behind him the stream runs on into the future.

What are the patterns Chinese people discern as they look upstream toward their past, and how do these patterns inform their understanding of the present? As in many ancient cultures, the patterns are as much myths about Chinese history as they are accurate accounts of past events. Common wisdom about the Chinese past is that China has always been a strong, unified state headed by a single, powerful individual, a minimal state with maximal reach: that is, a relatively small state apparatus that succeeded in extracting substantial revenues and labor from a large population. The bureaucratic system undergirding the state is believed to have been remarkably stable, having functioned without significant change for two millennia from its founding in the second century B.C. to its demise at the turn of the twentieth century. And the changes that did occur over this extraordinarily long span of history are believed to have been cyclical rather than linear; the system evolved, but it evolved through a series of deteriorations and restorations, as new dynasties looked to re-create the system as it had existed in a more perfect form at some point in the past, not to build a new order.

A key component in the Chinese view of their past is the idea of a unified state with a strong central government led by a single ruler exerting control over subordinate, weaker local governments and neighboring states. The geographical scope of this idealized state was very large: what the Chinese consider to have always been inalienable Chinese territory is in fact all the land inside China's borders when the reach of the empire was at its broadest, that is, in the eighteenth century A.D., during the middle years of the last dynasty. But when the contending principalities living in what is now Chinese territory were first unified under the control of the Qin emperor in 221 B.C., the empire occupied only a third of today's China—as far north as the Great Wall but not beyond. Its capital was in the city of Xianyang (present-day Xi'an), and its territory extended westward to the center of what is today Gansu Province. The first Qin emperor aspired to control all the land as far south as present-day Guangdong and Vietnam, but his armies' hold on that territory was tenuous at best.

The Chinese empire expanded and contracted, and the fluctuations were periodically interrupted by conflict and fragmentation. The Chinese may look on the latter as temporary aberrations from the unified, centralized imperial norm, but they in fact persisted for about a quarter of the time—five of the twenty centuries about which we are speaking. Nor were these times of regional fragmentation in the far-distant past. The century prior to 1950 was marked by a sharp decline and eventual collapse of central control and its replacement by dozens of heavily armed and contending satrapies.

Twice China was overrun by foreign invaders—once in the thirteenth century by the Mongols and again in the seventeenth century by the Manchus—and in each case the received wisdom would have it that the conquerors were engulfed and assimilated by their nominal victims. The Yuan and Qing dynasties, respectively, are made to fit the pattern of China's own dynasties; in fact it was under Manchu rule that the Chinese empire reached its maximal territorial grasp.

The island of Taiwan, for example, was brought under Chinese control only during the last dynasty in the late seventeenth century; Tibet, briefly under Chinese suzerainty during the Tang dynasty in the seventh century, also came under the tenuous hold of Chinese authorities at about the same time. When officials in Beijing speak of Taiwan and Tibet as always having been an inseparable part of China, they conveniently ignore these facts.

A dominant thread in this pattern from the past is the strong emperor. There were norms for the emperor to observe and rites to perform but only two real constraints on his power: his personal capacity, and the size of the empire under his rule and the necessity it imposed on him to make use of others to carry out his wishes and his will. And the proof of the pudding was always in the eating. If the dikes were mended, the borders secure, the people well fed, and commerce thriving, the emperor was ipso facto doing his job. A bad harvest, a natural disaster, a foreign threat, or hard times, by contrast, were signs that there was trouble at the center, under which circumstances those adversely affected might well consider mounting a rebellion aimed at displacing the incompetent monarch. But this was an extreme solution to the problem of misrule and occurred only a dozen or so times over two millennia. Most of the time an arbitrary emperor was restricted only by the length of his reach.

In China's traditional domestic sphere, a minimal state structure effectively controlled a massive society by making only limited demands on it, expecting society to control itself through its strong family system. The traditional order consisted of four interdependent elements: the family; the upper class, or gentry, as it is most commonly known; a group of bureaucrat-officials who were recruited to office by means of a civil-service examination; and the imperial throne itself. And it endured for so long because it involved a carefully constructed division of labor and a finely calibrated balancing of power and authority among these four elements.

The foundation of traditional Chinese society was the family, ideally consisting of several generations united under a single roof. But this ideal was feasible only for the best off in the best of times; for most people most of the time, the family was two parents and their children.

The Chinese have taken relationships within the family as paradigms for relationships within society and, indeed, for China's relationships with the world beyond its borders. They were described and subsequently canonized in the works of Confucius, the great scholar-teacher who died just a little less than a decade before the birth of Socrates. Confucius, an ethicist, not a metaphysician, argued that there were more than sufficient problems to address in this world so he had no time to devote to issues about the next world. Comfortable in his position on the banks of the stream of events and looking upstream, Confucius, as a teacher, aimed to find a way of restoring harmony to human relations

The paradigmatic relationship in Confucius's mind was that between father and son, and he depicted it as reciprocal. It is the responsibility of the son to obey and respect his father in all circumstances, of course, but the father, too, has obligations. The father must serve his son as a moral exemplar, to teach moral behavior by modeling rather than by relying on rules and harsh punishments. Confucius then applied this model of reciprocity to other relationships within and outside the family—between siblings, between marriage partners, and, ultimately, between ruler and subject.

The father-son paradigm also informed China's sense of its relationship to the outside world. Just as the father's authority is based on his superior grasp of and ability to exemplify ethical principles, China's authority among its neighbors was believed to be based on its superior grasp of ethical principles and its monopoly of a civilization that exemplified them. By these lights, China was the center of the civilized world and owed its neighbors the obligation of sharing its civilization by example, just as its neighbors owed it obedience and respect, which was symbolized by an elaborate ritual of bringing tribute to the emperor at various intervals. This Sinocentric worldview made

for great stability in East Asia for a very long time. It also made it difficult for China to take seriously the notion that there might be value in
ideas or approaches outside its own sphere of cultural influence.

The relationship between the commoner family and the gentry
class was also a reciprocal one. The family was responsible for providing for its own subsistence, and beyond that, it was relied on for a
surplus of both labor and product that could be tapped by the gentry
for its private purposes and by the government for its public purposes.
It was also expected to instill in its younger members a respect for order, discipline, and hard work.

Although the nuclear family was theoretically self-sufficient, in
practice there were situations in which it needed to call upon external resources. In normal times, this might take the form of mutual-
assistance arrangements with one's neighbors; in hard times, there
was the extended family and, beyond it, the clan. Exploring the fa-
milial web far enough, one might well encounter a relative, however
distant, who had secured membership in the gentry class: the resources of the extended family, especially where there were gentry
connections, might be tapped for financial assistance in straitened
times, for providing an education to a promising young scion, or for
adjudicating a civil dispute that had turned uncivil.

Defined in narrow terms, members of the gentry class were those
men who had passed a civil-service examination and had thus received a degree. Degree holders numbered, on average, about a half
million men. If we add the members of their immediate families, the
gentry class would have numbered no more than about 5 million in a
society that grew gradually from about 50 million to about 100 million people.

As we have seen, the gentry as a class depended on the nuclear
and extended families into which all Chinese society was organized,
and they, in turn, depended on the gentry. Similarly, the gentry and
the bureaucracy were engaged in an interdependent and reciprocal
relationship. Although gentry membership, strictly speaking, required a civil-service degree, landownership and the revenues derived
therefrom were the gentry's economic mainstay. The imperial bu-

reaucracy relied on the gentry to manage the local agrarian economy in such a way as to make available to the state the revenues and labor power it needed for public works and payroll. Also, by virtue of its monopoly of knowledge of the canon on which the examination system was based, the gentry identified and instructed future recruits to the bureaucracy. Finally, for reasons we shall explore in a moment, local representatives of the bureaucracy were strangers in the territories they administered and thus depended on local gentry for the information needed to administer successfully.

But the gentry were equally beholden to the bureaucrats. While receipt of a degree entitled a man and his family to membership in the gentry, every degree holder aspired to hold an office. A position within the bureaucracy not only enhanced the status of the gentry family but added significantly to its wealth. Beyond this, the bureaucracy's monopoly on political power was a necessary complement to the gentry's economic power. It was the bureaucracy that organized and supervised the public works—roads, dikes, and canals—on which the successful functioning of each local economy depended.

The bureaucracy was composed of men who had been appointed to their official positions by the throne. Its size varied substantially over time, but a reasonable figure to keep in mind is about thirty thousand officeholders. The lowest level in the bureaucratic hierarchy was the county magistrate, of which there were some two thousand. A magistrate, assisted by a staff of clerks, runners, and personal servants, would have been responsible for governing on average between twenty-five thousand and fifty thousand people. It was his responsibility to investigate crimes and prosecute criminals, adjudicate civil disputes that could not be resolved within the family system, collect taxes, mobilize a workforce for public works, and raise a temporary militia in times of civil unrest.

Because he set examinations, awarded degrees, and appointed officials, the emperor legitimated and controlled the bureaucracy, but the bureaucrats were the eyes, ears, arms, and legs that made it possible for him to govern China's vast territory and to control and extract tax revenues from its large population. From the emperor's perspective, the danger lay in the possibility that the bureaucracy would come to rule in his place rather than in his name. A carefully constructed system was devised to prevent local alliances from forming that might impinge on the power and authority of the center. To be avoided at all costs was a confluence of political, economic, and military power held simultaneously by men with strong ties to a particular territory. The law of avoidance, designed to prevent such a confluence, proscribed bureaucrats from serving as officials in their home locales. A newly appointed magistrate thus arrived at his post as a stranger. With no local ties and more often than not speaking a dialect different from that of the staff and clientele at his new post, the magistrate came to rely heavily on the local gentry (with whom he could communicate in Mandarin) for intelligence about the community.

State bureaucrats held a monopoly of political power within each local community. Although officeholders profited from their offices through legitimate and extra-legitimate emoluments, local economic power rested securely in the hands of the gentry. And though the local magistrate was authorized to call up a militia, once the disturbance was extinguished militia members returned to their civilian pursuits. A standing army was the exclusive purview of the throne. Political, economic, and military power were thus controlled by three separate and interdependent elements of China's society.

A key ingredient in the glue that kept this carefully balanced traditional system together over so long a period was the idea that one's position in the social order was not fixed for all time. A limited amount of social mobility was endemic, but more important to the system's stability was the pervasive *myth* of social mobility. The fortunes of many families—whether rich or poor—in fact remained much the same across many generations. (As in our own highly mobile society, there were obstacles to overcome in moving up and advantages to being on top.) But the myth held that a family's fortunes were likely to change radically every fourth or fifth generation: a peasant's great-great-grandson might well become a bureaucrat, and the bureaucrat's great-great-grandson might well end up tilling the fields. To sort out the myth and the reality of social mobility, we need to take a closer look at the rungs of what one historian called the "ladder of success in imperial China."

To begin the process of upward mobility, a commoner family needed two things: a son with intellectual promise, and enough wealth and labor power to do without him in the fields. The next step would be to find a teacher to assist the son in the tortuous process of becoming literate and acquiring an introduction to the classics on which the examination system was based. Here a family connection to the gentry—however attenuated it might be—was of great value. The teacher in all likelihood was himself a recent product of the examination system, a degree holder but not yet an officeholder who might well spend years training others before securing his own position in the bureaucracy.

The young man's education was largely a matter of modeling and memorization. One learned to write characters by reproducing perfectly and frequently models of calligraphy. One learned the classics by committing them to memory. One prepared for the examination by repeatedly practicing the complicated, formalistic essay style in which answers were to be couched.

Examinations were given at the local level every three years. Those who passed were granted the degree that brought elevated status and respect. The top few candidates in the local examinations were then admitted to examinations administered by the central government; successful passage of these brought still higher degrees and greater likelihood of appointment to office. Those who failed the local examination were entitled to take it again . . . and again. Those whose persistence exceeded their proficiency might well continue to sit for examinations into late middle age.

The successful scholar, degree in hand, would then begin what for many was a long, often tedious process of securing office. Respected for his intellectual attainments, he might find employment as a tutor or, even better for his résumé, as the secretary to an official. In this latter capacity, the scholar would encounter for the first time the practicalities of governance, which neither his education nor the examinations had been concerned with. Whatever extra income he had would be invested in buying more land, for it was in his capacity as a landlord and lender that a member of the gentry who did not hold office was able to advance his family's interests.

Office holding, when it finally arrived, was the capstone on the upwardly mobile scholar's career. His status and that of his family were enhanced and their wealth augmented by the emoluments of office—both legitimate and illegitimate ones (commonly known as "squeeze"). Once again it was additional land into which that wealth was most likely to be invested.

The reverse process, the descent of the ladder of success, was predicated on two important features of China's state and society: the first, a political feature, held that with the exception of that of the emperor himself, no position was hereditary; the second, a social feature, was that primogeniture was not practiced and a father's estate was divided equally among his sons. Given these facts of life, a son had to go through the same process his father had gone through—education, examination, and appointment to office—in order to hold on to the family's position in society. Of course, the deck was stacked in favor of the already well-endowed, and the chances of success were much greater for the scion of an elite family than for the scion of a commoner family. On the other hand, wealth and status often encouraged an effete lifestyle that dulled interest in and ability for a classical education. Failure to pass an examination put the entire generation at risk. Without income from office holding, the family would be hard put to maintain the extravagant lifestyle of China's upper elite, and landholdings, rather than being augmented with the investment of a surplus, would be sold to make up the deficit. Also, with the passing of each succeeding generation, landholdings were equally divided among the sons; the progeny were likely to find themselves obliged to work for a living until such time as, with a combination of wit, drive, and a cash surplus, the family might begin the process of ascent once again.

Marxist historians in China have worked hard to persuade themselves that the system described here was feudal in character and thus that Chinese society was moving through the same historical stages that Marx and Engels used to describe European history. As is clear from this brief description, however, the Chinese experience differed significantly from that of feudal Europe (or feudal Japan, for that matter), where a family permanently retained its status in the social order. Though fact may have fallen far short of myth, there *was* mobility in the Chinese system, and status was ultimately based on achievement, not on birth and only indirectly on wealth. Moreover, estates were more likely to be dissipated when all the sons were obliged to share the bequest with their male siblings.

In the same way that the fortunes of a Chinese family might rise and fall over time, the fortunes of an imperial dynastic house would wax and wane. To give a sense of continuity over a vast span of history, these changes were seen as fitting a cyclical, not a linear, pattern. Throughout, a Confucian set of ideas about governance, with a strong emphasis on the value of restoring an ideal system of right rule from which actual practice had slipped over time, dominated this cyclical pattern.

The idea that the imperial family had the "mandate of heaven" as its source of political legitimacy dates from as early as the Zhou dynasty in the twelfth century B.C. The idea of an anthropomorphic deity had been dominant during the Shang dynasty, which preceded the Zhou, and it gave way under the Zhou to the vaguer concept of "heaven" as a "supreme spiritual reality," as one student of Chinese philosophy describes it. It was heaven that bestowed the right to rule, and the ruler and his offspring retained that right or mandate so long as they ruled virtuously and effectively. A lapse in virtuous rule meant that the mandate would be withdrawn and placed in the hands of another, more virtuous emperor.

A corollary to the idea of the mandate of heaven was the "right to rebel." Under circumstances of misrule, since the mandate was about to be withdrawn from the ruler anyway, it would not be wrong to speed the process by mounting a rebellion. This "right," however, was granted only in retrospect—that is, if the rebellion was successful, it proved ipso facto that the mandate was about to be withdrawn, and if it failed, its very failure demonstrated that heaven was not ready to shift the mandate.

With nine major dynasties and numerous minor ones over two thousand years of Chinese history, the mandate shifted many times. Intriguingly, however, the new incumbent on the imperial throne, whether rebel or foreign invader, invariably made it his business to restore the system to the way it had existed at some better point in the past and never undertook to change it in any fundamental way. No doubt this had something to do with the strong restorationist theme in Confucianism, which served so effectively as the basis of the state ideology, but it also had to do with the fact that the carefully articulated and balanced social-political system had proved such a remarkably effective and efficient form of administration for a large, unwieldy empire.

The apex of the dynastic cycle was marked by good times, when the central government was at its strongest, taxes were collected, and the appropriate sum of tax revenue made its way to the capital. China's borders were secure, public works were undertaken and maintained, and the baneful effects of natural disasters were effectively addressed. In short, the economic health of the empire was sound, and the authority of the central government relative to that of local officials and the gentry was strong.

Conversely, at the nadir of the cycle, marked by bad times, the empire's economic health was seriously threatened, poverty was widespread, and the people were underfed, overworked, and overtaxed. The central government was weak and ineffective, tax revenues were insufficient, and a disproportionate share of them stayed in the hands of local officials and never got to the central coffers. External threats to the empire were not effectively repulsed. Natural disasters occurred with what appeared to be increasing frequency, and their devastation of the lives and livelihood of the people went unmitigated by government action. With the authority of the central government weakened, local power holders were emboldened, and their excesses went unchecked. Superstition surged: since heaven was known to express its dissatisfaction with the unvirtuous ruler through natural signs, people anticipated floods, droughts, earthquakes, and—everyone's favorite among the portents—birds flying backward. At this point, the mandate was transferred through rebellion or invasion, and the process of restoration and rebuilding began again.

Because restoration occurred with such unvarying regularity, one might have expected it to occur once again when the authority of the Qing dynasty began to wane in the mid-nineteenth century. How do we explain the fact that the Qing was replaced, when it finally collapsed in 1911, not with another dynastic cycle but with a long, intensely painful period of linear change—a period that has yet to draw to a close?

One very important feature of China in the nineteenth century that had not been an issue at the time of other dynastic nadirs was the size of the population, for its population growth rate had remained constant and very low for centuries. Estimates of the population in early times are, naturally, subject to large errors, but historians generally agree that the population in the Han dynasty (at the beginning of the Common Era) reached about 60 million people; a thousand years later, at the time of the Song dynasty, it passed 100 million; and five hundred years thereafter, in the middle years of the Ming dynasty, it stood at perhaps 150 million. During the course of the Qing dynasty, which ascended to the throne in 1644, China's population roughly trebled, and it stood at close to 450 million by the late nineteenth century.

Historians attribute this population surge from the mid-seventeenth to the mid-nineteenth centuries, which mirrors a growth in world population during the same period, to advances in agricultural techniques that permitted higher yields from the land. It had to do as well with the introduction of new crops, including corn, the sweet potato, and the peanut. Whatever the cause, the result of this extraordinary spurt of growth was that China's population quickly exceeded the capacity of the land to produce an adequate food supply; the development of a transportation network lagged far behind the growing population, and a food shortage in one area could not easily be relieved by shifting surpluses from another.

A second new factor was a series of steps taken by the throne to put down a virulent rebellion that came very close to overthrowing the dynasty. Rebels, led by a group claiming to have Christian connections, proposed to replace the Manchu dynasty with a "heavenly kingdom of great peace." So serious was the threat from these Taiping rebels that the throne agreed to undo the careful separation of political, economic, and military power that had given China such remarkable stability. Responding to the demands of a capable general, Zeng Guofan, the throne agreed to suspend the law of avoidance and the prohibition on mounting a permanent military force under local command. Zeng Guofan succeeded in defeating the Taiping threat but in the process became the first in a long sequence of local warlords who held full political, economic, and military authority over a discrete piece of Chinese territory.

A third factor in the nineteenth century was the arrival on China's shores of Western powers intent on opening it up as a source of raw materials, labor power, and new markets, and using weapons and technology that gave them significant advantages over their Chinese adversaries. The defeat of the defending forces time and time again at the hands of foreign powers discredited the central government, reminding its subjects of the foreign origins of the Manchus and sapping their authority.

Along with their guns, and later their railroads and factories, Westerners brought their ideas. The first response of Chinese intellectuals was to accept the guns, railroads, and factories and reject the ideas—the scientific and philosophical systems—that had given rise to them. Maintaining a "Chinese essence" while borrowing "practical things" from the West was a last-ditch defensive stance against the threat of wholesale Westernization. It was quickly overwhelmed, and Western ideas about social and political relationships soon damaged the credibility of the Confucian canon to the point that it could no longer serve to underpin the mounting of a new dynasty and the restoration of the old order. Instead, restoration gave way to a long, intensely painful process of revolution.

The uniquely long history of Chinese civilization is looked on by most Chinese as a source of great pride. Much effort was expended in an attempt to preserve this heritage in the face of changes encountered as China has entered the modern world. But more and more, others in China look on themselves and their compatriots not as enriched but rather as imprisoned by China's past. Perhaps the most vivid version of this counterview was a film series aired on Chinese television in the summer of 1988 titled *He Shang* (River elegy, or River dirge), which used familiar images from China's past—the Yellow River, the Great Wall, the dragon—to symbolize the restrictions and limitations imposed by tradition and juxtaposed these earth-tone images with that of the blue Pacific, symbolizing the freedom of the outside world. Only by looking beyond China and its past to the world outside, the series said, could the restrictions of that past be overcome and the country's great potential realized. Even those Chinese who agreed with the film's premises found the starkness of the images disturbing, and those who disagreed were vitriolic in their condemnation of such an attack on China's splendid past.

III

CHINA'S POLITICAL SYSTEM:
THE PARTY-STATE AND THE POWER GRID

AMERICANS LIKE TO THINK of the Chinese political system as the opposite of the U.S. system. Ours is a democracy; theirs is authoritarian or even totalitarian. Ours is a rule of law, theirs a rule of men. Ours protects the rights of the individual; theirs regularly infringes on these rights. In some instances, these generalizations are supported by strong evidence, but in others, they obscure similarities and common problems. In still others, they fail to take account of the substantial changes that have occurred in the past twenty years. But in each instance, the comparison is made between an American ideal (often very different from American practice) and Chinese practice (often falling far short of Chinese ideals).

When, as students, Americans learn about their political system, they are taught to think about four relationships: that among the executive, legislative, and judiciary branches of government; that between the federal government and state and local governments; that between political parties and the government; and that between civilian and military authority. Civics texts refer to the system of checks and balances that governs and regulates the relationship among the three branches of the federal government, designed to prevent any one from assuming an inappropriate ascendancy over the others. Laid out in our Constitution, these checks and balances have been elaborated and refined over time, with the three branches pulling and tugging, each trying to influence the other two.

The relationship between the federal government and state and local governments is still in flux. The idea of states' rights is an active political rallying point, reminding us that local governments existed before the federal one, which was created through an agreement reached among them. The terms of that agreement, spelled out in detail in the Constitution, include the important provision that what is not specifically set out as the prerogative of the federal government remains that of the states. Two hundred and more years of practice, a range of issues inconceivable to the framers of the Constitution, and the addition of thirty-seven new states have all served to modify the balance between federal and local power.

The relationships between our political parties and the government and between (or among) the political parties themselves postdate the framing of the Constitution, and custom more than law regulates them. Though there is an ideological core in each of the two major parties, they are not particularly ideological and play to the middle when they are out to win elections. Also, they are not selective: voters are free to choose (and to change) their party affiliation or to participate in the electoral process as independents. Each party tries to control the government by getting its candidates elected to the presidency or to a majority in Congress, but its ability to do so is limited by the actions of the opposition party. The existence of a vital opposition is critical to our definition of an effectively functioning democracy.

As for the relationship between civilian and military authority, we accept that our system is based on the principle that military forces must always be subordinate to civilian leadership. So ingrained is this idea in our political process that although we go through periodic bouts of concern over military spending or over the influence of the Pentagon on our foreign policy, intervention by our armed forces into our political life has never been a serious threat.

Considering these four relationships in the Chinese political system, we find similarities—many superficial—and profound differences. China's political system has three branches—a legislature, an executive branch, and a judiciary—but in practice there are really two, since the Chinese judiciary functions more as a department of the executive than as an independent check on the other two arms of the government. Similarly, the legislature has only very recently come to see itself as a potential check on the operations of the executive branch and the judiciary. The branches are not equal partners, and there is no provision in the Chinese constitution for checks and balances to maintain an equality. Indeed, the constitution itself and its function in the political system reveal perhaps the most important differences between the two systems. China has had five constitutions since the People's Republic was founded in 1949, and the document is probably best understood as a mission statement or policy platform with a finite duration. It was not intended, nor does it function, as a set of fixed principles against which specific laws and practices are measured and overturned if found to be at odds.

In general, the Chinese system relies much less on relationships fixed by law, constitutional provisions, or regulation. Rather, negotiated relationships between and among individuals and organizations dominate the political landscape—which helps to account for the very different relation between the national government and regional and local governments. China's is not a federal system, and the central government deals with provincial and municipal governments by means of myriad ad hoc agreements made after complex bargaining negotiations.

In practice, the center-local relationship is a power grid in which the vertical elements are the bureaucratic departments of the central systems and the horizontal elements are the provinces and cities. In many if not most instances, the vertical and horizontal elements work at cross purposes, stymieing rather than facilitating political activity.

The most important difference between the American and the Chinese political system concerns political parties. The key function of setting government policy in China since 1949 lies outside the government entirely and is monopolized by the Chinese Communist Party (CCP). There is no interaction among or between political parties, for the CCP succeeded long ago in eliminating its rivals and has effectively prevented the emergence of any force that could even begin to be a nucleus for political opposition. Indeed, most recently, more than a dozen individuals in cities across the country were given prison sentences of up to thirteen years for their roles in attempting to organize and register a new China Democratic Party.

A selective organization, the CCP chooses its members on the basis of their suitability for leadership in its political life. One in every twenty Chinese are Party members, for a total membership of about sixty million. (In contrast, roughly one in every two Americans is registered with a political party, and the total party affiliation is roughly double the size of the CCP.) Functioning somewhat like a board of directors for the country, the CCP defines its function as that of making all the critical decisions, which the government must then carry out. Unlike a board of directors, however, the CCP has created an organizational structure operating in parallel to that of the government bureaucracy, so that Party members oversee the work of the bureaucrats at every level.

With respect to the relationship between military and civilian authorities, there are, once again, substantial differences between the two political systems. Like the United States' Founding Fathers, the leaders of the newly formed Chinese state in 1949 had been active in the revolution that brought them to power, but unlike our Founding Fathers, the Chinese revolutionaries were slow to distinguish between military and civilian authority. The blurring of the lines was especially acute in regional and provincial governments, where, in most cases, the officer who had "liberated" an area stayed on as head of the new government.

As military and civilian authority gradually became differentiated, the Party continued to exert control over the army in the same way that it exerted control over the government bureaucracy. Twice, though, as we shall see, it found itself obliged to call on the army to intervene on its behalf in civilian affairs, in the aftermath of which the armed forces retained a hand in political decision making.

Today, because of the effectiveness of the Party's efforts to eliminate any organization that might challenge its monopoly on political

life, the People's Liberation Army (PLA) is the only organization in
China with a nationwide reach that can pick up the pieces if the
CCP should falter. For all these reasons, any account of the power
grid in China must include a careful look at the PLA.

The Party likes to think of itself, ideally speaking, as an elite organization that selects its members from the best that Chinese society has
to offer. Selection criteria have changed over the years, but political
correctness—a knowledge of the current line and an ability to apply
it to day-to-day decisions—has been a constant despite many changes
in the current line. Currently the Party also emphasizes technical
competence, managerial skills, and entrepreneurial ability. Its legitimacy is based on its monopoly of these desirable leadership qualities
and of the policies that derive from them.

But the reality is quite different. Although Party membership is at
an all-time high, members are unequally distributed among the population, with a substantially heavier concentration in the city and a
sparser concentration in rural communities. Moreover, the Party is
having difficulty attracting China's best and brightest. Although it is
true that for every thirteen individuals who apply for Party membership, only one is accepted, the quality of the applicant pool is not
what the Party would like it to be. There also is evidence that the applicant pool is artificially inflated: individuals who have no intention
of accepting an offer of Party membership are induced to apply to
fulfill their employer's quota. Party membership is no longer the exclusive avenue of upward mobility. An ambitious young Chinese
with imperfectly developed entrepreneurial skills and business contacts can get a leg up in career advancement by joining the Party,
thereby acquiring political clout that might be translated into economic gain. But for those with a full set of skills and contacts, Party
membership is superfluous, and the CCP does not attract the most
successful of China's young entrepreneurs.

But this should be no surprise, because the Party's political authority has been progressively undermined over the last forty years by

the irrationality of its policies, the corruption of its leaders, and its failure to put forward a compelling vision for China's future. It came to power in 1949 with a reputation for honesty and a promise to end inflation. It set up a government that contrasted with its predecessor's in its dedication and in its young officials' freedom from corruption. Inflation had been brought under control by 1952, and prices remained quite flat for thirty years. The substantial changes brought about in Chinese society and economy in the first years of the CCP regime appeared reasonable to most Chinese people and helped to improve the welfare of the vast majority.

Within a decade, however, people began to question the probity of the Party's leaders. The Hundred Flowers Campaign was the first of a number of events that undermined the Party's legitimacy. Confident of its achievements and its reputation, the Party called in 1957 for criticisms of its first eight years in power: "Let a hundred flowers bloom!" Mao cried. The attacks on those who responded to this invitation—imprisonment and forced labor for thousands of so-called Rightists—seemed irrational and out of proportion. Then the further excesses of the Great Leap Forward in 1958 and the destructive anarchy of the Cultural Revolution thereafter took even more of a toll on popular confidence in Party leaders.

One would assume that the considerable successes of the economic reforms undertaken after Mao's death would have restored at least some of the Party's lost legitimacy. Interestingly, this does not seem to be the case. The Party is not given credit for the transformation of the Chinese economy and its subsequent rapid growth, perhaps because they are the results of the effective abandonment of the Marxist-Leninist principles on which the Party rests. At best, the Party is credited with stepping out of the way and giving people with entrepreneurial skills free rein.

Paradoxically, it is not what has happened in China but rather what has happened in Russia that has bolstered the CCP's somewhat shaky position. Many Chinese people see the economic chaos and near anarchy of Russian society today as resulting from the collapse

of the Communist Party in the Soviet Union; to avoid the same outcome in China, they are willing to put up with a corrupt and discredited Party.

According to the textbook description of the relationship between
the Party and the government in the Chinese political system, the
Party proposes and the government disposes; the Party makes policy,
and the government carries it out. In real organizations, things seldom function according to the textbook, and the line separating policy making from policy implementation is often difficult to draw.
Certainly, the reality of the relationship between the Party and the
government in China shows this confusion, since all the key Party
leaders also occupy senior positions in the government. Decision
making is monopolized by a handful of powerful individuals; although the Party's constitution provides that the Party Congress is responsible for setting political policy, in fact that authority rests with a
half dozen or so Party leaders who, at any given time, are members of
the Standing Committee of the Political Bureau of the Party's Central Committee. In the recent past, even this small group had to refer all major decisions to retired elder statesmen, notably to Deng
Xiaoping as the primus inter pares of that group.

The Party has two means for ensuring that its policies are implemented by government officials. First, it has the power of appointment, since at each government level appointments are the
responsibility of the Party organization at the level just above.
(Provincial officials are appointed by the Central Party organization;
provincial Party organizations, in turn, appoint officials at the county
and city level.) Second, the performance of officials appointed by the
Party is then monitored by Party organizations. In organizations and
enterprises at each level of the government, a Party committee monitors political correctness and ensures that policies are carried out. It is
thus next to impossible to separate the roles of policy making and
policy implementation.

During the early 1980s, the goal of the political reform movement
that went hand in hand with economic reform was to address and
rectify this situation. Party and government were to be separated

and double-hatting eliminated wherever possible. The functions of and relations between the two structures were to be clarified, with the government acting independently in day-to-day affairs and the Party confining itself to broad policy making. But these efforts at reform came to an abrupt halt in 1989 when, in violation not only of the principles governing Party-government relations but also of Party rules for decision making and discipline, Deng Xiaoping moved from behind the scenes to mobilize support for the declaration of martial law in Beijing and, subsequently, to use the army to clear demonstrators from its streets.

Several factors have conspired to keep the reform effort on hold since then: the siege mentality brought on by the domestic and international reaction to the massacre in Tiananmen Square; the mounting concern over the imminent passing of the elders responsible for that episode; and the lessons drawn by Party leaders from the collapse of communist parties in Eastern Europe and the Soviet Union. Indeed, the principal task since 1989 has been to maintain Party control at all costs.

The CCP's dominance of China's political system has led many observers to favor the term "Party-state." It seems useless to try to distinguish Party from government when the government is so lacking in independent authority. And many in China agree, finding it futile to draw distinctions when they are so blurred in practice. On the other hand, some in China have begun to demand that the rule of law be extended and that the Party and its leaders be subject to it, which implies the idea that the blurring of functions is inappropriate. Indeed, one could argue that a strong state, operating with an effective legal system and set on eliminating political corruption, would have significantly greater legitimacy than the Party currently enjoys. But until that goal of eradicating corruption is addressed effectively, it makes sense to continue to use the term "Party-state" to describe China's system.

The executive branch of the Chinese government is headed by the State Council, a cabinet, whose members are the heads of the twenty-nine commissions and ministries that make up the 4.5-million-strong central bureaucracy. The focus of most of the ministries and commissions is the economy, its reform, and its relations with the world economy. There are, in addition, ministries devoted to noneconomic issues, such as public health and foreign affairs. In principle, commissions have a more comprehensive function than ministries, and some are intended to coordinate the work of several ministries.

Each ministry or commission stands at the top of a system of bureaus and offices located in provincial capitals and county seats. In all there are probably some ten million bureaucrats in these vertical systems, each of which has a specialized function, overseeing a narrow sector of the economy or society. The smooth operation of these vertical systems is complicated by the fact that bureaus and offices of central ministries and commissions report not only to them but also to the local government of which they form a part. The Shanghai education bureau, for example, reports both to the Shanghai municipal government and to the Ministry of Education in Beijing: its staff appointments are made by the latter, but its budget is set by the former. When push comes to shove, the interests of the local government often take precedence over those of the central ministry or commission.

In theory, communication flows smoothly and regularly up and down each system. Communication between systems, however, is often difficult or impossible to arrange except at the uppermost reaches. A construction project in a county seat, for example, requires the approval of a number of local bureaus of different systems, and the project manager will find it hard to get officials in one to talk to those in others; it seems much more effective to refer the question up one or two levels in the bureaucracy—in some cases, even as far as the central government itself—where differences between systems can be hashed out and approvals coordinated.

China's unicameral legislature, the National People's Congress (NPC), is routinely described in the Western press as a rubber-stamp parliament. In fact, until very recently, every proposal initiated by the

Party and drafted by the executive branch was given unanimous approval by the three-thousand-odd delegates to the NPC at their annual meetings in March. This led observers (and presumably many of the delegates as well) to wonder what purpose was served by their being regularly called together.

Early in his career, Mao was a great believer in citizen initiative. Defining what he called the "mass line," he said that correct ideas originate among the people, ideas that are then refined by those with a full command of and adherence to ideological principles. These refined ideas, now policies, must then be taken back and explained to the people, who were their original inspiration. So legislatures in the Chinese political system embodied this principle. Congressional meetings gave leaders the chance to hear what delegates had to say, and delegates, in turn, could have policies explained to them by the central authorities. Rather than a group of representatives brought together to *initiate* laws and policies, the NPC was conceived of as a group of representatives who would *learn about* laws and policies. While this exercise may have been educational, it was certainly not legislative in the sense we use the term in our own political arena.

Delegates to the NPC now seem less and less willing to accede to this narrow definition of their function. Since the early days of the post-Mao reform period, the NPC, through its Standing Committee, has actively participated in drafting the new laws needed to introduce a full-blown legal code for Chinese society. Increasingly, they have taken to speaking out during NPC meetings, and at their 1998 session, close to half of them abstained or cast negative votes—once an unheard-of act of defiance—to express their disapproval of the government's handling of the mounting crime rate. Although these are important steps in the development of an independent legislature, one should not overemphasize the progress made to date. Casting a vote against a government minister's annual report or against the candidacy of a new vice premier is a far cry from having routine oversight and comprehensive budgetary control over the work of the executive branch of the government.

Delegates to the NPC are elected to five-year terms but not directly by the constituents whom they represent. The process is indirect: delegates to people's congresses at the city or county level are directly elected by constituents, and in addition to these, congress delegates are selected to represent local organizations and interest groups; these local congresses elect delegates to provincial congresses; and delegates to the NPC are elected by these provincial congresses or by national organizations and interest groups.

The trend of legislators' taking their jobs seriously affects congresses at all levels. Indeed, delegates to local congresses, who are in frequent face-to-face contact with their constituents, are even more serious than their national counterparts about securing the initiative in local political battles. In this connection, a precedent was set in the fall of 1999, when the Guangdong Provincial People's Congress became the first legislative body in China to hold a public hearing on a piece of proposed legislation.

China's judicial system was not intended to serve as a check or a balance on the bureaucracy or legislature, nor does it so function. Its principal purpose is to serve as part of the apparatus of social control, alongside the police and the prosecutors' offices. Substantial changes were made to the criminal procedure law effective at the beginning of 1997. Before that, criminal cases were not brought to trial until the defendant had been proven guilty to the satisfaction of the court and the prosecutor, who worked closely together in investigating crimes. At trials, evidence was heard, and a panel of judges, some of them drawn from the local community, rendered its decision. Only at this point did the defense make its case, which was generally limited to presenting evidence in mitigation prior to sentencing. The new procedures have introduced the presumption of the defendant's innocence until proven guilty and have enhanced the role of the defense lawyer in criminal trials. Now, as before, the public is encouraged to attend most court proceedings, which are intended to provide uplifting lessons in civic behavior.

Verdicts are subject to appeal, and the Supreme People's Court is the final court of appeal. It is not the function of the Supreme People's Court or of any lower court, however, to rule on the constitutionality of the law violated by the defendant in the case. Hence, the court cannot serve as a check on the work of the government or legislature. The court system's principal function is, rather, to apply policies, laws, and regulations to specific cases.

China is divided into several regional systems. The seven military regions are features of the military command structure with no equivalent in civilian affairs, where the pyramid goes from the top—the central government headquartered in Beijing—to the provinces. There are thirty-one governments at the provincial level (thirty-two if one chooses, as does the government in Beijing, to regard Taiwan as a province), twenty-two of which are provinces; four city governments (Beijing, Tianjin, Chongqing, and Shanghai); and five "autonomous regions." Autonomous regions are province-like units, the population of which includes substantial numbers of non-Han people (there are also smaller "autonomous" units within several provinces), but these ethnic minorities' autonomy from central control is largely fictive. Most of their local officials are drawn from the minority populations, the minority languages are used in government and education, and the populations are exempt from the one-child policy. On the other hand, though the ethnic-minority population as a whole is quite small, the autonomous regions are strategically located, many of them contain important deposits of oil and minerals, and Beijing worries about ethnic ties that cross China's national boundaries. So, many Han people have been moved into the autonomous regions, the regions are heavily garrisoned by the PLA, members of the ethnic-minority elites are brought into China's central and coastal provinces for schooling in political orthodoxy, and Beijing is quick to suppress any expressions of genuine autonomy.

Provinces are divided into counties and cities. The average Chinese county, of which there are approximately two thousand, is about a third larger than the average American county, of which there are approximately three thousand. Counties in China are administered from a county seat and are divided into townships, each of which is made up of a number of villages. The cities are similarly divided into districts, and districts into neighborhoods.

At the lowest level of the political system is the *danwei*, usually translated as "unit." In its heyday in the 1960s, the unit was a key element in the CCP's system of social control, and virtually every Chinese person was affiliated with a unit. The workplace was the unit for fully employed people; the school, for students; the neighborhood, for the unemployed. The unit was supposedly nurturing: its function was to provide for all the needs of its members. But it was also the job of the unit to keep tabs on the lives of its members, and files on unit members contain biographical data, employment history, criminal records, and information on political attitudes. Moving from one unit to another almost never happened, and when it did, approval in advance from both the old and the new unit was required, and the person's file was transferred as well.

With the gradual emergence of a labor market, more and more Chinese find themselves cut loose from both the support and the watchful eyes of their units. Today 100 million or so floating workers are not affiliated with units, nor are the approximately 25 million who work in the private sector. Even those who remain formally enrolled in a unit find that it is much less encompassing than it once was. The weakening of the *danwei* system is a major reason for most Chinese feeling that their government is less intrusive in their daily lives than it once was.

There is no formal division of authority between the center and the provinces or between the provinces and their counties and cities. Instead, the relationship among central, provincial, and local governments is thrashed out in case-by-case agreements that are subject to renegotiation as conditions and needs change.

In theory, certain powers are vested in the superior level over its subordinates. The most important among these is the power to appoint and dismiss officials. Here the dilemma for the central authorities is analogous to that confronted by the throne in earlier times: an outsider in a given locality is more likely to be loyal to the central-government officials who appointed him but less likely to have the connections that will make him effective in office, while the reverse is true of a local person.

Second, the government at each level reserves the power to draw up budgets and levy taxes in its subordinate units. The central government determines what is taxed, the rate at which it will be taxed, the proportion of tax revenue that will go to the provinces, and the government expenditures for which local authorities will be responsible. Provincial governments do the same for counties and cities under their jurisdiction.

Third, the central government reserves the power to allocate and redistribute resources among the provinces; provincial governments do the same for counties and cities. Certain key resources—energy important among them—are allocated in this way. Governments in well-off provinces are taxed to help less-well-off regions. This Robin Hood function of the central authorities was used most actively under Mao Zedong, among whose first principles was that of equality of opportunity for rich and poor regions of China.

Local governments, on the other hand, are not without resources of their own. First, they have the choice of cooperating with or making life impossible for appointed officials. Second, though the central government levies taxes and determines the distribution of revenues, until very recently local authorities actually collected the taxes and forwarded a portion to the central government.

Third, and most important, local officials can thwart central directives by inaction. When local officials engage in this tactic, China's power grid experiences gridlock. As those who have had dealings with Chinese bureaucrats know, no phrase comes quite so quickly to a bureaucrat's lips as *kaolu yixiazi* ("I'll have to look into that a bit") or *yanjiu yanjiu* ("That needs some further study"). As we shall see presently, the bureaucratic style favored by the Chinese tends to result in a glacial pace of decision making and execution.

Writing in the middle of the Chinese Communist revolution and the war against Japan, Mao described the relationship between military power and political power: "Political power grows out of the barrel of a gun, [but] our principle is that the Party commands the gun and the gun must never be allowed to command the Party." Control of the People's Liberation Army in China today rests in the hands of the Party's Central Military Commission, under which the Ministry of National Defense exercises operational and administrative control.

The Ministry's General Staff Department has operational command over the approximately three million active-duty troops via seven military regional commanders. Administrative command is exercised by the General Logistics Department. The General Armaments Department is responsible for weapons development and procurement. Finally, the General Political Department stations political officers at each level of command to ensure that "the Party commands the gun."

This relationship among Party, government, and Army fundamentally altered on two occasions. At the height of Red Guard activity during the Cultural Revolution, the situation became anarchic, with both Party and government under attack and in no position to restore order; the PLA restored order and then set up and continued to participate in new political structures—revolutionary committees, as they were called. The year 1969 marked an apex of military involvement in China's political system, with military officers exercising political control at every level of the system, including the Party's Central Committee. Some officers no doubt enjoyed their foray into politics and were reluctant to return to their barracks when, in the early 1970s, the regime tried to demilitarize the political system. But many others were eager to relinquish their political responsibilities, realizing that they were discharged at the expense of military readiness: China's poor showing in a border war with Vietnam in 1979 proved their point.

In a second moment of Party weakness during two incidents of civil unrest in 1989, the armed forces again intervened in the political realm. In Lhasa in March, when Tibetans demonstrated against Chinese control of their region, which had been complete since 1951, and interference with their religious practices, the Army put down the demonstrations and martial law was declared. Two months later, Party officials, unable to respond effectively to the challenge posed by massive numbers of students and workers occupying the streets and central square of Beijing, once again asked the Army to intervene. But the military involvement in politics that had followed the earlier episode was not repeated in the 1989 aftermath; the only evidence of a shift in the balance of power was in the military budget, which increased significantly each year thereafter. Today, however, many of China's neighbors are concerned about evidence of Chinese military expansionism and believe that the PLA and not the Foreign Ministry is calling the shots in China's foreign policy. They attribute the Party's inability to control the PLA to its indebtedness to and continuing dependence on it.

This, then, is the grid of political power in China: imperfectly formed branches of government with significantly unequal power and with no effective balance or check on one another. Within the bureaucracy, the highly specialized and vertically structured departments are incapable of communicating with one another easily. Meanwhile, the crosshatched horizontal elements of the grid— provinces, counties, and cities—though unable to defy the central government openly for long, can at least stick wrenches in its wheels and stall forward movement. Overlaying everything, and active at each node, is the Party, which regularly oversteps its bounds, lacks the confidence of the people, and is utterly unwilling to submit itself to criticism, opposition, or legal regulation. Finally, waiting in the wings, a highly patriotic army may find itself, *faute de mieux*, holding China together if political authority collapses.

Four characteristics of the political process in China are especially to be noted: consensus, bargaining, networking, and saving face.

Americans seem very comfortable with a simple majority— whether in a Supreme Court decision, a vote in Congress, or a local referendum on a school budget. Although as individuals we may not be satisfied with a given outcome, we tend to regard it as legitimate if a majority has decided it. The Chinese vastly prefer consensus to a simple majority, and they prefer that this consensus be achieved at the lowest possible level in the political hierarchy: if one level finds it impossible to reach a consensus, the decision is bumped up to the next level. Although strategies for building consensus are much the same as those for building a majority, it usually takes longer.

Bargaining is an almost universal characteristic of political interactions. In American political life, bargaining usually focuses on issues that will have to be voted on: "I need your vote and this is what I'm prepared to do to get it." In the Chinese context, where voting is less common than consensus building, bargaining is more diffuse: "I will be more inclined to lend you my support on your issue if you agree to lend me your support on mine." Given the scarcity of goods and an imperfectly developed market, exchanges of goods and services as well as support are also subject to political bargaining. Political bargainers in China pay careful attention to their relative rank and status, which affect both the process and the outcome. Political transactions often seem to be conducted with all the attention to protocol of an ambassadorial dinner party or a military change-of-command ceremony, and politicians seem to relish the bargaining. Case-by-case bargaining is almost always preferable in China to applying a uniform rule to every case.

Networking, too, a practice common in both American and Chinese political contexts, is vitally important. Businesspeople new to China are taught the word *guanxi* (relationships), as though it were a powerful mantra unique to the Chinese setting. But "whom do I know who can . . ." is a formula that springs as quickly to the mind of a Westerner as it does to that of a Chinese. The difference is the degree to which it is appropriate to be proactive: a skillful practitioner of *guanxi* actively cultivates relationships that might be helpful at some unknown point in the future. Westerners may look on someone who does them an unbidden favor with some suspicion, but a Chinese person is likely to greet the unbidden favor without surprise and to assume that a request for a quid pro quo cannot be far behind.

Students of the Chinese psyche conclude that Chinese people

have a greater aversion to conflict and disorder than do Americans. And it is unquestionably true that finding oneself shamed in public — losing face — is for a Chinese person an experience to be avoided if at all possible. Because open conflict is likely to result in loss of face for one of the parties, passive resistance accompanied by a perfectly opaque demeanor is the weapon of choice for the conflict-averse Chinese.

As a result of all these characteristics, the political process in China may often seem agonizingly slow and mystifyingly obscure to Westerners. Americans have a reputation for being blunt and impatient even among Europeans; it is no wonder they find it hard to make sense of Chinese bureaucrats.

The Chinese political system, then, far from being the well-oiled totalitarian machine it was once reputed to be, is a highly complex and inefficient structure that tends to thwart much more than foster effective governance. The central authority is meant to be ascendant over regional authority, and Party authority is meant to be ascendant over government authority, yet the system operates with a substantially weakened central authority and a party whose power and legitimacy are seriously eroded. Unless it changes significantly, the system will continue to lack the capacity to address and resolve the many serious problems confronting it.

IV

CHINA'S ECONOMY:
WHO OWNS WHAT, WHO WORKS WHERE,
AND WHO MAKES THE DECISIONS

IN THE EARLY 1960s, an ideological controversy erupted into public view after simmering bitterly within international communist circles for years. A year before he was overthrown, Soviet premier Nikita Khrushchev scoffed at his erstwhile Chinese allies' view of communism:

> To follow their line of thinking, it transpires that if a people walks in rope sandals and eats watery soup out of a common bowl that is communism, and if a working man lives well and wants to live even better tomorrow that is almost tantamount to the restoration of capitalism!

Mao Zedong denounced Khrushchev as a proponent of what he sneeringly labeled "goulash communism."

Twenty years later, however, Deng Xiaoping struck a remarkably Khrushchev-like note when he described the rationale behind his economic reforms:

> Socialism means eliminating poverty. Pauperism is not socialism, still less communism. The superiority of the socialist system lies above all in its ability to develop the productive forces and to improve the people's material and cultural life.

Deng's first priority was to reform the Chinese economy so as to improve the standard of living. A second priority, always at a significant distance from the first, was to reform the political system. He was not an ideologue. He often sounded more like an American pragmatist than a Chinese revolutionary. His approach is encapsulated in his comment "It does not matter whether the cat is white or black; if it catches mice it is a good cat." During the Cultural Revolution, the regime denounced him as one of those who would abandon socialist goals and take China "down the capitalist road." Still needing to protect himself against such charges when he returned to a position of authority in 1977, he enunciated what he called his "four cardinal principles." They were, he said, the irreducible nucleus of what had been the full-blown (some might well argue overblown) ideology of his predecessor, Mao: any reform measure was acceptable so long as it did not call into question the leadership of the Communist Party, the dictatorship of the proletariat, the correctness of Marxism-Leninism, or the goal of socialism.

In practice, Deng operated with just two principles that became, if anything, more fixed as he aged: reform measures were legitimate if they promoted rapid economic growth and if they did not weaken the Party's control of the political system; everything else was subject to compromise. This was particularly true with respect to the "socialism" of the fourth cardinal principle, which, in Deng's hands, became "socialism with Chinese characteristics."

As it exists today, "socialism with Chinese characteristics" is an economy moving rapidly and sometimes painfully from central planning to market decision making. It is an economy with a large but shrinking state-owned sector, a substantial and growing collective sector, and a rapidly burgeoning private sector. Liberal use has been made of capitalist methods to jump-start and then fuel truly remarkable growth since the reforms began.

The government is still the most important player in the Chinese economy, with about sixty thousand state-owned industrial enterprises employing a workforce approaching thirty million. These enterprises operate as small, semi-independent communities within China's cities, the largest including as many as a half million people if managers, workers, service personnel, dependents, and retirees are taken into account. These state-owned factories were once all directly controlled by one or another government ministry. In the mid-1950s, ownership of most of them was turned over to provincial or municipal governments. Management schemes for them have come and gone over the years. At certain points, the factory manager has been given decision-making responsibility; at other times, his authority has been eclipsed by that of the factory's Party secretary. Today, as a result of reforms initiated in the mid-1980s, the factory manager is usually under contract to produce a given level of profit for a fixed period of time.

Prior to the beginning of the reforms, all profits from all enterprises reverted to the government at year's end. In cases where the enterprise had a deficit rather than a profit, the deficit would be made up with a government subsidy. With the reforms, the remittance of profit was abandoned and replaced by taxes, the rates set so as to leave a portion of the profits with the enterprises, and managers were permitted some flexibility in deciding how after-tax profits should be distributed. At the same time, the subsidies to make up deficits were replaced with bank loans on which interest is charged.

The state sector also includes about two-thirds of China's wholesale distributors, two-fifths of the country's fourteen million retail outlets, and all but a handful of banks, schools, and hospitals. Most urban housing stock is owned and managed either by individual enterprises and units or by municipal governments. Finally, although the state sector is all but completely absent from the rural economy, about two-thousand-odd state farms employing some four million workers account for two million acres—about 2 percent of the total land under cultivation. These farms are mostly in remote areas where land is being reclaimed for cultivation and people are being resettled—in some instances for disciplinary reasons, in others to alter ethnic balances.

Despite the positive effects of the recent industrial reforms on productivity, the state sector is in trouble. So serious is the deterioration that many argue that a political and economic crisis will result if it is not immediately and effectively addressed. The state sector's share of industrial output is declining each year, slipping in 1993, for the first time in forty years, below 50 percent. Although figures vary, at least half, and probably closer to two-thirds, of the state-owned enterprises are operating at a loss. To avoid putting its workforce into the ranks of the jobless, the state is subsidizing these losses rather than allowing the enterprises to go bankrupt.

A collective enterprise, in Chinese parlance, is one owned and managed by the people who make up a *danwei*, a workplace or residential unit. Rural townships own the largest number of collective enterprises, but collectives are also found in schools, neighborhoods, and even army units. There are about twenty-five million collective enterprises in China, with a workforce of some 450 million people.

The business of the collective enterprise may be farming, manufacturing, transportation, or commerce. Resources are mobilized, the enterprise established, and the product produced and sold on the basis of decisions the group makes on its own. Members are also responsible for deciding how profits are to be divided—how much will be reinvested and how much distributed as compensation. Finally, they also decide how members are paid—whether on the basis of the amount of their initial investment, the level of their skills or expertise, the amount of work they do, or the difficulty of the tasks they perform.

In legal terms, title to the assets of a state-owned enterprise is vested in "the whole people"—all the citizens of the country (or province or city). Title to a collective's assets is vested in its members. The collective is licensed and taxed by the local government. It may or may not have business relations with state-owned enterprises, either buying its raw materials from or selling all or a portion of its product to them. In some cases, collectives have been formed within state-owned factories in order to diversify their product lines, to provide work for the underemployed, or to augment sagging profits. A more radical solution to the problem of losses in state-owned enterprises is to sell off a losing enterprise to its workers.

Virtually all agricultural production in China is collectively owned and managed, but reforms have rendered the collective nature of these arrangements ambiguous at best. The more than 95 percent of cultivable land in China that is not controlled by state farms is collectively owned by citizens of villages and townships where the land is located. The "household-responsibility system," initiated as one of Deng's first economic reforms in the late 1970s, called for leasing the right to use plots of this land to individual households according to a contract stipulating the amount of grain to be produced on the plots. Contracts were awarded on the basis of the household's probable ability to fulfill the terms given its size and its number of able-bodied workers. Everything produced on the leased plot over and above the contractual amount can be disposed of by the household as it wishes—sold to the state (ordinarily at a higher price than that received for the contracted grain), sold on the free market, or consumed by the family.

Contracts were initially signed for a one-year term. To encourage farmers to invest in improving the land, the terms were extended to three, five, fifteen, and, in some instances today, even fifty years. Contracts can be inherited, bought, and sold. With key decisions thus being made at the household level and with the distinction between use rights and ownership rights blurred as a result of the extension of contracts over long periods, the "collective" nature of this economic activity becomes attenuated indeed.

There are some twenty-six thousand townships in China. The average township has about 850 collective enterprises, 7 of which are involved in agricultural production, 275 or so in industrial production, 350 in the service sector, and the remainder in construction and transportation. In addition, just under two million collectively owned industrial enterprises are located in China's cities, and probably an equal number are engaged in service trades.

Although still small in terms both of number of workers or enterprises and of output, the private sector is the fastest growing part of the Chinese economy. Close to a million and a half private enterprises are located mostly in China's cities. They employ, on average, fewer than fifty workers each and hold less than forty thousand dollars in registered capital, though a few are much larger.

Also included in the private sector for statistical purposes are the more than 225,000 foreign joint ventures. By the end of 1998, the cumulative total of foreign investment in China had reached $250 billion, and, most significant, goods produced by foreign-invested firms accounted for more than 40 percent of China's exports.

Furniture, personal effects, and individual bank accounts are all privately owned by both rural and urban Chinese. In addition, rural residents own their own homes, though they have use rights, not title, to the land they live on.

As is shown in Table 3, about 70 percent of the Chinese population live in the countryside. Among these 910 million people, there is a workforce of about 580 million, up to 100 million of whom elect to seek temporary work in the city. Of the 480 million who remain in the countryside, close to 70 percent are employed in agriculture (including farming, forestry, fishing, and animal husbandry). These 325 million agricultural workers are almost all under contract in the household-responsibility system and are thus part of the collective sector. The remainder work on state-owned farms. There is a substantial surplus of labor in Chinese agriculture: it is estimated that at least 100 million workers could be redeployed with no reduction in agricultural output.

In part to absorb some of this surplus labor, in part to raise household income, and in part to boost the production of manufactured goods, reformers have actively encouraged opening up collective factories owned and managed by township and village governments. There are now nearly twenty million of these township and village enterprises (TVEs), employing a workforce of more than 125 million. They tend to be small outfits with low capitalization that are thrown together quickly with little or no regard for their ill effects on air and water.

The private sector in the countryside is less well developed than it is in the city. About seven million rural residents are employed in

Table 3
EMPLOYMENT IN CHINA

Total = 1.3 billion people

Urban
30% = 390 million

136 million workforce

State	**Private**	**Collective**	**Unemployed**
90 million	20 million	20 million	6 million
(Of which 30M superfluous)			(Official figure; actual number may be as high as 15–20 M)

Rural
70% = 910 million

580 million workforce

State	**Private and self-employed**	**Collective**	**Migrants**
5 million	45 million	430 million	100 million

Industry	Agriculture	Other
40 million	325 million	65 million
	(Of which 100M superfluous)	

	State	Private	Collective
Percent of employed workers (excluding migrants)	16	11	73
Percent of output	18	25	57
Rate of growth in 1999 (%)	7.9	12.5	8.2

(Source: *China Statistical Yearbook 1999*)

privately owned enterprises. Another thirty-eight million are self-employed, primarily in handicrafts and other sideline activities.

Many rural households find that it makes good economic sense to keep a hand in several sectors. Holding on to the farming contract means access to fresh food and a certain amount of security, but a household's income can be significantly augmented if one or more of its members works in a TVE or a privately owned enterprise and further augmented, with luck, if a family member moves to a city and finds a job as a day laborer in construction, transportation, or a service industry.

In real terms, rural income has increased nearly fivefold since the reforms began in 1978. This exceeds the threefold increase in urban incomes during the same period, but urban income is more than two and a half times greater than rural income, and, in terms of spending power, the gap between city and countryside is ever more pronounced and aggravating to rural residents. Moreover, rural amenities by no means match those available in the city: schools are poor, and the tuition, while reasonable enough, is an expense that many find onerous. Medical care is less accessible than it once was and has significantly increased in cost. Finally, because they are a part of the collective sector, very few rural residents are covered by retirement programs and must rely on their children to support them when they leave the workforce.

The remaining 390 million Chinese people are urban residents. About 136 million of them are in the workforce, and, according to official figures, 6 to 10 million are unemployed. About 65 percent of urban workers work in the state sector: 30 million in state-owned industrial enterprises, another 50 million in the commercial, construction, transportation, and service sectors, finance and banking, education, and health care, and approximately 10 million as government and Party bureaucrats. Among the many problems plaguing the state-owned industries is excess staff. Some estimates place the number of surplus workers in state-owned factories as high as 30 million.

Jobs in the state sector used to be much sought after because of good pay, excellent fringe benefits, and a tenure system that made it virtually impossible to be fired. Workers receive a wage based on an eight-grade scale set by the state; during the last fifteen years, wages have been augmented by bonuses designed to reward productivity and performance, though in practice they are often given to workers regardless of their output. In addition, state-sector employees receive heavily subsidized housing, health care, primary and secondary education for their children, stipends that help to offset living costs, and generous retirement packages. For most factory managers, coordinating this benefits package is as great a responsibility as overseeing the production process. In addition to supervising an assembly line, managers must also oversee schools, clinics, housing blocks, and retirement communities. Covering the costs of this generous benefits package has pushed many state-owned enterprises into the red.

Collective enterprises in China's cities employ about 20 million workers. The remaining 20 million work in the private sector, 3 million of them in foreign joint ventures. China's collective and private enterprises have considerable flexibility with respect to whom they hire or fire and how much they pay their workers, but most of these enterprises offer no fringe benefits, and when they do, it is much less than state enterprises offer. To attract qualified workers, they must offer higher wages. Because a nationwide social-security system has yet to be implemented, only state employees are guaranteed retirement incomes. Some of the most profitable collective and private enterprises offer retirement packages, but most do not.

In recent years, China's urban population has been augmented by nearly 30 percent with the arrival of as many as 100 million floating workers. Until the mid-1980s, moving from countryside to city was virtually impossible, given a rationing system initiated in 1959 that limited any person's access to necessities, such as grain, cooking oil, and cotton cloth. Every household had an officially registered residence, and ration coupons were issued at one's place of residence and could only be redeemed locally. When economic reform made these necessities available on the free market, the rationing system no longer worked as a means of controlling geographical mobility, and a small but rapidly expanding labor market was born in which enterprises can recruit freely and people can choose where they work.

Rural residents who go to China's cities in search of more lucrative employment tend to take the first jobs they find. Most employment is short-term, and, although quite high paying, there is no job security and, of course, no benefits package. Moreover, the floaters are not officially city residents and hence have no claim on public services. Because they cannot live in regular housing, most of them go to squatter settlements in the suburbs. If they fall ill, they must cover the costs of their own health care. Many of them have come to the city alone; those who bring their families cannot put their children in public schools. Their presence in the cities is tolerated because they are a relatively low-cost and obligation-free labor force for the burgeoning construction projects under way everywhere, but they are potentially disruptive.

In his pursuit of economic reform, Deng Xiaoping had an opponent with a great deal less faith in the virtues of market forces. Chen Yun, an advocate of the centrally planned economy, is famous for his description of the economic plan as a birdcage and the economy as a bird within the cage. Chen believed in enlarging the birdcage to allow the bird more room to move about, a pragmatic approach to economic problems that at key points in his career enabled him to help bring China back from the brink of economic disaster. Still, it would never have been acceptable from Chen's point of view to open the door of the cage and allow the bird to fly free.

Chen's influence was at its height during the 1950s, at which time the Chinese economy, like the Soviet one after which it was modeled, operated under a comprehensive plan. In any economy, decisions have to be made about how national resources—land, raw materials, labor, and capital—are allocated. In an ideal market economy, these decisions are made on the basis of supply and demand; in an ideal planned economy, they are based on the plan.

The Chinese economy has never been wholly governed by plan,

in part because of a lack of experience and expertise, in part because of a lack of solid statistical data, in part because of a bias in favor of decentralized decision making, and in part because of a proclivity to throw the plan aside periodically in bursts of ideological fervor. Nonetheless, the State Planning Commission drew up annual, five-year, and in some cases ten-year economic plans embodying decisions about the allocation of national resources. Flexibility was limited by China's "givens." In 1949, with the triumph of communism, the new regime found itself with a reasonable resource base and a surplus of unskilled labor, but China had a shortage of land, capital, and skilled labor. Land, as a resource, was taken out of play in the plan, inasmuch as title to all of it was vested in either the state or the rural cooperatives and no rents were charged for it.

The principal focus of the plan was on state-owned industry, which, at the height of Chinese central planning in the late 1950s, accounted for nearly 90 percent of industrial output. The plan stipulated the amount of raw materials to be extracted and processed, the amount of energy to be generated, the amount of manufactured goods to be produced, the prices at which producer goods and products would be exchanged, the allocation and wages of the labor required to achieve these goals, and the amount and destination of investments. But agricultural production, too, was governed by national quotas, in turn divided into provincial, county, and, ultimately, commune or collective quotas: the prices at which quota grain was purchased and sold were determined by the plan; state-owned enterprises conducted the wholesale and retail trade.

Peasants also had private plots, on which they were allowed to grow goods for their own consumption or for sale on the rural free markets once they had fulfilled their obligations to produce for the state quotas. Handicrafts they produced as a sideline were either sold on the market or distributed through the collective. Rural free markets were subject to close regulation and during the high tide of the Great Leap Forward were shut down entirely.

Functioning on the margins of the economic plan were collective enterprises, which had gradually increased their share of industrial output from one-tenth to nearly one-quarter of the total by the late 1970s. The small private sector had been largely eliminated by the late 1950s and was reborn only after the reforms were launched.

A labor market was almost completely eliminated in China in the late 1950s. Skilled labor was scarce, and if their movement had not been subject to government regulation, workers would have bid up the cost of their services to unacceptable levels. Also, since unskilled labor was overly plentiful, particularly in the rural sector, and per capita income was consistently higher in the urban economy than in the rural one, free movement of labor would have resulted in a massive immigration of rural workers into the already crowded cities.

The shortage of skilled labor was addressed by expanding gradually the secondary and postsecondary training facilities for scientists, technicians, and skilled workers. Through a job-assignment system, graduates of these institutions were channeled into the state sector, where they were needed. Once assigned, employees were given what amounted to lifetime job security, but the quid pro quo was that lateral moves were virtually impossible to effect. Meanwhile the risk of urban in-migration by underemployed rural workers in search of higher pay was avoided by implementing the rationing system described above. Permission to shift one's household registration from the countryside to the city was almost never granted: where you were born was likely to be where you spent your life; where you began working was likely to be where you retired.

This centrally planned economy was by no means a total failure in its three decades from 1950 to 1980. In fact, economic performance in China was worst during the Great Leap Forward and the Cultural Revolution, when the plan was set aside and a campaign mentality replaced it. The economy grew at an average annual rate of 8.6 percent; industrial output led this growth with an average annual rate of 10 percent; agricultural output, growing more modestly, was outpaced by population growth. Still, the end result was an abysmally low per capita gross national product and a living standard that fell far short of the expectations aroused by promises of a bright socialist future. When he launched his program of economic reforms, Deng

Xiaoping proposed to expand that portion of the economy in which market forces were decisive while at the same time keeping the central plan for the state sector. He hoped that a vibrant, rapidly growing market-driven sector would, by its success, persuade his skeptical colleagues and potential successors of its merits.

Agriculture was the first to experience the introduction of market forces. Deng's household-responsibility system re-empowered the household, giving it the authority to decide how to use its labor and strong incentives to increase productivity. But prices and production quotas were still in government hands: like all commodities, grain had had a very low price, limiting the exposure of the government, which supplemented the urban population's income by selling grain below cost; without quotas, this low price would have encouraged farmers to turn to more lucrative crops.

There have been recent experiments with allowing the market to determine grain prices and allowing prices to determine the amount produced. But this strategy resulted in a very sharp rise in the price of grain—a more than 50 percent increase in 1994—that seriously exacerbated urban inflation. Regulating grain prices helps to reduce inflation, but overregulation undermines the incentive needed to increase grain production. Today more agricultural produce is traded on the free market than in state stores. Free market prices are higher, but the quality, supply, and variety of fresh meat and produce available to city dwellers have increased markedly over the last decade.

The success of the household-responsibility system in increasing agricultural output was useful to the reformers in building support for their efforts when they turned to China's cities. The straightforward solutions that had worked so successfully in the countryside were, however, ill-suited to the complex urban economy. Among the first reform steps was permission to revive the private sector. Very small privately owned enterprises in the service sector were the first to appear: food stands, tailor shops, cigarette vendors, and the like. These small businesses gave jobs to many people returning to the cities after having been sent to the countryside during the Cultural Revolution and provided goods and services that were unavailable in state-owned stores and restaurants. At first, there was a limit on the number of nonfamily members each business was permitted to hire, though exceptions were made where needs existed that were not being filled by state-owned enterprises. But soon there were a number of very large enterprises, some of them operating under the same name and management they had had thirty years before.

The collective sector was encouraged to expand as well. Workers in state-owned enterprises, schools, hospitals, and government offices were encouraged to form collectives that, because of their smaller size and greater flexibility, could develop new product lines, employment practices, and markets. Their immediate success promoted the merits of the market to otherwise conservative skeptics and encouraged them to explore the ways the state-owned businesses could take advantage of it.

By the mid-1980s, reform of the state-sector economy had begun in earnest. At this point, taxes replaced the remission of profits, and enterprise managers became responsible for their profits, losses, and investment decisions. These reforms were interrupted by the retrenchment measures taken to slow the overheated economy in 1988–1989; efforts to revive them in the early 1990s were hindered by mounting losses.

Meanwhile, the Chinese economy was being opened up to the outside world. Trade expanded rapidly, and the government actively encouraged foreign investment. China's experience in the world economy had been very limited, self-reliance having been a guiding principle and foreign trade having been closely controlled by the central government and confined, for the most part, to the socialist world. Although trade in the mid-1950s had amounted to nearly a quarter of China's national income, the proportion had sunk to a mere 6 percent by the end of the Cultural Revolution in 1970.

The "open policy" of the reform era called at first for substantial importation of technology, which would be funded by the export of oil. When China's oil reserves proved insufficient for this, and exploration and drilling operations too time-consuming, the strategy shifted to encouraging technology transfer through foreign invest-

ment in joint ventures; special economic zones were set aside where
preferential regulations were put in place to attract this investment,
the first four in Guangdong and Fujian Provinces in 1979; similar
arrangements were extended to fourteen coastal cities and to the island of Hainan five years later. (The most recent addition to the list
of zones and regions is the Pudong area in the city of Shanghai.) The
third stage in this process was a substantial expansion of production
for export, led by the foreign-invested industrial sector.

We can see, then, that the critical decisions about allocation of
land, raw materials, labor, and capital, once made by the Party-state
and incorporated in an economic plan, are being made, after more
than twenty years of reform, by the market. Contracts involving use
rights to agricultural land can now be bought and sold, so there is the
beginning of what amounts to a real-estate market in the countryside.
State-owned enterprises and governments in the cities are selling
housing stock to tenants to reduce the heavy burden of providing
subsidized housing. Use rights and sometimes title to land are also
involved in some joint-venture contracts. In the case of deficit-
producing state enterprises where the only attractive asset of value is
the land on which the factory is located, foreign investors, after signing a deal, level the factory buildings in order to put the land to more
profitable use. In effect, the state is raising capital by liquidating
some of its landholdings and, in the process, creating a real-estate
market for the first time in more than forty years.

The dual-allocation system for raw materials—a portion allocated
by the government, a portion allocated on the basis of supply and demand—has been dismantled, and today the market determines commodity allocation. Only a few key commodities—steel, coal, oil, and
electric power—are still allocated to state-owned enterprises, and
even here the prices, held artificially low to maximize industrial profits, are gradually being raised to the world-market level.

Price reform is of course a sensitive issue in an economy as vul-
nerable to the effects of inflation as China's. Nonetheless, 95 percent
of retail prices, 90 percent of agricultural prices, and 85 percent of
capital goods prices are now market determined, though when, in

the late 1980s and early 1990s, urban inflation got out of hand, the government stepped in to regulate food prices, since the price of food accounts for as much as half of the consumer price index.

The government has been reluctant to give up control of allocating labor, and a genuine labor market has been slow to develop. Nonetheless, decisions about movement in the workforce are much more likely to be made outside the government than they were twenty years ago. Though it is still very difficult for anyone to move from one job to another within the state sector (those with scarce skills or good performance records find their current employer reluctant to let them leave, and those without these qualifications are unlikely to find a new employer willing to agree to their transfer), many workers have chosen to leave the security of their state-sector position entirely and *xia hai*—plunge into the sea of private or collective enterprises. Of course one loses the benefits package, including access to housing, a health plan, and a retirement plan, but the advantages are higher salaries and greater freedom to change jobs or even residence.

Others seek to have the best of both worlds by keeping their state-sector position and taking a second job in the collective or private sector. Factory workers, many of them involuntarily placed on short hours or on furlough, find part- or full-time work in private or collective enterprises; doctors with positions in hospitals or medical schools take on private patients; government employees, capitalizing on their access and connections, set themselves up as business consultants, moving, sometimes with less than perfect precision, along the fine line that divides ethical practice from corruption. And this tendency to function in several sectors is as common in the countryside as it is in the city: moonlighting has so many advantages that it would not be surprising to find that most Chinese families today have more than one employer and a foot in more than one sector.

Capital allocation is the last decision to be opened up to market forces. As a part of the urban reforms, state-owned enterprises were to be weaned from their dependence on subsidies to cover deficits or to fund expansion: government funds would continue to be available

but only in the form of interest-bearing loans, for the eventual repay-
ment of which enterprises would be held accountable.

The subsequent poor performance of most of China's state-owned
enterprises and the government's unwillingness to suffer the political
consequences of adding the employees of bankrupt businesses to the
ranks of the disgruntled unemployed effectively rendered this reform
moot. Subsidies continued to flow into state-sector businesses. Nominally called loans, they accumulated as uncollectible assets in the
banking system, precluding more productive use of capital. In early
1999, these nonperforming loans amounted to 25 percent of the port-
folios of the four major state banks, according to official figures. According to foreign observers, the proportion was closer to 40 percent,
or $240 billion.

A reform of the banking system aimed at addressing this problem
was undertaken as early as 1993. Zhu Rongji, then serving as vice
premier, was dissatisfied with its implementation, dismissed the head
of the People's Bank of China, and temporarily took over its administration himself. The goals were to make the People's Bank of China a
central bank and to create a series of policy banks that would direct
the flow of credit away from speculative projects and toward projects
that would serve the development of the overall economy.

To address the problem of uncollectible loans in the system as a
whole, Zhu, now serving as premier, directed the formation of four
"asset management companies" beginning in early 1999, each of
them affiliated with one of the four major banks. Reminiscent of the
Resolution Trust Corporation (RTC) established by the U.S. government to address the collapse of the American savings and loan industry in 1989, the asset management companies trade debt for equity in
the borrowing firms. Just as the RTC worked to sell off the real estate
held by savings and loans as collateral against their nonperforming
loans, the asset management companies are attempting to recoup
their assets by the sale or restructuring of the deadbeat firms.

Although the RTC ultimately cost the U.S. government some
$450 billion, four times what was estimated at the outset, that figure
amounted to only about 6 percent of gross national product. Nonper-

forming loans in the Chinese banking system amount to a quarter of gross national product, result in the four major banks having a negative net worth, and, unless effectively addressed, threaten, in the words of one observer, "a lower pace of economic growth, a declining rate of job creation, and thus an even greater challenge to political stability."

What, exactly, is socialist about "socialism with Chinese characteristics," then? A cold-eyed response to the question would have to be "Not much at all." The elements most commonly associated with a socialist economy are public ownership of the principal means of production, economic activity largely determined by government decision as contained in an economic plan, a heavy dose of egalitarianism, and a high level of government attention to the welfare of the working population. All these elements are in the process of being dismantled in China under the current program of economic reform. And however negative the consequences, there is little likelihood that China will return to socialist solutions.

V

THE CHINESE ARMED FORCES

THE PEOPLE'S LIBERATION ARMY (PLA) is a major force in the Chinese economy, a potential participant in its politics, and a growing cause of concern to other nations in Asia.

The nominally civilian hand that controls the gun in China is that of the Central Military Commission. In the restructuring of the political system that occurred in the mid-1980s, it was anticipated that there would be both a Party and a government military commission—the one to oversee military policy, the other to implement it. But in fact there is a single seven-member Party commission, which was chaired by Deng Xiaoping himself until 1989, when he relinquished the position to Jiang Zemin. The commission hardly constitutes *civilian* control, given that all its members save Jiang Zemin are uniformed officers and include the minister of national defense.

Taking its orders directly from the Central Military Commission, the Ministry of National Defense is divided into four major departments: the General Staff Department, which has operational command of the three million active troops and takes responsibility for operational planning, intelligence, and procurement; the General Logistics Department, which is responsible for finance, supply, maintenance, and transport; the General Political Department, which ensures the political correctness of the military forces, drafts regulations, and runs personnel matters—assignment, promotion, and retirement; and, newly established in the spring of 1998, the General

Armaments Department, which is responsible for weapons development and procurement. In addition, there are a Discipline Inspection Commission and a Commission on Science, Technology, and
Industry for National Defense.

As in the civilian political structure, where provincial and local
government officials often thwart the implementation of directives issued by the central government, regional commanders and their subordinate garrison commanders often thwart the commands issued
by the central military authorities. In the first twenty-five years of the
People's Republic, the regional commanders were the generals
whose troops had been responsible for "liberating" the areas under
their command. Concurrently holding positions in local Party and
government organizations, they became well-connected fixtures, ad-
vantageously placed to implement, modify, or ignore central directives.

But this monopoly of local power was broken by Premier Zhou
Enlai, who shortly before his death in 1976 reassigned most of the regional commanders to new posts. Such reassignments have recurred
periodically since then, and they reduce the resources with which
the regional commanders are able to resist central directives, though
not their tendency to try to do so.

The PLA, including the army, navy, and air force, has a troop of
about 2.8 million men and women—about two-thirds of the force
level of the late 1970s, when the PLA had been increased in size in
anticipation of a 1979 border war with Vietnam. Since 1985, approximately a million and a half troops have been demobilized, returning
the Army to its pre-Vietnam size. This force is somewhat less than
twice the size of the U.S. military, which as of 1997 had about 1.5
million people in uniform. And beyond the uniformed personnel,
the Chinese military establishment includes about 4 million military
dependents and several million civilian employees and workers. Also,
the People's Armed Police (PAP), administered as a branch of the
PLA and having 1.8 million members, is the first line of defense in
the case of civil unrest. (It was because the PAP was so unsuccessful

at this in the spring of 1989 that the PLA was called in.) In the aftermath of the Tiananmen massacre, the PAP was strengthened substantially, its budget augmented, its riot-control equipment upgraded; and a large number of demobilized PLA troops were reassigned to the PAP.

China's armed forces and the military budget that supports them are among the world's largest, and the budget has been expanding rapidly. A portion of the funds has gone for new equipment from foreign suppliers, including planes, submarines, and, perhaps, an aircraft carrier, and other Asian powers naturally see this upgrading of the Chinese arsenal as related to a possibly aggressive and expansionist new policy.

The military budget passed annually by the National People's Congress alone is insufficient to underwrite the modernization of China's armed forces, and indeed it accounts for only a portion of the revenues available to the PLA, which uses its extensive system of factories not only to meet its own logistics needs but also to produce weapons for sale abroad and consumer goods for domestic sales, profits from which supplement the official budget.

The official budget is seven times larger today than it was before the reforms of the late 1970s, and now stands at just under $15 billion per year. Factoring in the effects of inflation, however, the military budget in 2000 was twice what it was in 1978 in real terms. In recent years, it has stabilized at about 9 percent of the total national budget and just over 1 percent of the gross national product.

Some have argued that the large budget increases accorded the PLA between 1989 and 1994 constituted a quid pro quo for services rendered when the PLA came to the aid of the Party elders, but others take a longer view, seeing that expansion as compensation for the 1980s, when military budgets shrank in real terms. The reform goal had been described as the "four modernizations"—of agriculture, industry, science and technology, and the armed forces—and Deng told the PLA that he took the sequence in which these were listed seriously: military modernization had to wait until Chinese industry and technology could supply the needs of the PLA. Past experience, with the armed forces heavily dependent on Soviet equipment, training, and technical assistance, was not to be repeated. So the military budgets of the 1980s reflected these priorities, first decreasing after the post-Vietnam demobilization, then averaging less than 4 percent annual growth while the national budget increased at three times that rate. Taking the effects of inflation into account, one can see that the PLA actually lost ground over the decade 1978–1988; prices doubled while military expenditures increased by only 25 percent, giving a net effect of a 2.3 percent loss per year.

Another way of putting it is to say that budget increases between 1989 and 1994, which averaged a bit over 16 percent, did no more than allow the armed forces to recoup their position at the beginning of the reform period. An index of real growth in military expenditures using 1978 as 100 shows a figure of just 103.05 for the year 1994.

As one might imagine, this decline in military expenditures had a serious effect on morale, as military pay fell seriously behind civilian wages. In 1988, an officer earned only a little more than half of what an average urban worker earned; a new conscript's pay was a fifth of that. This discrepancy naturally affected military recruitment. Once, the PLA had been a highly desirable avenue of advancement for rural young people, offering training, good pay, and, perhaps most important, geographical mobility, and there was stiff competition to get in, so recruits tended to be very capable young people. Today, with so many lucrative employment opportunities in the countryside, and the freedom to move to the city to find even better paying work, few qualified young people are attracted to a military career.

The official military budget tells only a part of the story—by far the smaller part, some argue. The "real" Chinese military budget is harder to estimate because it is not a matter of public record, and, depending on the accounting practices one employs, the numbers vary widely. A figure of $36 billion, roughly the midpoint between the lowest and the highest estimate, is accepted by most foreign observers.

On the expenditure side, this real budget, larger than the official budget by a factor of more than two, includes a range of goods, ser-

vices, and even salaries that are usually included in the reporting of
military budgets in other countries. (For example, research and development—estimated by some to be as high as $5 billion per year—
is not included in the official budget.) Some observers have assumed
that procurement of military equipment from foreign suppliers—a
major item in recent years—is also off-budget, but more recent research indicates that it is included in the official budget.

The PLA has two major sources of income, not reported in the official budget. The first, the sale of weapons to foreign purchasers, is
estimated to have been nearly $2 billion annually in the late 1980s.
With the end of the Iran-Iraq War, to both sides of which China supplied arms, and with pressure from the United States and other nations to restrict these arms sales, China has reduced the volume, but
they probably continue to generate up to $1 billion annually. Profit
from the second source of off-the-books income for the PLA, the sale
of civilian products produced in military-controlled factories, may
until very recently have contributed as much as an additional $4 bil-
lion per year to PLA revenues.

The armed forces are responsible for some ten thousand factories
that employ about 700,000 workers. Most of these are administered
by the General Logistics Department, others by the General Political, General Armaments, and General Staff Departments. This network of military factories is the legacy of Mao's policy initiative to
make the Army self-sufficient in food and supplies and to promote
the development of China's hinterlands. Locating military factories
in remote areas had two advantages: the Army's sources of supplies
would be dispersed and thus more impervious to enemy attack; and
industrialization of the hinterlands would contribute to Mao's para-
mount goal of egalitarian development of China as a whole. At the
peak of its expansion, this so-called third line of defense-managed
factories numbered thirty thousand and employed nearly three million people.

Today enemy attack is a less-than-present danger, and the goal of
egalitarian development has been abandoned in favor of a policy
of "building on the best," so the third-line factories seem more a lia-

bility than an asset. Efforts have been under way for some years to re-locate them nearer lines of communication, redirect their production, restore their profitability, and close those that cannot easily be transformed. During the 1980s, the central military authorities inaugurated a range of new enterprises, among them a commercial satellite-launching service. Their expanded economic activities not only augmented the lean budgets of that period but also gave work to some of the one million soldiers demobilized then.

Of the ten thousand PLA-managed factories, probably a third are losing money each year—a performance record significantly better than that of the rest of the state sector. Those that are turning a profit sell to civilian consumers. At the beginning of the reform period, about 8 percent of the output of military-managed factories was destined for the civilian economy, but by 1992 the proportion had risen to 65 percent and is currently 85 percent. One estimate has placed the market share of these consumer goods at 20 percent and has suggested that the PLA has set a 50 percent market share as its target.

In addition to these state-sector factories, a plethora of collective enterprises attached to regional and local military commands and operated by uniformed troops or their dependents have been spawned by the armed forces. Profits from these enterprises, impossible to calculate, generally go directly to the command under which they operate and are mostly used to augment the pay and benefits of the troops.

Finally, the PLA is not immune to the attraction of foreign joint ventures. There are currently more than two dozen such foreign-invested military firms.

The most immediate effect of all this economic activity, a substantial augmentation of the funds available to the military, is difficult to assess. A 1994 study of the PLA concluded that the net effect of off-budget income and military expenditures debited to other accounts in the official budget increases China's military spending fivefold; projecting that figure forward to 2000 yields approximately $75 billion per year. Were this true, it would place China second after the United States or third after Russia in military spending, with its military outlay at 7.5 percent of gross national product, a rate nearly twice that of the United States. Others more cautiously argue that the PLA does not have direct access to all the profits from production attributed to its enterprises and suggest that the real military budget is somewhat more than twice the official one—about $36 billion per year, or 3.6 percent of gross national product.

Whatever the total revenue generated by military entrepreneurship, it is clear that only a small portion is being allocated to upgrade and expand the Chinese arsenal. Most of the off-budget income is used, instead, to augment military pay, so as to offer a marginally competitive standard of living for military personnel and to help ward off the effect of inflation on their real income, and in investment to expand the already huge PLA-controlled economic empire, for example in Hong Kong real estate.

The Army's economic activity has important unintended effects. First, it enmeshes the armed forces deeply in China's new market economy and its connections with the world economy, and where they were once regarded as a conservative force opposed to economic reform, many military officers would now find their personal and professional interests seriously prejudiced were the reforms to be reversed. Second, it affects combat readiness; time, energy, and thought spent managing businesses are time, energy, and thought not spent in military training. The PLA's capability to defend China's borders and its national interests is, then, hardly strengthened by encouraging the military to augment its revenue through entrepreneurship. As one foreign observer of the Chinese military commented, "At the end of the day, this is an army that is more interested in making money than it is in being the guardian of the national interest."

With this concern in mind in the summer of 1998, Jiang Zemin, in his capacity as chairman of the Central Military Commission, ordered the PLA to divest itself of its non-military-related industrial and commercial interests. His instructions were part of a broader effort to reduce the degree to which government agencies were dabbling for profits in the fast-growing economy. The military establishment was slow to comply with Jiang's order, off-loading primarily its low-end, debt-ridden enterprises onto the reluctant shoulders of local govern-ments. A year later, the process appeared to have ground to a halt. In reaction to the NATO bombing of Kosovo, the Chinese military es-tablishment determined that its first priority was to upgrade signifi-cantly its equipment and technology. Any move that reduced military revenues was deemed inappropriate, and indeed the central govern-ment made a onetime $1.2 billion grant ('Taiwanese sources put the figure at $7.3 billion) to the PLA for weapons acquisitions. For the near term, at least, it appears that the PLA will continue to be a ma-jor player in the civilian economy.

The term "praetorian rule" is sometimes used to describe a situation that results from a nation's military force seizing control from a gov-ernment it regards as inept or corrupt. Under what circumstances might the PLA be tempted to establish praetorian rule in China, and how capable would it be of doing so?

The Party has been very effective in preventing the emergence of any national organization that could mount strong political opposi-tion. There is no church, no labor union, no political party in China that could do what these organizations did in eastern Europe and the former Soviet Union when Communist Party control unraveled. The Chinese people, told that their choice is between Party rule and an-archy, have reluctantly but firmly chosen Party rule. But in fact, there is a third choice: the PLA could step in should the Party collapse in the same fashion that the Communist Party of the Soviet Union col-lapsed in August 1991.

The Army has a number of characteristics that lend themselves to its serving as a praetorian administration. Most important, of course, is its arms. It is also highly patriotic, and its intense patriotism could motivate it to intervene politically were there a real danger of the col-lapse of central authority and a breakup of the Chinese state into competing regional entities. And the PLA enjoys credibility. While many people in China have come to question the credibility of the Party, fewer question the legitimacy of the Army. As a corollary, the PLA has a reputation for being less corrupt than the Party.

In 1989, the military rallied in Beijing to enforce martial law and save a regime on the brink of collapse because of its commanders' personal loyalty to Deng Xiaoping. It is highly unlikely that they would agree to do so again on the same terms. No other political leader has personal connections equivalent to those that Deng used to secure its compliance, and the negative consequences of the 1989 intervention were very serious, losing the PLA respect in the eyes of many of China's urban population and highly valued contacts with foreign military leaders as well. The next time out, it will be patriotism rather than loyalty to the Party or to particular leaders that brings the military into the political arena. Although they could use new Party leaders as a cover for their actions, they would function as an alternative to the existing Party, not as a crutch for it.

But could the PLA succeed in restoring central authority? The PLA and the PAP have a virtually total monopoly of armed force in Chinese society. As the legitimacy of the Party and the central government has declined and the independence of local and regional governments has increased, the implicit threat of the use of this armed force has become politically more and more important. But the PLA was ill-equipped and ill-trained for what it did in the streets of Lhasa and Beijing in 1989. Upgrading the PAP in budget, equipment, and training after those episodes was intended to rectify its shortcomings in civil enforcement, but it is easy to imagine the 1.8-million-strong PAP, backed by the 2.8-million-strong PLA, stretched very thin were it forced to restore and maintain order over any significant portion of China.

Public respect for the Party and the PLA derives from their having fought a successful revolution. Respect for the Party seriously eroded over decades of disastrously counterproductive economic and social policies, but respect for the PLA suffered no such decline in the 1950s and 1960s—indeed, its reputation was enhanced by its effectiveness when the Cultural Revolution threatened anarchy. But China's urban population lost respect for the military at the time of the Tiananmen massacre; that this loss of respect did not go beyond the cities was due to a surprisingly effective propaganda blitz about the "counterrevolutionary incident," which portrayed the PLA as victim rather than perpetrator. Hence, while in the cities neither Party nor Army is popular, in the populace as a whole respect for the PLA almost certainly outweighs respect for the Party.

From early on, this has been based in great part on the PLA's reputation for scrupulous honesty, tight discipline, and incorruptibility, especially during the revolution and civil war but after 1949 as well. As corruption has come to taint China's politics more and more, and as politicians have failed to curb it, the PLA's reputation for honesty has frequently been called to public attention. But unfortunately, that reputation is not what it once was. During the Cultural Revolution, the PLA became deeply involved with national and local political machines, which gave it new opportunities to engage in corrupt behavior. More recently, corruption is flourishing where the political realm intersects with the economy, and the PLA's heavy involvement in entrepreneurial activity is the source of most of the current perception of corruption in the ranks.

In some respects, the PLA is ill-suited or ineffective as a praetorian force. It is a specialist organization, not an organization of generalists, and it is short on experience in civilian administration. Although it is reasonably unified, exercising the responsibilities of civil administration would very likely divide it along several fault lines. Because national defense is its mission, there is no reason to expect that its officers would be especially good at directing economic development or political and economic reform. There is no question that a military caretaker government in China would look after the interests of the armed forces, but there are serious questions as to its ability to look after the national interest.

The PLA has had more experience than some armies in civil administration, but that experience is now thirty years old, and only a handful of officers on active duty remember it. One could argue that since economic issues dominate China's political agenda and since the PLA is acquiring substantial managerial experience in business, it is better suited to be a caretaker than it was during the Cultural Revolution. Still, a PLA-led regime would have to depend on the technical and managerial expertise of those on whose behalf it was caretaking.

Also, within the officer corps there are strong differences of opinion over whether the PLA should ever take on political assignments. There are, in addition, divisions of the kind found in most military forces: rivalries among the services and differences of viewpoint based on age, rank, and time in service. Finally, the central military authorities and the regional military commands are divided along lines parallel to those of the center-region political divisions.

The long-standing division between so-called reds and experts in the PLA dates from the immediate aftermath of the Korean War, when some officers began to argue for a new strategy to replace the guerrilla doctrine of the revolutionary years and for a new professionalism to accompany the transition from guerrilla band to national defense force. Mao disagreed. He argued that the strategy of drawing an invading enemy into the heartland of China and defeating it by guerrilla warfare was still appropriate. Moreover, he believed that the Army was, most importantly, a paragon of political virtue to be emulated by society; yet to emphasize professionalism, he thought, was to undermine political correctness, for expertise was acceptable only if matched with and tempered by "redness."

The PLA's military professionalism was, perforce, ignored during the Cultural Revolution, when it was involved in politics for a decade. Many officers attributed its miserable performance in the border conflict with Vietnam in 1979 to that involvement. They argued that the PLA could become an effective national defense force only if it attended exclusively to training, developing new strategy, and updating and upgrading its arsenal. (Their case was strengthened during the Gulf War in 1991, when Iraqi troops were defeated so rapidly and their equipment, some of it supplied by China, proved so ineffectual against American weapons.) Their position is that the PLA is not now combat-ready for the kind of conflicts in which it is likely to find itself engaged. To them, any expenditure of time or money that does not directly enhance combat readiness is inappropriate, whether spent on managing a factory or doing the job of a provincial Party secretary.

These professionals in the PLA are interested in defining as sharply as possible the respective roles of China's armed forces, Party, and government and working to ensure that each confines itself to its designated part. They appreciate the benefits of having contacts with the military establishments of other countries, and they are eager to maintain these, since they provide the PLA with access to technology, training, and strategic and tactical thinking; they tend to be less xenophobic than some of their colleagues.

The PLA's "nonprofessionals" (for lack of a better term: certainly "reds" is no longer appropriate) take a more benign view of noncombat-related military activity. Some of them are nostalgic for the heady days when the government called in the PLA to restore order, wield political power, and pull China back together, others have a strong personal and professional interest in being economic buccaneers, and they don't mind blurring the roles of Party, government, and Army. They see more to be lost than gained by the PLA's having contact with foreign military establishments: for them, to respond to the Pentagon's request for mutual "transparency" in military affairs is to reveal state secrets in a treasonable fashion.

The professionals' hesitation to intervene politically might in a given circumstance be overcome by patriotism, were the situation sufficiently dire and the alternative sufficiently unsatisfactory. But any eagerness to divest themselves of political responsibility as quickly as possible would put them at odds with their more politically inclined colleagues.

To a degree, the split between professionals and nonprofessionals parallels a split among the services. Interservice rivalry, which after all is found in most military establishments, is encouraged to the extent it builds loyalty and enhances morale; it is played out through strategic-planning bargains and, more sharply, around the table when military appropriations are decided on. In the case of the PLA, the army is by far the largest service, with 2 million soldiers; the air force numbers about 470,000, and the navy some 260,000. As one might expect, the technological level of the weapons and equipment used by the navy and air force is far higher than that of the ground forces, and so is the educational level of their soldiers and officers. Troops assigned to the ground forces are generally more conservative and less professional than their navy and air force colleagues.

Current strategic doctrine in the PLA calls for rapid deployment forces capable of responding quickly to domestic or international incidents. This doctrine, relying heavily on the navy and air force, has given these two arms prominence and necessitates the upgrading of their equipment and training. Moreover, they appear to have strong and effective spokesmen at the highest level. Admiral Liu Huaqing, once head of the PLA navy, occupied influential positions on the Politburo Standing Committee and served as vice chair of the Central Military Commission until his retirement in 1997.

Divisions along lines of age, rank, and time in service are more acute in the PLA than in other, more established armed forces. For one thing, the PLA has only quite recently implemented a regular retirement system for senior officers, and there is a greater age spread between the oldest and youngest soldiers than in the Pentagon, for example. Also, because of the significant difference in military operations during the revolution and civil war, during the Korean War, in the border conflicts with India and Vietnam, and in the more recent attempts to intimidate Taiwan, the military "generations" in the PLA have had substantially different experiences.

Ranks and rank insignia were eliminated in the PLA prior to the Cultural Revolution, so as to level differences among the troops and emphasize the belief in the virtue of egalitarianism. Lip service was paid to equality, but the absence of formal designations and badges had little lasting effect, and the ranks were restored in 1988.

The fissures between the authority of China's central military and that of the regional military commanders weakens the PLA's ability to staff any caretaker government needed in the future to help mend a regionally fractured state. The regional commanders' habit of ignoring directives that run counter to their local interests, very like the habits of civilian authorities at the provincial level, will significantly reduce the adhesive properties of the caretakers' glue.

In sum, were civil authority to collapse or a regional breakup threaten, along with a loss of central government control, the PLA would very likely intervene to form a caretaker government. It would do so out of patriotism and knowing that, as the only national organi zation capable of taking the place of the CCP, anarchy might result if it did not. Once in power, it would be likely to rule in the name of a purged and revivified Communist Party and to pursue a policy of continuing Deng's economic reforms and his open policy toward the world economy, since its officers would consider their own economic interests served by these policies. But there would be strong pressure to make the caretaker government a short-lived affair from the pro-fessional officers, who would consider the adverse effects on combat readiness and be sensitive to international pressure to restore civilian rule. Rebuilding confidence in China's central authority would be the major undertaking, with an effective crackdown on corruption and the equal enforcement of laws and regulations as important first steps. But apart from its possibly greater discipline, there is little to in-spire confidence in the PLA as a better problem solver than those whom it would replace.

The Gulf War in 1991 and the NATO bombing of Kosovo in 1999 have given rise to new strategic thinking in the PLA. "Asymmetric warfare" that makes use of "pockets of critical technology" is seen as an alternative to the all but hopeless task of across-the-board military modernization. Some even argue that the Chinese, having entered the arms race so late, are at an advantage, since they are able to pick and choose what advanced technology they acquire. Picking and choosing, however, presupposes an effective strategy that combines a close working relationship with advanced foreign military establish-ments—primarily that of the United States—and an ambitious pro-gram of weapons purchases, which to this point have been primarily from a cash-hungry Russia.

U.S. policy makers are divided in their response to China's interest in what the Clinton administration called a strategic partnership between the two nations. One school of thought, noting the written work of Chinese strategists, argues that China is a potentially threatening military rival of the United States. Another school dismisses these writings as jingoistic saber-rattling and points out that the gulf in military capability between the two nations is unbridgeable for a long time to come.

It was in the context of this debate that widespread allegations arose that the Chinese were illicitly acquiring U.S. military technology and data through commercial technological transactions and through scholarly exchanges between technicians and scientists. Congressional concern resulted in a Select Committee investigation headed by the Republican congressman Christopher Cox of California. The Cox Report, released in 1998, depicted numerous examples of lax security on the American side and an intense interest in acquiring advanced technological information by whatever means on the Chinese side. Critics of the report called its language inflammatory and its charges unsubstantiated.

The situation was complicated by the discovery that Admiral Liu Huaqing's daughter, Liu Chaoying, herself a military officer serving in Hong Kong with the China Aerospace Corporation, had attended a $25,000-a-plate fund-raiser for the 1996 Clinton campaign and had subsequently arranged a $300,000 gift to the campaign allegedly from a high-ranking Chinese intelligence officer. Critics of Bill Clinton's loose-handed fund-raising habits saw this as a clear-cut case of accepting campaign funds in exchange for according China's armed forces favorable treatment with respect to military technology.

The Pentagon believes that military-to-military contacts between China and the United States can give Americans firsthand insights into Chinese military strategy and policy and avenues of communication that will help to defuse tensions arising from misunderstandings. The Chinese see these contacts as a way of getting up-to-date information on U.S. strategic thinking and the deployment of military technology. Contacts began in the late 1980s, were interrupted in protest against the Tiananmen massacre in 1989, were renewed in the mid-1990s, and were interrupted again, first by Chinese military action in the Taiwan Strait at the time of the first presidential election on the island in 1996, and then after the bombing of the Chinese embassy in Belgrade in 1999. The Cox Report findings notwithstanding, military-to-military contacts between the two countries were renewed early in 2000, the Pentagon arguing that their value outweighs the risk involved and that it would be cautious.

The PLA is actively trying to acquire foreign military hardware. During the 1980s, it was told that upgrading its equipment had to wait until China's own industries could supply the new equipment; the policy was implemented by an initial reduction in the military budget and then only very small annual increments to it, which, given the effects of inflation, did not offset the continued downsizing of the military budget. But two events at the beginning of the 1990s turned this situation around: the PLA began to augment its budget through arms sales abroad and through production for the domestic civilian market; and the collapse of the former Soviet Union put large quantities of military equipment on the market. The PLA took full advantage of this coincidence of events: it signed contracts with Russian suppliers to buy one hundred S300 missiles, seventy-two Su27K fighter aircraft, and four Kilo-class and two Typhoon-class submarines; conversations were also held about the purchase of SS-18 nuclear missile technology; the cost of these acquisitions is approximately $5 billion to date, part of it paid in cash, part in barter arrangements. In addition, China has made substantial purchases of arms and equipment from Israel, including laser-guided armor-piercing warheads; electronic fire-control systems; optics and cannons for tanks; night-vision, communications, and radio equipment; antitank missiles; artillery ammunition; and AWACS (airborne warning and control system) equipment. The bill for this equipment over the last ten years is estimated to be another $4 billion. The United States has lobbied hard to curb Israel's sales of military equipment to China, arguing that some of it might jeopardize Taiwan's security.

Before he retired, Admiral Liu Huaqing long sought to add aircraft carriers to the Chinese navy. Some years ago, he negotiated the purchase of an Australian carrier, which was then dismantled in order to duplicate its design. Since even with this assistance it is estimated that it will be 2005 before China is capable of launching its own carrier, Liu began negotiations to purchase one under construction in the Ukraine. His negotiations apparently came to fruition in the spring of 1998, when a Hong Kong company with connections in China acquired the carrier *Varyag* for $20 million. Although the company claimed that *Varyag* would be converted to a floating hotel or resold for scrap, it was widely assumed that the ship would end up in the hands of the PLA navy.

The PLA argues that these acquisitions are meant simply to update its antiquated arsenal, but China's neighbors see evidence of expansion, not simple replacement. And they relate this expansion to actions taken to strengthen China's military position outside the national borders. An agreement was signed with Burma in 1994 by which, in exchange for sending military equipment to the Burmese army, China would have access to naval facilities in the Bay of Bengal. A year later, China extended its position in the South China Sea by occupying the Mischief Reef, just 135 miles off the coast of the Philippines. Alarmists saw these events as evidence of a pincers movement designed to encircle and control Southeast Asia. But the Chinese government depicts the two events as unconnected and defends the actions in the South China Sea as intended exclusively to protect Chinese territory.

One can plausibly argue that the PLA is engaging in these actions simply to justify an expanded military budget. But whatever its motivation, the key question is whether its actions are proceeding under a plan drawn up by civilian authorities and implemented under civilian control or whether the PLA is doing the planning and controlling. There is evidence to suggest that the latter is the case.

Military officers who enjoyed close personal ties to Deng and his senior colleagues occupy key positions in the highest circles of power in the Party and the armed forces. Their influence is enhanced because, as we have seen, the Party-state is heavily dependent on the PLA and the PAP. When Chinese arms sales abroad have become an international issue, the foreign minister has left the impression that he has only very indirect and ineffective control over the military corporations making these sales.

In arguing for a larger share of the national budget, the PLA takes advantage of its position of influence within the triangle of Party, government, and military authority, using the resources available to it to upgrade its arsenal, adopting a new strategy that takes account of the structure of power in East Asia and the Pacific, and lobbying effectively for a strong assertion of Chinese sovereignty broadly defined.

VI

SOURCES OF RURAL DISCONTENT

THE SHEER SIZE of China's rural population is one of its most arresting features—910 million people, close to three and a half times the total population of the United States. Even when it was only a third of its present size during the civil war, China's rural population was recognized by Mao Zedong as a singular resource that could give the Communist Party the leverage it needed to defeat the city-based forces of the Nationalist Party. And so he set aside the conventional Marxist-Leninist canon and focused his attention on peasant grievances: their desperate poverty and their concern about the depredations committed by the Japanese forces seizing and occupying so much of China's territory. Attending to these concerns, the Chinese Communists mobilized their overwhelming social force and with the help of the peasantry brought about the victory of the Communist revolution in 1949.

By means of land reform and the creation of collective farms in the years immediately following the Communist victory, rural incomes were equalized and raised. But in other ways, the exploitation of the rural population continued. Keeping the price it paid for grain artificially low, the government turned a profit at the expense of the peasantry and then used this profit as the source of capital for industrializing China's cities; city dwellers also got government subsidies for housing and food that were unavailable to the rural majority. And it was the rural population that suffered the most serious consequences of China's disastrously misguided agricultural policies during the late 1950s. In the twenty-five years prior to the reform period, per capita income in the countryside increased less than 50 percent.

Deng Xiaoping began his economic reforms in the countryside for two reasons: he knew that reforming agriculture would be much easier than reforming industry; and if the reform of agriculture were successful, Deng could use that success to persuade his skeptical colleagues to take on the more complicated tasks of reforming industry.

Indispensable to the success of agricultural reform was the household-responsibility system, which had originated as an experiment in the early 1960s, when Deng and his colleagues were looking for ways to alleviate the disaster brought on by the Maoist excesses of the Great Leap Forward in the late 1950s. In the experiment, land was taken out of the collective and given to households to farm; what any one household produced over the quota set by the local government, it was permitted to sell on the rural free market. The experiment had been successful, but it was abandoned once the disaster abated, and Mao later denounced it as unacceptably capitalist in spirit.

The household-responsibility system was resurrected in 1978, once again as an experiment in one or two locations. But almost overnight it was adopted by farming communities throughout China. The incentives it incorporated quickly boosted productivity, output, and household income. When these increments began to slow seven years later, a further round of reform stabilized the contract system and opened the door to the proliferation of small-scale industry in the rural economy.

The combined effect of these reforms was to raise rural incomes by a factor of three over the first twelve years of the reform period. A lot of publicity was given to the first "ten thousand *kuai* households" (households whose annual income had reached twelve hundred dollars). When news of this new phenomenon reached city residents, they found themselves envious of their country cousins for the first time in memory and were more than ready to see replicated in the city some of the entrepreneurial opportunities available beyond the suburbs. And given their significantly improved standard of living,

China's rural residents were generally quite satisfied with their lot at the end of the 1980s. They were somewhat insulated from the inflation that loomed large in the cities, and corruption, which was the second most frequent complaint of city dwellers, had yet to become fully visible in rural communities. This helps to explain why the slogans and speeches of students and workers who rushed into the streets of every major city in China in the spring of 1989 fell on deaf ears in the countryside, why there was so little sympathy among country folk for the demonstrators' demands, and why the demonstrators made virtually no effort to arouse the support of people living outside the cities.

During the 1990s, this quiescent satisfaction in the rural community disappeared. Urban reforms eliminated the small entrepreneurial advantages that rural residents enjoyed over their urban compatriots, and today the gap between rural and urban living standards is growing rapidly. The rural majority is reacting to this situation in two ways: they are taking advantage of the relaxed restrictions on geographical mobility in record numbers, and some 100 million underemployed workers have left their rural homes in search of temporary work in China's largest cities; and those who stay in the countryside are nursing their grievances and, increasingly, acting on them. Given their new attitudes and habits, it seems unlikely that they will sit on the sidelines the next time political dissatisfactions spill into China's streets.

Until the 1980s, the Chinese countryside was organized into large collective enterprises called communes, a unit (or *danwei*) typically incorporating the people of what had been several villages before collectivization began. The average commune, with about two thousand households, was divided into brigades, each made up of a population roughly equal to that of the average village, or about two hundred households; the brigades, in turn, were divided into production teams of twenty to forty households. The production team or, in some cases, brigade held title to the land and equipment for which it was responsible; members received their work assignments from the production-team leader. Individual householders owned their houses (but not the land on which the houses were built) and personal effects and had use rights to a "private plot" of land on which produce or animals could be raised for home consumption or for sale on the rural free markets.

Compensation within the commune system was based on work points. Work points were assigned based on the difficulty of the task, the capability of the worker, and the amount of time spent at work. Men, who were considered more capable than women at working the land, routinely received more work points than women for performing the same task for the same period of time. After the harvest, grain was sold to the state according to predetermined quotas, and work points were totaled; whatever amount of the team's profit it had agreed to set aside for compensation was then divided by the total number of work points earned by all the team members. This fixed the value of the work point, and team members then received compensation based on the total points. Only the largest, richest communes could offer their members retirement plans, but all of them offered medical care and primary education at nominal cost.

This compensation system gave peasant households fairly secure if very low incomes, but it provided no incentive to work hard or efficiently, and Chinese agricultural production was essentially stagnant. Productivity was very low, and the growth in total output did not keep up with the growth in population.

During the first years after the Communist revolution, ownership of land and equipment and the power to make decisions about production were removed from individual households and vested in progressively larger and larger units—first the mutual-assistance team, then two stages of cooperatives, and finally the communes. In this process, the size of the decision-making unit in the rural economy grew from a household to an entity encompassing, on average, more than five thousand households. But after the failure of the Great Leap Forward, this process was reversed. Beginning in 1959, ownership and decision making were shifted downward, first to the brigade and subsequently to the production team. The cycle was completed with the reintroduction of the household-responsibility system in 1978. With it, the individual household was re-empowered and once again serves as the locus of production decision making and de facto landownership.

Village governments, which took the place of production-team management groups, put the new system in place. They evaluated their land and divided it into parcels, each parcel containing non-contiguous pieces of good land and less productive land. Households were allowed to bid for use rights on these parcels; better-off families with more able-bodied workers were rewarded with use rights to the larger, better parcels. Team implements and draft animals were sold at auction to householders.

The village authorities and successful bidders signed contracts that stipulated three "fixed items": the price the household would pay for inputs, including seed and fertilizer, which were rationed based on the size of the contracted parcels; the expected output of specific commodities, such as grain or cotton, to be produced on the parcel; and the price the state would pay for the contracted commodities. The initial contracts were written for one-year terms. Everything the household produced over and above the stipulated amount of the stipulated commodity it was free to dispose of as it chose—whether for personal consumption, barter, or sale. Sales could be made either to the state at a price higher than that paid for contract commodities or directly to consumers on the free market.

The rural working community responded to this new system's incentive for hard and efficient work. The increase in grain production was modest, but total agricultural output grew significantly. The average annual increase in the total amount of grain produced during 1970–1977 was 3.6 percent; it rose during the seven years following the introduction of the responsibility system to 5.5 percent; comparable figures for the total income from agricultural production are 3.1 percent and 13.9 percent. These figures reflect the fact that the contract system, which encouraged farmers to diversify their crops, led to the cultivation of fruit and vegetables, which were more profitable than grain.

Bringing industry to China's countryside was a goal that Mao pursued during the last twenty years of his life. He saw a number of advantages in doing so: peasants would be proletarianized by exposure to the industrial workplace; rusticating industry would bring factories closer to their source of supply and to the rural consumer; and China's national defense would be enhanced by making each part of the country more self-sufficient, so that the occupation or destruction of one area would not affect the economic viability of the rest of the country. Finally, opening up factories in the countryside would absorb the substantial surplus labor power in the rural economy.

The first step in introducing industrial practices into the rural community came during the Great Leap Forward, with the creation of what were called "backyard steel furnaces." Rural residents, like their urban compatriots, were encouraged to collect scrap metal (along with useful tools and utensils that were declared scrap in order to reach the inflated goals of the campaign) and to melt it down to help increase the nation's steel output. The campaign was a failure on all counts. Few proletarianizing lessons could be learned in these ad hoc workplaces, and the lumps of melted metal produced in them were largely unusable.

Alongside the useless steel furnaces, however, workshops and small factories were set up that began the process of creating a "cellular" economy in rural China. During the 1960s and into the 1970s, a major effort was launched to open new factories and to make China's more than two thousand counties as self-sufficient as possible. Some of these factories belonged to the state sector, many were owned and managed by the county government, and others were owned and managed by individual communes. In the mid-1970s, rural small-scale industry was producing about 10 percent of China's total industrial output; in certain lines, such as chemical fertilizer and cement, the small-scale factories accounted for more than half of the nation's total production. As we have noted, these efforts were augmented by the PLA, which was active in building a "third line" of factories in remote areas.

The most recent wave of rural industrialization began in the mid-1980s, when the initial surge of growth in rural per capita income brought on by the introduction of the responsibility system had begun to slow. Reformers now encouraged a rapid proliferation of new industrial enterprises under township and village management; these enterprises now have a workforce of forty million and account for nearly a quarter of China's industrial output, producing both for the domestic market and for export.

Unfortunately, there are negative consequences of this otherwise promising development. The little factories occupy what was once arable land and contribute to air and water pollution. Built with the lowest possible capitalization, very few of them conform to China's environmental protection regulations. Local officials eager to reap the benefits of rapid industrialization put pressure on the environmental protection officials to ignore violations or to grant waivers. In the trenches where the war between economic development and environmental protection is being fought, economic development is winning most of the battles.

The household-responsibility system increased farmers' productivity through monetary incentives. But the smallness of the contracted parcels severely limits the ultimate productivity. Actually, with so much underemployment in Chinese agriculture, inefficiency and lack of productivity are not the obstacles to increased production that they would be were labor scarce. Nonetheless, there is talk of rationalizing agricultural production by combining small contracted plots into larger, more efficient farms.

Some consolidation of parcels is occurring spontaneously. In some places, households pool their parcels, labor, tools, and animals and farm the land as informally constituted cooperatives. Since contracts are transferable, others have sold their contracts and left agriculture entirely. People buy up these contracts, hire a staff of farm laborers, and become large-scale agricultural producers, which can realize economies of scale with respect to inputs such as chemical fertilizer and insecticides. But large efficient farms turn underemployed farmworkers into unemployed ones. Their need for jobs frequently encourages local authorities to build more factories, which takes badly needed arable land out of cultivation, thereby reducing total production.

With the introduction of the responsibility system came a structural change in rural administration in which the township took the place of the commune as the lowest level in the government structure. On average, each township is approximately twice the size of a former commune, and its administration serves as the local government, supervising the civic life of the two dozen or so villages under its authority, and as a production company, overseeing numerous collective enterprises (the average township has more than seven hundred of these). The production company is organized into agricultural and industrial departments and perhaps others with responsibility for commercial activities, transportation, and the like.

A second stage of structural change has been proposed. The goal is a bold one: to shift the rural-urban population ratio from its current 70:30 to 50:50, which would require a vast expansion of existing rural villages. Facilities and services will be needed for the more than 300 million people to be relocated from their villages to new, more urbanized residences. The purpose behind this radical social restructuring is to transfer rural Chinese underemployed workers into industries based in the countryside. And it is proposed that once this plan has been implemented, rural town governments will take responsibility for administration of their neighboring townships; since there are roughly half as many towns as townships, this consolidation means that the lowest level of rural administration will be roughly twice its current size.

Meanwhile, the countryside is the site of what one observer has called "creeping democratization." Beginning in the late 1990s, elections were held on an experimental basis at the village level. A village committee of three to seven members is directly elected on the basis of open nominations. While the authority of the committee is limited, voter turnout is typically high. Village elections were sanctioned in a new law adopted by the National People's Congress in 1998. By 2000, more than half of China's one million villages had elected committees, and the experiment had been extended to the township level. Foreign observers of village elections have found them to be open, honest, and boisterous events.

Whereas in the past the Chinese government could count on peasant acquiescence and could focus on the more volatile political behavior of workers, students, and intellectuals, today it can no longer take for granted the passivity of the peasant.

The most serious problem the government faces in the countryside is underemployment, perhaps better conceived of as hidden unemployment, affecting nearly one-third of the rural workforce: the direct cause of the outflow of 100 million people into China's major cities. A first priority is to find a way of providing housing and social services for that proportion of the floating labor pool that is actually needed in the urban economy. Its second, more complicated priority is to find jobs to attract the floaters who are not needed back to their homes in the countryside.

Other problems are related to the task of ensuring a sufficient food supply for the Chinese people. The task is best thought of as a fraction, with the numerator food supply and the denominator population, the aim being to increase the numerator as much as possible while simultaneously controlling the growth of the denominator.

The first aspect of this task is to ensure a steady increase in the production of grain, cotton, and other agricultural commodities, without which the Chinese economy would grind to a halt. The market solution—raising the price paid to the farmer to encourage him to produce more—threatened to create as many new problems as it solved old ones. Under the commune system, farmers had little or no choice as to what to grow, to whom to sell their produce, and at what price. Natural disasters and sloth were the only obstacles to the state's realizing its quotas each year. Natural disasters are a constant, of course; reform policies largely eliminated sloth by means of material incentives. But these same policies created a new hurdle for the government to surmount: producing the basic agricultural commodities became a money-losing proposition for the farmers. Almost anything the rural household planted on its contracted land would yield a better income than grain, given the prevailing prices the state was willing to pay for it.

The situation is comparable in cotton production. Raising cotton on contracted land and selling it to the state at the state's artificially low price produced only about one-fifth of the income that vegetables brought in. Peasants obliged by contract to grow cotton took to selling it on the black market for three times the state's price and claiming a shortfall in the harvest when state purchasers came to claim their contracted amount. Were the government to raise cotton prices, it would increase costs for the textile plants, most of which are state-owned enterprises already teetering on the brink of bankruptcy.

As part of its package of perquisites for city dwellers, China in years past purchased grain well below market prices then sold it in the cities at an even lower price, absorbing the difference as an expense item in the national budget. Similarly, as part of the package of subsidies for state-owned textile factories, cotton was purchased at below-market prices from the farmer and sold to factories at an even lower price. When these expense items grew, the state decided no longer to subsidize grain and cotton and to allow prices to rise to market levels: in 1994, the price of grain in city markets rose by 50 percent, and another 30 percent the following year, a major factor in driving the urban inflation rate to 25 percent in 1994 and 17 percent in 1995. Meanwhile, the price of cotton increased 60 percent in 1994 and another 30 percent in 1995, thereby exacerbating the already precarious fiscal health of the textile industry.

These radical measures (abetted by favorable weather) appear to have been effective. Grain production reached a record output of 504 million tons in 1996 and has remained close to that level in the years since. Cotton production, too, has increased since 1994, though at a more modest rate. Meanwhile, the runaway inflation of the mid-1990s has been brought under control, and grain prices in the cities have stabilized at a level approximately 75 percent higher than that of 1994.

Increasing the numerator of the food supply–population ratio is all the more difficult because of the declining supply of arable land. Every day decisions are made in rural communities that reduce the already scarce amount of land available for cultivation. China has about 20 percent of the world's population and only about 7 percent of its arable land: currently about 366,000 square miles, which is 80 percent of the 1950 figure. This means that over the past five decades China has endured a net annual loss of about 1,800 square miles despite its vigorous efforts at reclamation; and the rate at which land has been taken out of cultivation since the reforms began is about five times that average.

Yet land is being withdrawn from cultivation for good cause. Rural factories produce goods that augment the gross national product and give jobs to workers who would otherwise leave the countryside or be unemployed. But factories occupy land that could be cultivated, and they need raw materials and markets, which means expanding the highway and rail network, eating up still more land. As rural incomes rise, people are eager to expand their living quarters, and although local regulations restrict the proportion of land in a community that can be devoted to housing, these are often stretched or violated. Land is also taken out of cultivation for uses with little or no value for economic development: many odd schemes have proliferated recently, the most egregious of which are two dozen golf courses laid out in 1994.

In the mid-1990s, some foreign demographers and agronomists issued dire predictions about China's ability to feed its population over the next thirty years. Given the current growth rate of the Chinese population and its changes in diet, they estimated that it would take more than 600 million tons of grain to feed that population in 2030. Not only will there be more people to feed, but as household income increases, so does consumption of meat, poultry, and eggs. Grain production in 1996 reached the record level of 504 million tons. To reach 600 million tons by 2030, production must annually increase by 3 million tons. But, with land taken out of cultivation more and more quickly in the late 1980s, conservative projections showed a drop in grain output of up to 20 percent over the next thirty-five years, which would result in a grain deficit of more than 300 million tons in 2030. The total world grain surplus available for export in 1993 was only about 220 million tons, and many other countries are dependent on that surplus. "What will happen when China becomes a grain importer on a massive scale?" they asked.

The Chinese government at first ignored these dire predictions, then began to take them very seriously. A land-use law that came into effect at the beginning of 1999 severely restricts the conditions under which land can be taken out of cultivation. Transfers of up to eighty acres of agricultural land to nonagricultural use are subject to approval by provincial authorities; transfers of more than eighty acres are subject to approval by the central government. Land taken out of cultivation must be compensated for by an equal amount of land reclaimed. Speaking directly to the question of China's grain self-sufficiency, Chinese agronomists pointed out that not only is the country very close to completely self-sufficient in grain but average annual per capita grain consumption, at 330 kilograms, exceeds the world average, as does per-unit grain output, at 1.8 tons per acre.

Assuming that these measures will result in continuing growth rather than a decline in grain production over the next thirty years, state planners project an annual increase of between 2 and 3 million tons to a level of about 570 million tons. They estimate the need for grain at some 630 million tons in 2030 and argue that imports should be relied on to make up the shortfall of 60 million tons. They contend that the drive for grain self-sufficiency has resulted in stockpiling, corruption, and a new price structure that puts domestic grain prices higher than world prices without significantly increasing farm incomes.

If the dire predictions were overly pessimistic, these new Chinese government projections seem overly optimistic, given the difficulties in enforcing the new land-use law and the strong economic incentives to disobey it, as well as the lingering economic disincentives to devote land and labor to grain rather than to more lucrative crops or enterprises.

The goal of controlling the growth of the denominator of the food supply–population ratio is equally daunting. China's efforts to limit population growth to one child per family have fallen short of their target. The average number of children in China's cities is very close to 1 per family, but the national average is 1.84. Rural resistance to the birth-control program is attributable, on the one hand, to tradition, which dictates a preference for a male heir to carry on the family name (multiple births in one family frequently being the result of repeated attempts to have a male child), and, on the other hand, to the economics of the rural reforms. The household-responsibility system rewards big families in which there are many workers. Because girls cease to contribute to their parents' exchequer once they marry and leave the household, boys are considered a better source of income. And since there are no retirement plans in the vast majority of rural collectives, a couple's only source of old-age security is a large family. The birth-control program is successful in the Chinese countryside only when it is enforced with draconian measures, such as forced abortions or sterilizations or the destruction of homes and property. But such measures further alienate the peasant community.

A final source of government dissatisfaction with the rural population is the very high rate at which they withdraw their children from school. Census figures in 1990 revealed that 205 million people, or 18 percent of the Chinese population, were illiterate or semiliterate, of which 90 percent were rural residents and a startlingly high proportion were females under the age of forty. This is precisely because Chinese families will withdraw children, particularly girls, from school before they have completed their education.

Schooling is not free in the countryside. The tuition is nominal, amounting to about two dollars per term, but informal ad hoc charges can mount to twenty-five times that—a sizable amount when the average household income is less than eight hundred dollars per year. Most parents see little to be gained by paying for a high-school education for a child, since what the child is likely to learn seems largely irrelevant to his or her earning capabilities. This is especially so for girls, whose only chance to make money for the family is during their teen years. Only as the economy diversifies and becomes more complex will this shortsighted attitude give way to an appreciation of a high-school education as an appropriate investment. The government's providing truly free schools in rural communities would help to speed this change of attitude.

But rural people have as many reasons to be dissatisfied with their government as the government has to be dissatisfied with them. They face more and more problems that local authorities are unwilling to address or unable to resolve. In some instances, the local authorities themselves are the problem.

Among the most serious sources of dissatisfaction is excessive taxation. There is a cap of 5 percent on the amount of rural household income that can be taken as tax by the government, but in practice, local officials impose fees, tolls, fines, special levies, and charges that in most areas add up to 15 percent or more of household income, in some cases as high as 50 percent. Were this revenue used to pay for public services and improved infrastructure, rural taxpayers would no doubt continue to grumble but would at least enjoy some benefit. In fact, a substantial proportion of the tax revenues goes into the personal accounts of local officials, along with their take from bribes, graft, and profiteering. All too often this ill-gotten gain is consumed in conspicuous displays of personal excess—lavish banquets, expensive automobiles—that only inflame resentment. Indeed, this corruption is itself a potentially explosive source of rural discontent. Those who lived through the final days of the Nationalist government in the 1940s—days marked by rampant corruption—claim that the situation is worse now than it was then. The situation is particularly aggravated in the province of Sichuan, which has been the site in recent years of any number of violent demonstrations by rural residents protesting excessive taxation. Employing a different form of protest, two thousand Sichuanese households took advantage of the 1990 change in the legal code that permits citizens to sue the government and successfully litigated against local officials for levying taxes in excess of legal limits.

Unfortunately, three aspects of Chinese society today combine to create a climate particularly conducive to corruption. The first aspect is a mind-set inherited from the Confucian tradition and its emphasis on understanding society as a web of mostly hierarchical relationships. To make one's way through this web one is supposed to cultivate relationships (*guanxi*) that are likely to be helpful. This practice of *guanxi*, just as vital in contemporary society as it was centuries ago, lends itself all too easily to bribery and political corruption. The line between the legitimate cultivation of reciprocal friendship and the corrupt practice of bribery is difficult to draw, especially where there is the tendency to inflate the cost of the former.

A second element that encourages corruption is the experience of forty years of socialist rule. The Yugoslav author Milovan Djilas, writing in the 1950s, was among the first Communists to describe a "new class" of privileged bureaucrats to which socialist society could give rise. Mao Zedong took up the same theme in his criticisms of the Soviet Union under Khrushchev, and he subsequently applied these criticisms to China itself on the eve of the Cultural Revolution. As managers of state resources, bureaucrats in a socialist system monopolize and misuse those resources for their own advancement. And because they control education and recruitment into the political system, they can perpetuate their personal control by favoring their own choices or indeed their own offspring. Mao argued that this process of embourgeoisement—creating a new bourgeoisie out of corrupt proletarians—could be controlled only by means of a "continuing revolution" that takes power away from the privileged class. The "new bourgeoisie" in China was seriously undermined during the Cultural Revolution, though the perpetrators of that movement abused their power just as much as or more than the targets of their persecution. Many who were victimized during the Cultural Revolution then returned to power under the aegis of Deng, himself a target of the movement, and they seem to regard the comforts of their current station in life as fitting compensation for what they sacrificed

during the earlier thirty years. Deng and his immediate circle of senior colleagues avoided an extravagant lifestyle, but their sons and
daughters are infamous for taking advantage of their parents' positions to acquire personal wealth and influence.

A third element of Chinese society that is conducive to the growth
of corruption is the economy's current state of partial marketization.
Most decisions about allocating resources are made by the market,
but decisions about allocating certain critical resources are still made
by Party and state officials. The sharp competition among the state,
the collective, and the private sector has raised the ante in decisions
about who gets what quantity of critical items in short supply, a situation rife with opportunities for corruption.

Corruption, the kudzu of contemporary China, is intractable because the legal system is not able to establish a standard against which
to measure it and the political system lacks an independent agency to
attack and control it. Central authorities launch periodic anticorruption campaigns, but the agents on whom they rely to implement these
campaigns are the very officials who are their most eligible targets. At
best, one or two scapegoats are prosecuted and lose their jobs, but the
problem grows worse. In the summer of 1993, Jiang Zemin, calling
on his authority as president of the PRC and general secretary of the
Party, announced a campaign to end corruption; two months later,
People's Daily, the organ of the Party's Central Committee, editorial-
ized that "a certain amount of corruption in our system is inevitable."
Needless to say, Jiang's campaign did not achieve its goal.

Another source of rural dissatisfaction with the government is the
periodic cash flow crises. Eager to take advantage of promising if
highly speculative investment opportunities and not always successful in collecting tax revenues, local governments often find themselves strapped for cash just when the farmers are ready to sell their
grain to the state and thereby fulfill their contracts. Rather than getting cash for their grain, farmers have got IOUs redeemable when the
government's cash-flow problem is resolved. So serious was the cash
shortage in 1994 that stories were told of floating workers in China's
cities who purchased money orders at municipal post offices and sent

the money orders home to their families, who, when they tried to cash them at local post offices, were given IOUs instead.

One source of dissatisfaction, perhaps not felt by rural residents in their daily lives, is over the long term perhaps the most serious of all: the gap between rural and urban incomes. For a brief time in the early 1980s, economic reforms in the countryside resulted in the income of rural households growing much faster than that of urban households: in 1980, rural incomes were only one-third of urban incomes; by 1985, when reform of the urban economy began, they had at least grown to one-half of the average urban income. But after 1985, the gap began to widen again, and, in monetary terms, it is sixteen times what it was in 1978.

The average urban household income in China's cities stands at about $3,000 per year; the average rural income is somewhat less than $950 per year. Three percent of the Chinese population is living in poverty (defined as a per capita income of less than $220 per year), and the vast majority of these are rural residents. And the situation is getting worse. The overall growth rate in the urban economy is more than 10 percent, and in the rural sector only about 6 percent. Foreign economists estimate that the gap between the poorest of the rural poor and the richest of the urban rich is now as great as that in any country in Asia and surpasses that in the United States and in western Europe.

In the past, this rural-urban gap didn't matter a great deal. The state's control over the flow of information and the almost complete absence of geographical mobility meant that much of China's rural population was ignorant of city conditions, and even if they were aware of the differences in living standards, there was nothing they could do. Today the situation is very different. Information about conditions in China's most highly developed cities is trumpeted in the official media, and a large number of rural families have one or more members who are floating workers temporarily living in cities.

Another aspect of the rural-urban gap, of which individual farmers may be less aware but which seriously jeopardizes their long-term interests, is that the rate of capital investment in the industrial sector is substantially higher than that in the agricultural sector. In the early days of the People's Republic, it was very different: investment in agriculture constituted nearly a quarter of total investment in China in the late 1950s and early 1960s. By the late 1990s, however, that proportion had dropped to 2 percent, the rationale being that the rural collective sector, powered by reforms, was generating enough capital to allow local governments to take over agricultural investment. The fact of the matter is, however, that this local government investment also declined precipitously during the 1980s, from nearly 40 percent of total local investment to under 10 percent by the end of the decade. Seeking a high return on each investment dollar, local governments are much more inclined to invest in new industries or even real-estate development than to settle for agriculture's low return.

Grain production in China totaled 444 million tons in 1994—a decline of 3 percent from what was then the record harvest of 456 million tons in 1993. Alarmed by this decline, the central government pledged to reverse it and to provide investment funds for agricultural infrastructure and for research and development of new seed strains, new fertilizers, and new pesticides. Although some additional investment has been made in the ensuing years, it has not been sufficient to reverse the continuing problem of underinvestment in the agricultural sector.

Several other problems have caused China's rural residents to lose confidence in their local governments. Environmental pollution is one of them. People in the countryside are the first to suffer when township and village industrial enterprises flout air and water pollution regulations. (Until very recently, China had no grassroots "green" movement pressuring the government to address these matters, but there are signs that a citizens' movement with an interest in improving environmental quality is coming together.) Also, crime is on the rise throughout China, and one form of violent crime endemic in the countryside is the abduction of women and of male children, the women to be sold as wives or prostitutes, the boys to be sold to families who have not produced a male heir. About fifteen thousand cases of abduction are investigated each year. Although the Public Security Ministry reports an increasing number of arrests and prosecutions in cases of kidnapping and abduction, the crime wave has sapped citizens' confidence in the local governments' ability to maintain civil order.

Inflation, a serious cause of urban dissatisfaction in the late 1980s and early 1990s, was a less serious issue in the countryside, since the rate of inflation there was consistently much lower than in the cities. Rural residents own their homes, and most of them produce at least a portion of their food, so they are insulated from the two major causes of fluctuations in the cost of living in the city.

As we have seen, rural China was largely inactive when students and workers in China's cities were demonstrating against the government in 1989; rural residents were generally unsympathetic with their demands for a more open, more effective government. But since 1989, as the sources of discontent described here have taken their toll on rural toleration of incompetent governance, the climate has changed. In 1994, the Chinese press reported more than a thousand instances of protest demonstrations involving the rural population. Public protests occurred in rural communities in more than half of China's provinces. The largest of these drew more than ten thousand rural residents protesting excessive and illegal taxes into the streets of a community near Chengdu, the capital of Sichuan Province. In the years since 1994, the official press has restricted its coverage of civil disturbances in the countryside. Human-rights monitors in Hong Kong, however, report that rural protests continue unabated in frequency and in numbers of protesters.

Mao's comment in 1930 on the volatile character of a discontented peasantry, "a single spark can start a prairie fire," vastly understates the amount of political mobilization and organizational work that it took for the Chinese Communist Party to launch the revolution that overthrew the old order in the Chinese countryside. A thousand protests do not a revolution make. On the other hand, 910 million people in rural communities who harbor serious doubts as to the capability of their government to address their pressing problems pose a serious challenge indeed to the central authorities in Beijing.

VII

CHINA'S CITIES: UNEMPLOYMENT, CORRUPTION, AND ANOMIE

MAO ZEDONG WAS DECIDEDLY not a city person. Born in a small village in rural Hunan, he spent his youth deep in the Chinese countryside. Having concluded that the Communist revolution was to be won in China by mobilizing the support of the peasants, he proposed to build a peasant army and, using guerrilla tactics, seize control of the countryside; once the Japanese occupation was over and Nationalist troops had been driven out, the Red Army would control the nation, for the cities, cut off from their sources of supply in the hinterlands, would of necessity fall to them. Having decided on this strategy, Mao and his colleagues threw in their lot with rural China for the duration of the revolution; doing so left a permanent mark on them, their party, and the policies they subsequently pursued.

Mao and his colleagues were of the opinion that the countryside was the seat of a kind of primitive virtue, the city, by contrast, the seat of decadence and corruption. During the 1960s and 1970s, the highly disruptive and apparently irrational practice of *xiafang*, or rustification—whereby urban residents were involuntarily removed and made to live in remote rural settings, some for a short time, others for years—was based on this opinion. It was taken as an article of faith that their rural experiences would cure city dwellers of their urban flaws and instill virtue in them.

But Mao's reading of Marx presented him with a picture of urban life that conflicted with his experience. He found persuasive the idea that the proletariat was formed in the industrial workplace, a process that, despite the pain inflicted by the capitalists in control, was salutary and necessary, for only the proletariat could lead the ultimate advance toward communism. Although he had limited experience outside China, Mao understood that modern societies are urban and industrial; for China to take its place in the world, preferably at the forefront of modernity, it must first clean up, then build up, its cities. So he looked for a way to resolve these contradictory views of the city. Bringing industry to the countryside seemed to him infinitely better than bringing the peasant to the city. The wave of rural industrialization now under way in China is, in effect, a realization of Mao's vision, though it has been undertaken for economic, not ideological, reasons.

Reforming the urban economy in China was significantly more complex than reforming agriculture. The initial changes in the industrial workplace, begun as early as 1979, were undertaken only on an experimental basis, and full-scale urban economic reform was postponed until 1984. By that time, the successes of the household-responsibility system in the countryside and the experiments in the urban sector had built a following for extending the reforms throughout the urban economy.

Reform in the countryside had been greatly facilitated by two factors: that agricultural production as practiced in rural China is a relatively simple enterprise involving little in the way of technology or specialized expertise; and that farm households live where they work and the family operates as a production unit. These features meant that the farm household was well suited and fully able to take on the responsibility for decisions about farming that had once been made by production-team leaders. Once re-empowered, the household willingly took on this new role. Spurred on by effective incentives that soon raised household income, agricultural workers worked harder and more efficiently, and farm output increased.

Although some city families live and work in circumstances quite similar to those of a farming family—with all the employed family members working for the same enterprise and living in housing provided by that enterprise—for most city dwellers the situation is very different. People work for different employers and are very likely to commute to their workplaces, where the labor is complex. A household lacks the qualifications to make decisions in the production process, since, except in the smallest workshops, industrial production requires collaboration, coordination, equipment, and technology.

The goal of urban reform also differed. Although no one in a position of authority in China would be rash enough to say so, the goal of the rural reforms had really been to restore private enterprise to family farms. Fictions were devised to make this goal conform to "socialism with Chinese characteristics" (for example, households were given use rights but not title to the land in order to preserve the appearance of collective ownership), but despite these fictions, the practical effect was to privatize agricultural production and to supplement it with collectively owned industrial enterprises.

Full-scale privatization of industry was neither the spoken nor the unspoken goal of urban economic reform. Reformers encouraged the growth of private and collective enterprises in order to increase the supply and variety of goods and services available to city dwellers and to give them more jobs, but privatization was intended not to supplant but rather to supplement a core of revivified state-owned industrial complexes. Hence, while analogies could be drawn from the agricultural reforms and applied to the urban reform process, they were only analogies, not models.

The urban reforms outlined in a document adopted by the Third Plenum of the Twelfth Central Committee in October 1984 set out to change three key relationships of state-owned enterprises: those with the state, with employees, and with customers.

The relationship between the enterprise and the state prior to the reforms was one of total dependence: the state owned the enterprise and managed it with goals and targets set in the national economic plan; the enterprise itself had no incentive to maximize its profits and minimize its losses. Profits were recouped in their entirety by the state, and operating losses were made up by state grants.

Drawing an analogy from the distinction between landownership and land-use rights, the urban reform document distinguished between an enterprise's ownership, which would remain in the hands of the state, and its management, who would have full responsibility for running it. In the past, factories were virtual government agencies; once reformed, they would be independent legal entities with the power to transform and develop and with the responsibility for their own profits and losses. Managers were responsible for planning, supply, production, and marketing, for appointing supervisory personnel and recruiting workers, for determining wages and rewards, and for setting prices on their products. At the same time, they were told to trim the bloated workforce and increase productivity.

To establish each enterprise's economic independence, the state proposed that they all pay a fixed-rate corporate tax rather than turn over profits to the state at year's end. It would be up to the manager to decide how much to reinvest and how much to put toward wages and benefits for the workforce. Similarly, the state would no longer subsidize enterprises that operated at a loss, though loans would be available, within limits. The responsibilities of the state were thus limited to appointing managers, levying taxes, extending credit, establishing new enterprises, and consolidating, closing, moving, or transforming enterprises that failed.

Sweeping changes were also called for in the relationship between the enterprise and its employees. Until very recently a position in a state-owned enterprise was highly coveted, for the average annual wage, though only about seventy-five dollars at the current rate of exchange, was better than what workers received in other sectors. Actual wages were based on seniority; there was no relation between remuneration and performance. Job security and the benefits packages were also unparalleled elsewhere in the economy, since workers in state-owned factories enjoyed lifetime tenure, popularly known as the "iron rice bowl": once a worker was hired, it was next to impossible to dismiss him or her except in the case of a criminal conviction. The benefits package met virtually all a worker's needs: housing at a rent so low that it did not cover the cost of maintaining the housing stock; subsidies to help with food and transportation; free medical care; and China's only full retirement plan. The national average annual per capita expenditure for housing in 1998 was just under fifty dollars, accounting for 9 percent of total household living expenses. (The comparable figures in the United States are thirty-five hundred dollars and 13 percent. Further comparisons are shown in Table 4.)

Table 4

AVERAGE ANNUAL PER CAPITA LIVING EXPENSES
CHINA (1998) AND UNITED STATES (1997)
(IN DOLLARS)

	China		United States	
	Amount	Percent	Amount	Percent
Total	522	100	27,000	100
Food	232	45	3,510	13
Recreation, education, and culture	60	12	2,970	11
Clothing	58	10	1,350	5
Housing	49	9	3,510	13
Household	43	8	2,700	10
Transportation	31	6	2,700	10
Medical	25	5	3,780	14
Miscellaneous	24	5	2,160	8
Tax/pension	0	0	4,320	16

(Sources: *China Statistical Yearbook* 1999 and *World Almanac* 2000)

Until the costs of maintaining the benefits package became untenable, workers in the larger state-owned enterprises enjoyed what could be called, to borrow a term from American retirement homes, "total care"—child care at factory-owned crèches, education at factory-managed schools, medical care at factory-operated clinics, and access to tickets for entertainment and travel through factory-run procurement offices. Retired workers got pensions amounting to about three-quarters of their last wages, might go on living in factory-owned housing, and enjoyed virtually all the amenities provided their working colleagues. In addition, through a system known as *dingti*, they could get jobs for their children as they themselves left the workforce.

The 1984 reforms sought to improve the abysmally low productivity of the industrial workforce by introducing incentives. The tenure system would be phased out and new workers hired on limited-term contracts, renewable depending on performance. The standardized wage scale based exclusively on seniority was to be replaced by one based on productivity.

To change their relationship with customers, enterprises were given new authority to determine their products' prices. The reform document described a "chaotic" system of prices, in which variation in quality of goods was ignored, the prices of producer goods—raw materials and semi-processed goods—were artificially depressed, and the state absorbed the difference between the price that urban residents paid for food and housing and the actual cost of these items.

Creating order out of this chaos would inevitably be painful for city dwellers, so the decision was made to implement price reform piecemeal rather than all at once. Increases in living costs were to be partially offset by wage increases and special subsidies. Price reform was a highly sensitive issue, for it could cause inflation, and inflation, the government knew, would trigger a strong reaction among city dwellers.

Reform of the urban economy was launched in earnest in the spring of 1985 and proceeded with some success for three years. The inflationary effects began to be felt in 1988, and retrenchment measures were implemented in the fall of that year. When concern over urban inflation (among other issues) brought hundreds of thousands out into the streets in protest during the spring of 1989, reform of the urban economy was put on hold. It was revived again in 1992, but the old reform program was ill-suited to the new circumstances.

When the urban reforms were announced in 1984, it was noted that about a third of China's hundred thousand state-owned industrial enterprises were operating at a loss; by the early 1990s, that number had nearly doubled. Under these conditions, replacing subsidies with bank loans was impossible, for the banks had all but exhausted available credit and the state was once again in the business of subsidizing losses. Government support for state-owned enterprises amounted to nearly $50 billion in 1994, including, in addition to outright subsidies, "stability and unity loans," tax waivers, and supplementary payments to workers—a figure equivalent to half of China's total national budget. Beyond the enterprises' profit and loss statements the picture was even grimmer. One-third of the output of state-owned enterprises in 1994 remained unsold at year's end. In addition, those enterprises were very slow in settling their financial obligations among themselves. This so-called triangular debt among enterprises in the state sector had amounted to an additional $70 billion by early 1995. Nor did the situation improve in 1996. During the first quarter of that year, losses in state-owned enterprises exceeded profits for the first time; indeed, total net losses exceeded the entire equity of China's banks. In terms of industrial profits for 1996 as a whole, collective, private, and joint-venture enterprises accounted for 99 percent of the total, state-owned enterprises only for a tiny 1 percent.

A major reason for the unprofitability of China's state-owned enterprises is their burden of payroll and benefits. Enterprises are, on average, about 30 percent overstaffed, yet because the tenure system is still in effect for workers hired before the reforms began, it is very difficult to downsize the workforce. Nationwide, enterprises are responsible for the pensions of some eighteen million individuals, and the number is growing. The cost of health coverage for workers and retirees is also mounting sharply. With no health-insurance plans, enterprises are effectively self-insured, covering the medical costs of their employees as they are incurred; when the cost of medical care was very low, this was not onerous, but as the costs have increased, enterprises are limiting the coverage they offer. Lastly, housing is an additional financial burden, which is only increasing as housing stock ages and prices rise.

China's central government has acknowledged for some time that the state sector is in crisis. The current level of government financial support needed to keep state-sector enterprises afloat is untenable even in the short term. A logical, if drastic, solution is to allow the least successful state-owned enterprises to go out of business. With this in mind, and after extensive debate, the National People's Congress passed a bankruptcy law in early 1989. Yet implementing that law would send hundreds of thousands of workers onto the streets unemployed and angry, and the government regards this as equally untenable.

A number of proposals have been advanced to resolve this dilemma. One that gained some popularity in the early 1990s was that of creating "enterprise groups," in which a marriage would be arranged between a profitable, well-managed state-owned enterprise and an unprofitable, ill-managed one, the theory being that the successful one would, with its better management and new ideas, pull the unsuccessful enterprise up. In practice, the unsuccessful enterprise often served as a sea anchor on its more successful partner, thereby multiplying the effects of its failure.

Another solution is divestiture: the state sells its interest in the enterprise to the employees or to outsiders in the form of equity shares, the enterprise moves from the state to the private sector, and its new shareholders shoulder the burdens once borne by the government. A variation on this idea is to get a foreign investor to buy out some or all of the assets of an unsuccessful state-owned enterprise. But determining the value of state-owned assets has been problematical for many potential investors. Some enterprises are in such bad shape that their real-estate holdings turn out to be their only asset of any value. A divestiture plan was adopted at the Fifteenth National Party Congress in 1997 that called for selling off all but the five hundred largest state-owned enterprises. By the end of 1998, the number of state-owned industries had dropped by half; it has continued to decline, though more slowly, since then.

For the worst-off enterprises, bankruptcy is the only realistic alternative. A plan was announced in late 1994, designed to avoid some of the potential danger involved in putting state firms out of business, that would apply the bankruptcy law experimentally to enterprises in eighteen cities, cities that were to get central-government funds to assist in worker outplacement and to establish municipal social-security systems giving retirement support to those put out of work. Even with these built-in safeguards, the bankruptcy program is filled with political risk for local politicians. It is also highly unpopular among those who continue to believe that a large and vibrant state sector is the sine qua non of a socialist economy.

However the immediate crisis is addressed, over the longer term a solution must be found for lightening the onerous burden of the benefits package. Creating a government-funded retirement program was a first step. The system being put in place is based on worker contributions and managed by local governments. For the plan to succeed, a large infusion of government funds was needed up front, since contributions from the current workforce would not begin to cover the cost of even the existing pensions. The social-security line item in the national government budget is currently running at more than $20 billion per year.

Plans are also afoot to change the housing system. First, rents have been raised on factory-owned housing at least to a level that covers construction and maintenance costs. Although rents are still remarkably low, the current average urban household expenditure on housing is nearly ten times what it was in 1985. Second, enterprises have begun to sell off their housing stock to residents. This was not at first easy, for the prices were high and the quality low. There was little incentive for tenants paying low monthly rents to increase their out-of-pocket expenses and also take responsibility for maintaining their decrepit quarters. As a property market begins to be created in China's cities, however, the possibility of getting in on the ground floor of what might be lucrative real-estate investments is sweetening the deal in the minds of many tenants. And third, the number of new employees entitled to the full package of benefits has been reduced. Many of those newly employed in the state sector are hired on fixed-term contracts with limited access to benefits.

In the case of some foreign joint ventures, the state-owned enterprises have been split into two independent corporations, one a manufacturing concern, the other a service corporation providing employee benefits. A portion of the production company's profits is earmarked as a contribution to the service company, but the service company must find cost-reduction strategies and increase employee contributions to bring its operations into some approximation of fiscal balance.

The official figure for unemployment in the urban sector of China's economy is a modest 3.1 percent. Many of the unemployed are young people who have yet to start full-time work. (Indeed, the Chinese term for the unemployed—*daiye*—means "awaiting employment" and reflects the composition of the group.) Finding employment for young people entering the workforce—some twenty million annually—is a major task for the government. Nonetheless, were these the only urban residents whose livelihoods were at risk, China's leaders would have relatively little to worry about, particularly given the growth rate of the urban economy.

The official figure, however, is a far from perfect guide to the employment status of the urban workforce. First, it omits workers who have been laid off from state-owned enterprises. By the beginning of 2000, that number had reached twenty million, only half of whom had found new jobs. In addition, the unemployment figure does not include workers who have been put on furlough by state-owned enterprises, which, as we have seen, remain significantly overstaffed. Meeting the monthly wage bill is a major problem for many state-owned enterprises that are also trying to turn a profit at year's end; by the late 1990s, up to 10 percent of the state-sector workforce, or more than fourteen million workers, had been placed on unpaid furloughs or on reduced hours and reduced pay.

Second, the official unemployment figures do not mention the approximately 100 million floaters in the urban workforce. Those temporary city residents who do find work are employed only on a temporary basis, many of them work only intermittently, and millions are, in effect, unemployed. Because their legal residence is the rural communities from which they come, they are officially not city residents and have no claim on housing, health care, education, or social services. They have, in effect, slipped through the cracks of what was once a very tight system of social control. These floaters, living just beyond the long arm of the law, are able to flout birth-control regulations and may be major contributors to the increasing amount of urban crime. They are a current headache and a potential catastrophe for urban officials.

In an effort to control the influx of floaters and to offset the costs of genuine city residents, the Beijing government announced in late 1994 that it was instituting a new licensing system for floaters: job applicants were to be charged $5,600 for a work license. A firm seeking to hire floaters could cover the cost of a license, but then the rate would double to $11,200. These figures are so far out of line with anyone's ability or any firm's willingness to pay that one wonders how the regulation can possibly be enforced. Taking all these numbers together, China's cities have as many as 30 million residents, or a quarter of their workforce, who are not fully employed and up to 100 million nonresidents who are competing with one another for short-term low-end jobs. In short, there are a disturbingly large number of people whose economic needs are not being fully met; their dissatisfactions may manifest themselves in the very political instability the Party-state is trying so hard to avoid.

News reports from Beijing in the tumultuous spring of 1989 during the demonstrations in Tiananmen Square were often misleading: it was not, despite the general opinion in the West, a desire for democracy that brought demonstrators out. The students, the first to demonstrate, had very specific issues in mind: they were dissatisfied with the low quality of their university education and the crowded conditions of their dormitories and wanted them changed; workers and professionals who later joined the protests shifted their focus to the broader issues of corruption and inflation, particularly sensitive and long-standing issues in the Chinese political context.

Immediately following the Japanese surrender in 1945, the Chinese Communists gained public support by pointing to runaway inflation in the economy and rampant corruption in the political system, both of which they blamed on the Nationalist government, which, they argued, appeared powerless to control either. The Communists promised to put in place a scrupulously honest regime that would master the problem of inflation, and they did just that upon taking power in 1949. That regime had become hopelessly mired in corruption by the early 1990s, and after three decades of nearly stable prices, inflation reappeared, the unwelcome consequence of the economic reforms and recent rapid economic growth.

The average rate of inflation during the first three decades of the People's Republic was just under 2 percent; retail prices rose only about 65 percent in thirty years. In 1988, however, the retail price index increased by 18.5 percent, and even more for urban residents, and it continued to mount through early 1989. City dwellers found their decline in buying power and real wages alarming. Their alarm turned to anger as they realized that the government officials were not only incapable of resolving the problem but also insulating themselves from its effects through rampant corruption. It was this alarm and anger that brought them out in unprecedented numbers onto the streets of eighty cities in China in opposition to the government.

The retrenchment measures the government had put in place to slow economic growth and curb inflation in late 1988 were redoubled after the demonstrations had been put down in early June 1989. As a result, the overall inflation rate was reduced from 17.8 percent in 1989 to just a little over 2 percent in 1990. It began to rise again in

1993 and reached a new high of 24.2 percent in 1994 (35 percent in the urban economy).

Until 1995, the inflation rate in China's cities consistently exceeded the rate for the economy as a whole by several percentage points. Food expenditures account for a high proportion of urban household budgets, and food prices in urban markets increased 32 percent in 1994—partly because of the effort to bring the prices paid to rural producers closer to market levels and partly because of bad weather during the growing season.

The government had difficulty meeting the targets it set each year for bringing inflation under control because it was unwilling or unable to address the underlying causes. It solved its cash-flow problems by increasing the money supply, it used up bank credit to shore up the teetering state sector, and it failed to control local government speculation in property schemes. It seemed to harbor the hope that periodic wage increases would anesthetize the public to the effects of inflation.

In 1995, Zhu Rongji, then serving as vice premier, took a series of draconian measures to reverse these tendencies. Under his leadership, the government brought inflation under control, and by the end of 1997 the rate had been reduced to 2 percent. In subsequent years, indeed, deflation rather than inflation became the issue. At the beginning of 2000, the economy was experiencing its twenty-seventh straight month of a declining consumer price index, and the government was desperately seeking incentives to increase consumer spending.

If inflation was no longer aggravating the lives of China's urban residents, corruption was still omnipresent. China's city dwellers experience corruption in their daily lives no less than do those who live in the countryside, though differently. Rural residents are in closer touch with local government officials, and, as we have seen, it is very often the acts of petty corruption committed by individuals whom they know, at least indirectly, that aggravate them and undermine their confidence in the Party-state. China's cities are more tightly buttoned, and the opportunities for small-scale graft, bribery, and the like are relatively restricted, so urban residents experience corruption more indirectly, but on a grander scale.

Understanding the inherent dangers, Jiang Zemin responded to a petition drafted in February 1995 by twelve intellectuals and addressed to the National People's Congress calling on that body to mount a national campaign to stamp out corruption. Jiang's campaign began with a bang. Zhou Guanwu, chairman of the massive Capital Iron and Steel Corporation and a confidant of Deng Xiaoping, resigned suddenly and unexpectedly; shortly thereafter, his son, said to be a business partner of one of Deng's sons, was detained in relation to unspecified economic crimes. Two months later, the suicide of Wang Baosen, executive deputy mayor of Beijing, became public: he and others in the Beijing government had been accused of extracting bribes in conjunction with the granting of construction permits. Within a few weeks, Beijing Communist Party secretary Chen Xitong resigned under duress, tarred with the same brush. An ally of Li Peng, then serving as premier, Chen was later removed from his position in the Party politburo, dismissed from the Party, and, in 1998, sentenced to sixteen years in prison.

The attack on corruption in high places then moved quickly out of the capital and into the provinces. But just as quickly, it ground to a halt, for Jiang Zemin discovered that, unable to control a nationwide campaign, he risked losing supporters critical to his efforts at consolidating his position as Deng's successor. By September, the drive against corruption had all but ended.

It is a recurring pattern. A crackdown on smuggling was announced with great fanfare in 1998, designed to stop corrupt behavior on the part of government and military officials and, as a side effect, to recover lost tariff revenue on as much as $12 billion in imported goods each year. In the coastal province of Fujian, the campaign uncovered a ring of smugglers in the port city of Xiamen, more than 150 local officials were detained, and the ensuing investigation found evidence of more than $10 billion in smuggled goods. Lin Youfang, head of the Fujian Foreign Trade Corporation, was eventually implicated, but because Lin was the divorced wife of a politburo member who is a close associate of Jiang Zemin, the case against her went nowhere.

Other high-profile corruption cases have included the misappropriation of more than $40 million in flood-control funds, which, had they been put to their intended use, would have saved lives and property in the extensive flooding of 1998–1999. Similarly, Zhu Rongji accused local officials of misappropriating funds from the $11.2 billion budget for relocating individuals and enterprises from areas to be flooded by the Three Gorges Dam.

Each year the Party-state announces the number of corruption cases it has prosecuted—generally in excess of fifty thousand—and each year corruption continues to thrive. Chinese cynics believe that until the Party-state takes the unprecedented step of creating and empowering an agency independent of both the Party and the government to address the problem of political corruption, there is no hope of bringing it under control.

On a quiet spring weekend in 1999, the sidewalks surrounding Zhongnanhai, the walled compound that houses Party offices and officials in the center of Beijing, were quickly and quietly filled with more than ten thousand very average-looking citizens, who seated themselves on the ground and engaged in a daylong silent demonstration on behalf of their beliefs. It was the largest crowd that had assembled in the capital since students occupied Tiananmen Square ten years earlier. The protesters were members of a sect known as Falun Gong (usually translated "Buddhist Law"). Li Hongzhi, a former grain bureau clerk, founded the movement in 1993, capitalizing on the popular revival of *qigong*, traditional Chinese breathing exercises designed to focus one's energy, or *qi*, in order to heal one's body and mind. Li, who now lives in New York, claims to have as many as 100 million followers, most of them in China.

The protesters were dispersed, and they left peacefully, so the Party-state initially appeared ready to ignore this unusual event. Two months later, however, the politburo branded the movement a "superstitious cult" and banned it. Soon dozens were arrested and sentenced to long prison terms, and tens of thousands more were arrested, booked, released, and often transported back to their hometowns.

There are several explanations for the severity of the government's reaction to Falun Gong. First, it felt severely threatened by the discovery of an organization outside Party control that claimed a membership larger than that of the Party itself. Second, Jiang Zemin appears to have been particularly aggrieved that some senior Party leaders not only were members of Falun Gong but had urged their colleagues to join the movement. Finally, there are disturbing historical analogies: dynasties in decline were often threatened, some successfully, by millenarian movements with belief systems startlingly similar to that propounded by Li Hongzhi. Despite its severity, however, the reaction has had little effect on the movement. Although public practice of *qigong* has diminished significantly, protests occur regularly in China's cities.

Although Falun Gong is by far the largest and most public movement of its kind in China, it is by no means an isolated phenomenon. Officially tolerated religions claim 100 million adherents, and observers estimate that non-sanctioned movements, including Falun Gong, have twice that number. This surge in religious faith is symptomatic of a widespread quest on the part of many Chinese for a belief system to replace the now-discredited Marxist-Leninist-Maoist ideology of the past and the rampant self-seeking individualism of today. Some Chinese describe feeling rudderless and adrift on a fast-moving current of social and economic change. For some who are experiencing this anomie, superstition or genuine religious faith seems to offer relief. Others find appealing the individual empowerment encouraged by the self-help aspect of a movement like Falun Gong.

For its part, the Party-state has advanced nationalism as its remedy for rootlessness. Chinese nationalism first came to the fore as a reaction to Japan's incursions on Chinese sovereignty a century ago. Communists very effectively used anti-Japanese nationalism to mobilize popular support as they consolidated their position against the Nationalists in the 1930s and 1940s. And anti-Japanese sentiment is also part of the current revival of nationalism. Periodic efforts made by Japanese patriots to deny the atrocities committed by Japanese troops during what came to be known as the "rape of Nanjing" in 1937 evoke both official and unofficial Chinese outrage.

Anti-American nationalism, absent from the Chinese scene for thirty years, has reemerged as the United States, no longer rivaled by Russia, has undertaken what Jiang Zemin called a "global strategy for world hegemony." When NATO bombs hit the Chinese embassy in Belgrade in May 1999, killing two staff members, tens of thousands of urban residents in China turned out in violent and very well organized anti-American protests. The American ambassador was under virtual house arrest for five days in the embassy compound in Beijing as angry crowds—first spontaneous, later orchestrated—swirled past hurling rocks, bottles, and vitriolic slogans. Americans were stunned to find their Chinese friends utterly convinced that the bombing had been an intentional anti-Chinese act, though these friends were hard-pressed to explain the motive behind such a self-defeating action. And of course the United States is also deeply implicated in another issue that the Party-state has utilized to whip up nationalist fervor: the reunification with Taiwan.

But anti-American nationalism is itself a source of anguish for young Chinese. Many of those who hurled stones at the American embassy returned soon thereafter, this time to apply for visas that would permit them to study at American universities or look for jobs in Silicon Valley. And contemporary urban life in China is by no means immune from the dominant influence the United States has on popular culture worldwide.

Change is unsettling, and the Chinese people, particularly those who live in the largest cities, have experienced a sustained period of extraordinary change. The revival of *qigong*, on the one hand, and of

Chinese nationalism, on the other, underscores the dissatisfaction of many Chinese and the tendency to express that dissatisfaction in spontaneous, unpredictable ways.

Yet, for all the problems, China's cities are infinitely more interesting and pleasant places to live than they were decades ago. Foodstuffs, once available only in limited quantity, low quality, and no variety, are now abundant and of high quality and great variety. (A sign of this progress was a slump in the cabbage market at the beginning of the 1994–1995 winter. Chinese city dwellers had always bought great quantities of cabbage in the late fall for use during the winter, when no fresh vegetables would be available, and they stored it in every possible cranny in their cramped living quarters; then, day after winter day, they would pull out a head, peel off the decayed outer leaves, and boil up yet another monotonous meal. Today, with fresh vegetables available throughout the winter, cabbage growers have no market for their once essential product.) Consumer goods of all kinds are abundantly available in China's cities; domestic goods are also plentiful, much of them produced, as we have seen, in factories owned by the armed forces; and more and more imported merchandise is seen in city shops and department stores. Retailing has emerged as an area of joint-venture interest, and several large Hong Kong and Japanese retailers have flourishing outlets in China's largest cities.

Thirty years ago, China's city streets virtually closed down when the sun set: storefronts were boarded, crowds dispersed, and the sidewalks were only dimly lit. Today street life extends well into the night hours. Neon lights and illuminated storefronts beckon. Restaurants and fast-food outlets are abundant and their clientele numerous. Films, mostly domestically produced, attract large audiences, as do discos and karaoke bars.

For all these improvements, though, Chinese city life is not easy. Housing is still inadequate, most apartment buildings are old and in disrepair, and most urban families live in cramped quarters and must share bathroom and kitchen facilities with their neighbors. A major push to construct new housing has increased and improved the housing stock, and per capita living space in China's cities has doubled over the last twenty years, but people still have less than one hundred square feet, on average, of living space.

China's urban population has increased sixfold over the last fifty years, and this does not include the 100 million floaters. Shanghai's population per square mile, for example, is a third higher than that of New York City. The construction of urban infrastructure — roads, bridges, public transportation, sewers, water supply systems, and the like — has lagged far behind population growth, and getting from place to place, whether by bicycle, public transportation, or automobile or on foot, is most often slow. Moreover, air and water quality is seriously deficient in virtually all Chinese cities.

Add to these difficulties the insecurities brought on by unemployment, underemployment, corruption, anomie, and the lack of confidence of most urban Chinese in the capability of their government officials, and you have the potentially explosive mix that China's leaders must seek to defuse. These issues were cause for great concern to China's leaders as they approached the celebration of the fiftieth anniversary of the founding of the People's Republic in the fall of 1999. They were unable then and they have been unable since to put forward any viable solutions.

VIII

THE CENTRIFUGAL FORCES
OF REGIONALISM

OVER THE LAST DECADE, the authority of the Party and the national government it controls has significantly weakened, while provincial and local governments have become more assertive in advancing their interests, often at odds with those of the central government and of other localities. Will the central authority of the Chinese state collapse in the near term? Will the country break up into independent political and economic entities competing with one another for scarce resources?

In Chapter 1, we saw the differences in economic opportunity among three regions—the coast, the center, and the west. Although the provinces in each region have much in common, it is highly unlikely, were China to break apart, that these three regions would constitute the resulting pieces, for important interests are not shared among the provinces in each. This is perhaps most obvious along the coast, where the provinces compete for foreign investment and, in several instances, are closely linked with the economies of their principal foreign partners.

The anthropologist G. William Skinner, in a close study of the economic geography of nineteenth-century China, concluded that it was useful to consider China not as a single economic system but as divided into nine "macroregions." (Skinner's macroregions are shown on the map.) These macroregions are defined by their river basins

MACROREGIONS OF CHINA
IN THE MID-NINETEENTH CENTURY

OUTER MONGOLIA

INNER MONGOLIA

Manchuria

ZHILI

North China

Yellow River

SHANDONG

SHANXI

SHAANXI

Northwest China

ALASHAN

GANSU

CHINESE TURKESTAN

QINGHAI

TIBET

SICHUAN

Upper Yangzi

Yangzi River

JIANGSU

Lower Yangzi

ZHEJIANG

Southeast Coast

ANHUI

HENAN

HUBEI

Middle Yangzi

HUNAN

JIANGXI

FUJIAN

GUIZHOU

GUANGDONG

West River

Lingnan

GUANGXI

Yun-Kwei

YUNNAN

Source: G. William Skinner, ed.,
The City in Late Imperial China

and by the mountain ranges that serve as barriers to commerce and trade. Although economic activity within each region was intense, there was relatively little economic activity across the macroregional borders. The geographical features that divided macroregions are of course still in place, but much has changed in the Chinese economy over the course of the century and more since the period to which Skinner's data refers. Communications links have expanded. Railroads, air routes, and highways now connect places that were once isolated, and the economy is much more unified. Through the strenuous efforts of the Nationalist government in the years leading up to World War II and, later and more successfully, of the Communist government after 1949, the economy was centralized and came to be managed under a single, unified plan. And when the centralized and planned economy was subsequently decentralized once again, the units to which economic decision making was relegated were political, not physiographic or economic.

To gauge the realities of China's economic regions today, one would have to subject the contemporary scene to the same careful scrutiny that Skinner applied to economic interactions of a century ago. Short of this, we can speculate about the outcome of such a study. It would surely reveal additional macroregions: the far west is one, given the importance of the natural resources being explored there. A second might result from dividing North China into coastal and hinterlands regions. Study of the economic activity within the latter and of its links to the Lower Yangzi region might suggest a redrawing of macroregional boundaries in central China. But apart from these adjustments, Skinner's macroregions still cohere today, despite the many changes wrought by political integration, economic development, and technological modernization. Were China's central government to fail and a breakup occur, at least some of the resulting pieces would closely resemble these macroregions.

Chinese politicians have a strong preference for ad hoc arrangements that are negotiated case by case over formal arrangements applied uniformly. This preference is well illustrated by the messy web of relationships that link center and region in the Chinese political system.

The American federal system was created by local governments coming together and, after careful negotiation, surrendering certain powers to the newly created central government. The Constitution provides that all powers not specifically surrendered to the federal government remain in the hands of the states.

The Chinese system, by contrast, still contains elements of the traditional division of authority between center and regions, in which provincial and local officials were supposed to serve as agents of the central government. The carefully crafted arrangement put in place to ensure that these agents did not become advocates of local interests in competition with the interests of the throne broke down when the throne was weak, threatened, and in need of the assistance of local authorities to suppress the Taiping rebels in the middle of the nineteenth century. Thereafter China experienced nearly a century of fragmentation; local interests became strong and entrenched, and the central government had little or no power over them, finding that the best it could do was to negotiate among local warlords for their cooperation in projects benefiting the nation as a whole.

In the current relationship between center and region in China, there are echoes of both mandarins and warlords. The central government would like to think of provincial leaders as their agents, but very often it finds itself negotiating for their cooperation. Their relationship is the end result of a period of centralized decision-making authority and a subsequent one of intentional decentralization. The Chinese Communist Party and the Red Army worked closely together to unify the country after a century and more of war, civil war, and revolution. Military and civilian authorities shared in running the territories they had captured and then, as the new government was established in Beijing, handed over control to civilian authorities in the central and provincial governments.

Military regional commanders remained actively involved in Party and government affairs, however, and eventually became entrenched in the affairs of the territories under their command. To break up their strong regional identities, and to stop them from forming stable long-term local interests, the Party periodically reassigned commanders.

Once it had reasserted control after a century of regional fragmentation, the Party began to see the disadvantages of a highly centralized political system. It was impractical and inefficient to try to manage an economy as large and diverse as China's from a single command post, and Mao was mistrustful of the bureaucracy that was being created to do this management. Finally, he believed in the "mass line"—the idea that policy should reflect both central interests and local initiative—and he believed that decisions were best made at the level where they were most likely to express local initiative. So, beginning in the mid-1950s, the center began to devolve decision-making authority to local officials, selected for their loyalty to the interests of the central government, among other qualities. This was accomplished seldom by means of uniform provisions applying equally to all provinces or to all cities but rather by means of case-by-case negotiations, the outcome of which reflected the relative clout of the parties involved.

One of the Party-state's most important levers in controlling local officials is of course the power of appointment, and provincial officials are to some degree agents of the center. On the other hand, they are most likely to be effective if they have the confidence of the local community. It used to be the case that almost all of them were outsiders brought in by and thus beholden to the center. More recently, after a long history of loyal but ineffective appointees, Beijing has been appointing officials with strong local affinities to important provincial and municipal posts.

The power to levy taxes, the second lever the center uses to control local government, expresses a very concrete aspect of the center-region relationship—who determines the local budget and how the revenue for that budget is generated.

In the American fiscal system, the power to tax and the revenue generated from the tax are assigned, depending on what is being taxed, to different jurisdictions. Personal and corporate income, for example, is taxed by the federal government, by state governments, and by some cities. The sales of many goods are taxed by state and local governments, but certain items, such as alcohol, tobacco, and gasoline, by the federal government. Personal and real property is taxed by county, town, and city governments. Customs duties are collected by the federal government. (Table 5 compares tax revenue by source for the American federal and the Chinese central government.) Towns and counties must draw up expenditure budgets, the size of which is determined by their projected tax revenues. They are generally precluded from deficit spending, though they may borrow money for capital projects. The federal government, though, is permitted to spend more than it takes in in a given year, and, exercising that option, it has accumulated a national debt of $5.5 trillion. There are, in addition, transfers of funds from the federal government to state and local governments that can amount to as much as a quarter of expenditures for the latter.

Table 5

TAX REVENUE BY SOURCE, UNITED STATES AND CHINA, 1998
(IN PERCENTAGES)

	United States	China
Individual income tax	48.1	1.0
Corporate income tax	11.0	10.0
Social insurance taxes and contributions	33.4	
Industrial and commercial taxes		81.3
Customs duties	1.0	3.4
Agricultural tax		4.3
Excise tax	3.4	NA
Estate/gift tax	1.4	NA
Other taxes	1.7	NA
	100.0	100.0

(Sources: *China Statistical Yearbook 1999* and *World Almanac 2000*)

Prior to the economic reforms of the 1970s, China's Party-state operated on the assumption that all government revenues were its to distribute. Most revenue derived from state-owned enterprises. Corporate income was subject to taxation, and, in addition, as we have seen, the government recouped corporate profits from state-owned enterprises in the form of transfer payments. Besides industrial and commercial taxes, the government had the revenues from customs duties on imported goods, a tax on salt, and an agricultural tax. Neither property nor personal income was subject to taxation.

Although Beijing controlled the distribution of all tax revenue, it relied on local governments to collect the revenues, and until 1994 there was no central tax-collection agency. Local authorities collected taxes and corporate profits, then forwarded on to the central government a pre-agreed proportion of this revenue, retaining what was needed to cover their approved annual budget. The proportion forwarded to Beijing was subject to annual renegotiation; each province and municipality had its own negotiated rate, and these varied widely. For many years, the city of Guangzhou, for example, contributed only 10 percent of its municipal revenues to central coffers, while Shanghai during the same period was routinely turning over 90 percent.

Expenditure budgets for governments at all levels were determined in a highly centralized fashion, with the budget at each level being set by the level just above it: the center set budgets for provinces and the directly administered cities; provincial authorities set budgets for their counties and cities. While some effort was made to balance revenues and expenditures at the national level, nothing related provincial, county, or city expenditures to the revenues generated in that jurisdiction. Rather, wealthy areas were expected to spend less than they took in, and Beijing used a portion of the surplus to cover the deficit in poorer areas, which routinely spent more than they could raise.

In reforming the economy, the central government looked for new sources of tax revenue, as is shown in Table 6. In addition, the government began a scheme, known as "eating from separate kitchens," under which the provinces turned over a proportion of their revenues that was fixed for five years so as to allow them much-needed long-

term planning; they could set their own budgets, but on the understanding that the central government would no longer cover their
over-budget expenditures.

Table 6
CHINESE GOVERNMENT REVENUE BY SOURCE, 1978 AND 1998
(IN BILLION YUAN)

	1978	1998
Taxes		
Industrial and commercial taxes	45.1	762.5
Tariffs	2.9	31.3
Agricultural tax	2.8	39.8
Salt tax	1.1	0.0
Income tax of state owned enterprises	0.0	74.3
Income tax of collective enterprises	0.0	18.1
Revenue from enterprises	57.2	0.0
Subsidies to loss-making enterprises	0.0	−33.3
Other revenues	3.0	94.6
Total	112.1	987.3

(Source: *China Statistical Yearbook* 1996 and 1999)

Uniformity was the goal, but in practice many different arrangements were put in place under the rubric of "eating from separate
kitchens." Sixteen of China's twenty-seven provinces and regions
agreed to having title to some state-owned enterprises shifted from the
central government to them. Beijing got the tax revenue from its enterprises, while provincial governments got the tax revenue from
provincial enterprises. Other arrangements were made with other localities: Guangdong and Fujian Provinces agreed to lump-sum transfer payments, to remain unchanged for five years; Jiangsu Province
was assessed a percentage of its total revenue, fixed for five years; Beijing, Tianjin, and Shanghai were assessed percentages that were to be
renegotiated annually, as in the past. The eight poorest provinces and
regions, where revenues did not cover expenditures, were assigned
fixed subsidies, to increase annually by 10 percent for five years.

Total budgetary revenue increased steadily thereafter, but an unintended consequence of "eating from separate kitchens" was that the central government's share of the revenue shrank from nearly 60 percent in 1978 to close to 40 percent in 1993. In transferring title to state-owned enterprises, the central government had kept control of strategic but not necessarily profitable factories. As its revenues declined, it shifted entire categories of expenditure from the national budget to local ones, which put local governments in a bind: their revenues were fixed, but now they had to take on new expenditures. To solve this problem, they increasingly relied on extra-budgetary funds — every imaginable kind of fee, fine, levy, toll, assessment, commission, and tariff. At the beginning of the reform period, extra-budgetary funds amounted to no more than 20 percent of regular tax revenues, but by 1993 they had increased to more than 100 percent of regular tax revenues and were a particularly sore point with the people.

A second round of tax reform was put into effect on 1 January 1994. The economy was then growing with unprecedented speed, but tax revenue as a proportion of output was declining. (Whereas tax revenue amounted to about a third of the total output value of the economy in 1979, it had declined to about 15 percent by 1992. A comparable figure for Western countries is more than 40 percent of output value.) Moreover, state enterprises were draining resources from the central government rather than contributing substantially to its resources as they had been doing a decade earlier. The new reform created a central-government tax-collection agency with local branches. The reform set as a goal that 80 percent of all tax revenue would be collected by central-government agents and only the remaining 20 percent by local collectors, which, if successful, would reverse the situation in which most revenue was retained by the provinces. Under the new arrangement, the central government would get the lion's share of tax revenues and provide grants to the local governments where needed to cover their expenditure budgets. The scheme of distinguishing central from local government ownership of state-sector enterprises is to be universalized, with all enterprises paying both national and local corporate income taxes. A problem may well arise from the fact that those who staff the tax bureaus, though they report to the central government, are local residents with, we might assume, local interests at heart.

To date, the 1994 reforms have raised the central government's share of tax revenues from 40 percent to 50 percent, though tax revenue as a percentage of gross domestic product dropped further — from 15 percent to 12.4 percent in 1999. The government has set a goal of raising that percentage to 20 over the next five years.

As we have seen, Mao's egalitarian ideal had expressed a Robin Hood approach to China's provinces, with the central government taking funds from the wealthier provinces and cities and redistributing them to the poorer ones. His idea was that only when regional inequalities had been reduced could China move forward — slowly, but equally. But Deng Xiaoping rejected this egalitarian approach to development, believing that it kept the best-endowed regions from realizing their potential and made for unacceptably slow growth. He justified his new approach with what we often call trickle-down economics, arguing that letting regions with the greatest potential develop rapidly would eventually benefit the poorer regions as well. Using an analogy, he described the special economic zones along the coast as pivotal points of two fans, the one extending out into the world economy, the other extending westward into the hinterlands. Capital, technology, and new markets would be drawn to the coastal cities along the ribs of the outward-extended fan and, in turn, would spread into China's interior along the ribs of the inward-extended fan.

There are many Chinese who are not persuaded by Deng's argument. They either consider the trickle down too slow or dispute that there is one. China's experience during the past several decades suggests to them that a kind of center-periphery relationship is emerging, in which poorer provinces serve as suppliers of raw material, semifinished products, and labor power for the economic centers, which, awash in foreign capital and advanced technology, reap all the profits.

flow of foreign investment, while the provinces want the freedom to attract foreign investors and the authority to cut deals with them. The center sets restrictions with respect to the size and nature of investments that may be locally approved; the provincial governments then set about calculating how to circumvent these restrictions.

Yet another source of conflict between center and region is what in the United States would be called unfunded mandates. Like our own federal government, China's central government has had a habit of enacting laws and regulations that require local government action but provide no funds to cover the costs. For example, the central government, wanting to improve the quality of air and water, has a full set of environmental laws and regulations but gives little or no financial support to local governments to cover the cost of enforcing them. Similarly, it is actively engaged in a program to reduce the size of the Chinese population but vests responsibility for implementing this program with local governments and provides no funding to offset the costs involved. In education, too, the central government enacts programs for expansion and improvement, but it relies on the local governments for the funds to carry out this mandate.

Provinces and regions frequently find themselves competing with one another for the resources, benefits, and exemptions distributed by the central government, for foreign investors, and for opportunities to engage in lucrative foreign trading deals. To better their positions, they try to maximize their ability to make independent decisions, and, to promote their local interests, they rival one another in lobbying the central government and currying favor with its officials.

Occasionally competition among regions has taken the form of protectionism. Some years ago, state-owned department stores in Shandong Province, for example, launched an informal "Buy Shandong" campaign, agreeing to exclude merchandise from other provinces and to limit the stock in their stores to goods produced in Shandong. Similarly, when officials in Hunan Province concluded that they were on the losing end of an economic competition with neighboring Guangdong Province, where factories were buying goods from Hunan suppliers at low (regulated) prices and making finished products that they sold at high (unregulated) prices, they closed Hunan's border with Guangdong and stopped the flow of goods in both directions. Only when the central government intervened was the border reopened and cross-border trade resumed. (It was perhaps this episode that Nicholas Kristof had in mind when, in *The New York Times*, he wrote an article sketching out three scenarios for China's future, in one of which economic cross-border competition between Hunan and Hubei Provinces erupts into a civil war that an impotent central government cannot bring under control.)

There are other issues that set provinces and regions at odds with one another. Water and air pollution seldom affects only the immediate area in which the pollution occurs; provinces or regions responsible for enforcing environmental regulations find their efforts undermined by neighboring regions that are unwilling to undertake or are less responsible for enforcement. Similarly, major public-works projects like the Three Gorges Dam or the proposed South to North Water Diversion Project have consequences that benefit one region while harming another. (In the case of the latter, for example, the northern provinces will have more water, but the central-south provinces not only get no extra water but also must bear the cost of the land taken out of cultivation for the right-of-way.)

Finally, with a newly mobile population, the movement of workers is a source of conflict. More than 100 million people have left their original jurisdictions for distant cities. Is it the responsibility of the cities or of the rural communities from which they came to bring this population under control? A Wild West variant on this problem concerns the so-called Gold Lords, who staked out illegal mining claims in China's hinterlands, hired migrant rural workers as miners, and defended their claims against rival claimants (and local authorities) with massive arsenals. Here again, region is pitted against region: Is it the responsibility of Qinghai (where many of the claims are located) to control this "attractive nuisance" or of the regions from which the prospectors come to give them jobs and control their movement?

The means at the disposal of a province or a region for asserting and defending its interests are varied. The mildest form is the time-honored technique of persuasion through debate, jawboning, or lobbying. Local officials who think their interests are being threatened by the central government or by their neighbors will argue the case as persuasively as they can with the best-connected representative they can find. The central government seems to operate most comfortably by treating each case as sui generis and is least at ease when trying to enforce uniform regulations uniformly, which means that a region or province can quite easily make the case for being treated as one among many exceptions to a given rule or regulation.

If this argument falls on deaf ears, local authorities can resort to the next means at their disposal for asserting their interests, passive resistance; given the nature of China's political system, this tactic is perhaps the most effective. Paying lip service to the interests of the central government or of neighbors yet actively pursuing one's own plan is usually a highly effective way to stymie rivals. Bureaucratic practice is replete with methods for appearing to conform while not actually doing so.

If all else fails, active resistance is possible, but this third option is a dangerous strategy because of the possibility of violent retaliation. Whether setting forth new local regulations, encouraging local practices that directly contravene central directives, failing to collect or forward tax revenues due the central authorities, or closing one's borders to cross-border trade, a province must carefully calculate the capabilities and intentions of its opponent. Active resistance against China's central authorities has only been tried two or three times since 1949, and it was always unsuccessful, but that was when the central authorities were strong, unified, and credible.

For some years after the 1949 revolution, China's central Party and government enjoyed great credibility, central and regional interests were seen as united, and the united interests were contained in and explained by an ideology to which many were deeply committed. But much, if not all, of the credibility of the Party-state has now been lost, as a result in part of disastrously mistaken policies, bloated egos, pervasive corruption, and the collapse of ideology and its replacement with a shallow, self-seeking materialism. In the absence of credibility, China's central authorities have had to secure compliance with their directives by manipulation, persuasion, or coercion.

One method they use to further the cause of local compliance is to minimize the differences between central and local interests. An example of this strategy is the shift of policy after Deng's inspection trip in February 1993 to the Shenzhen special economic zone, where retrenchment policies adopted in 1988 to slow economic growth and cap inflation had been very unpopular but where a new policy of encouraging market reform won the immediate approval—and compliance—of all but a handful of local authorities. Still, local interests are diverse, not uniform, and bringing central policy into conformity with the interests of one region inevitably raises difficulties with the interests of other regions.

A second strategy that the center uses to secure compliance from local governments is to bargain, since it holds a limited but significant number of chips that it can use in the game with local authorities: items that benefit the individual official like appointments and promotions, and items that benefit the constituency like tax waivers or public-works projects. The process is akin to the pork-barrel politics with which Americans are familiar, though compliance, not votes, is the operative currency in the Chinese case. It is because of the advantages it gets from bargaining that the center is so reluctant to formalize, regularize, or "federalize" its policies vis-à-vis local governments.

Where compromise and bargaining fail, the center can always appoint or dismiss local officials. This power is somewhat limited, because effective local officials need the confidence of their communities as well as that of the center: the center can replace a rebellious official, but his replacement will be a success only if he gains his constituency's cooperation. As we have seen, the center appoints people with strong local ties more and more frequently, but this undermines its leverage.

As a final resort, local compliance can, in theory, be secured through coercion, as it has been in the past. The center has a nominal monopoly on the instruments of coercion—that is, the People's Liberation Army and the People's Armed Police. In practice, however, it would take a very flagrant example of a local government's flouting central authority to induce the center to send in troops. And then there is the question of whether the armed forces would obey such an order. Certainly there are reasons for military commanders to think twice before carrying it out. First, there is the question of where a commander's loyalties lie. Despite the Party's best efforts, the Army itself suffers from regional divisions, and one can imagine situations in which a regional military commander would see his interests aligned with those of the region where he is stationed and not with those in distant Beijing. He would also reflect on the negative consequences for the armed forces of its having obeyed the orders of the elders in Beijing in 1989. In short, there are reasons for the Army to doubt the wisdom of acting as the coercive arm of a tottering political authority.

Were it to do so, as I believe it well might, it would do so to end an interregional conflict threatening civil war or if it perceived that central authority had collapsed, as in the former Soviet Union in 1991. But intervening under these circumstances, it would see itself as a substitute for the paralyzed Party-state, not as its agent.

Given the divergence of interests between the central government and local governments in China and the relative weakness of the former, it is very likely that more and more decentralized political and economic systems will emerge. Given their rivalries and their growing ties with foreign economies, China's macroregions will act with greater and greater independence in determining the direction of their development. The central government will probably be unable to amass the authority, the bargaining chips, or the coercion to reassert its power in the near term.

IX

HAN AND NON-HAN:
THE DIVISIVE FORCES OF ETHNICITY

THE TERM "ETHNICITY" is not easy to come to grips with. People define themselves as an ethnically distinct group when they have in common a set of customs and characteristics, a language, a history, or a religion. And yet in China, people who identify themselves ethnically as Han—a group that makes up 92 percent of the population, or close to 1.2 billion people—have in common, as we have seen, neither spoken language, customs, characteristics, nor religion. Nonetheless, Han Chinese do think of themselves as ethnically distinct from the roughly 100 million people who are members of the fifty-seven other ethnic groups that make up the Chinese population. And those groups, as we shall see, do have languages, customs, characteristics, history, and religions that separate them from one another and from the Han majority.

Three cases illustrate the way in which ethnicity presents itself as a pressing issue in China today: Inner Mongolia, Xinjiang, and Tibet. Although none of the minority nationalities (as the Chinese commonly refer to ethnic groups) in these three territories is among the country's four largest, all three territories are home to ethnic groups that extend across China's borders into neighboring states to the north and west. All of them have experienced unrest inspired by ethnic separatist sentiments. And at least one of them—Tibet—receives extensive international support for its independence movement. Finally, although they are contiguous to one another (or nearly so) and were linked culturally in the past, they have quite distinctive histories and are dissimilar today in their ethnic composition, economies, and relations with Beijing.

Table 7

MINORITY NATIONALITIES IN THE 1990 CENSUS
(IN MILLIONS)

Zhuang	15.5
Man	9.8
Hui	8.6
Miao	7.3
Uighur	7.2
Yi	6.6
Tujia	5.7
Mongol	4.8
Tibetan	4.6
Kirghiz	1.4
Kazakh	1.1
Tajik	0.3
Uzbek	0.1
Other nationalities (44)	18.3
Total minority population	91.3
As a percentage of total population	8.1%

(Source: *China Statistical Yearbook* 1999)

We begin with a relatively benign case: Inner Mongolia. Both Inner Mongolia (today's Inner Mongolian Autonomous Region) and Outer Mongolia (today's Mongolian People's Republic, or MPR) were part of the Qing empire. Even before they established their rule over China proper, the Manchus defeated the Inner Mongols and, with their help, brought the Eastern Mongols (also known as the Khalkha tribe) under Manchu control as well. The Western Mongols (the

Dzungar tribe), by contrast, were an unruly lot never more than nominally governed from Beijing. The government set up a new office, the Lifan Yuan (literally, the "Barbarian Management Department"), with responsibility for Mongolia, Chinese Turkestan (modern Xinjiang), and Tibet. Indeed, Mongolia was already closely linked with Tibet by religion. That branch of Tibetan Lamaism currently led by the Dalai Lama had spread to Mongolia in the mid-seventeenth century, and a succession of religious leaders known as living Buddhas were based in the city of Urga (modern Ulan Bator).

Meanwhile Russia had expanded its influence in Asia, an expansion greatly facilitated in the latter years of the nineteenth century by the construction of the Trans-Siberian Railroad. In a 1907 agreement between Russia and Japan, spheres of influence were carved out: northern Manchuria and Outer Mongolia to Russia, southern Manchuria and eastern Inner Mongolia to Japan. Historians draw an analogy between this assault on China's "back door" and the pressure from European powers and the United States to open treaty ports at the coastal "front door." When the debilitated Qing dynasty collapsed in 1911, Outer Mongolia declared its independence. Russia refrained from recognizing the new government as fully independent, but its formula of Chinese suzerainty, Outer Mongolian autonomy, and Russian protection amounted to the same thing. When the Mongolian People's Republic was formally established in 1924, it was recognized immediately by Moscow but not until 1952 by a reluctant Mao Zedong.

Inner Mongolia, like the rest of China, came under warlord control after the fall of the Qing and, with the backing of the Japanese in the late 1930s, declared its independence as the state of Meng Jiang, closely affiliated with a similar puppet regime in Manchuria. At the Japanese surrender in 1945, a provisional government was formed under the leadership of Ulanfu, a Mongol who had allied himself with the Communist guerrillas. The Inner Mongolian Autonomous Region (IMAR) was established in 1947, two years before the founding of the People's Republic. By 1956, it had been expanded to include Mongol areas that had been under the administrative control of the former provincial governments of Rehe, Chahar, Suiyuan, and part of what is now the autonomous region of Ningxia. The term "autonomous region" was never more than a public relations gimmick designed to win the support of minority ethnicities for a Party-state that was always firmly in the hands of the Han majority. Lip service was and is given to ensuring representation of non-Hans in Party and government positions, but, with very few exceptions, leadership posts are occupied by Han Chinese.

By 1949, Mongols had quite literally become a minority nationality, even within the borders of Inner Mongolia. Although once an area closed to Chinese migration, in the declining years of the Qing, Chinese settlers had been encouraged as a counterweight to Russian influence. In 1998, only one in six of the IMAR population was Mongol, most of them engaged in raising camels and horses. Inner Mongolia is a high plateau at about three thousand feet, roughly three times the size of California, and mostly given over to grasslands, some of which are threatened by encroaching desertification. It stretches nearly sixteen hundred miles from its northeastern border with Russia to its southwestern border with the province of Gansu. In 1998, it had a gross domestic product of $14 billion, of which 68 percent was industrial production, 31 percent was transportation, commerce, finance, and the like, and only 1 percent derived from agriculture and animal husbandry. Like the other autonomous regions we will consider, the IMAR is heavily dependent on funds from the central government: regional revenues in 1998 totaled only $900 million against regional government expenditures of just over $2 billion.

Ethnic relations are considerably smoother in Inner Mongolia than in Xinjiang or Tibet, at least in part because of the heavy preponderance of Han Chinese. There have been few reported instances of separatist activities, and visitors have observed an attitude of mutual respect between Hans and Mongols in government and business settings. Pressed to define what "autonomy" means in practice in the IMAR, both Han and Mongol leaders say that, in fact, the term means little but is retained for "historical reasons."

Since the collapse of the Soviet Union, with which the Mongolian People's Republic had close ties, there has been considerable interest in the IMAR for cross-border trade with the MPR. In 1998, two-way MPR-China trade was just under $250 million, three-quarters of it Chinese imports of Mongolian goods, mostly timber and cashmere wool, and the Chinese have invested some $25 million in projects in the MPR. A substantial international economic collaboration was proposed in the early 1990s for the Tumen River area in Jilin Province. The United National Development Program project involving Mongolia, the two Koreas, China, and Japan called for a $30 billion trade and transport complex designed to expand the region's outreach to the international economy. The Asian financial crisis and ongoing problems in relations between the two Koreas stalled the project. Meanwhile there is some concern in the MPR over its growing economic dependence on China. Steps have been taken to limit exports, and, as a sign of its independence, Mongolia reaffirmed its historical ties to Tibet when it welcomed the Dalai Lama on a visit to Ulan Bator in 1995.

We move next to a significantly less benign case: Xinjiang. Unlike in Inner Mongolia, minority nationalities are in the majority of its population. Xinjiang is twice the size of Texas but has a population of only seventeen million, 60 percent of which is composed of ethnic minorities. Unlike Inner Mongolia, Xinjiang, lying athwart the Silk Road over which trade passed between China and the West for centuries, has always been open to interactions with countless ethnic groups and foreign nationals. Unlike in Inner Mongolia, violent protests organized by ethnic separatists occurred with increasing frequency after 1985.

The two areas that make up contemporary Xinjiang, the area around the Ili River in the north and the Tarim Basin in the south, were brought under what historians have called a "tenuous supremacy" of the Qing dynasty in the middle of the eighteenth century. These regions are home to at least five ethnic groups: the majority Uighurs, the Kazakhs, Kirghiz, Tajiks, and Uzbeks. These

groups are all Muslim (they are Shiites rather than Sunnis), and their languages, while distinct from one another, are all variations of Turkic, a member of the Altaic family of languages (which includes Mongolian and Manchu). With the exception of the Uighurs, almost all of whom live in what is now Xinjiang, the minority nationalities extend across national boundaries to the north and west into Kazakhstan, Kyrgyzstan, Tajikistan, and Uzbekistan. And increasingly, they are all subject to the appeal of Muslim fundamentalism.

The tenuous hold of the Qing over Xinjiang was interrupted in the mid-nineteenth century by a Muslim rebellion in the Tarim Basin led by Yakub Beg. Ten years later, when Russians occupied the Ili Basin, the dynasty debated whether the campaign to recapture Chinese Turkestan, as it was then known, was worth the doubtlessly daunting cost. Zuo Zongtang persuaded a reluctant foreign minister to undertake the campaign in 1873, though the empire was also under assault by foreign powers on its southern littoral, and against all odds, Zuo was successful: all of eastern Turkestan was retaken, with the exception of the Russian-occupied Ili region. But the latter was recouped under the Treaty of St. Petersburg in 1880, and Chinese Turkestan became the province of Xinjiang (literally, New Territories), with its capital in Ulumuqi (Urumqi).

Xinjiang, like Inner Mongolia, experienced a great deal of de facto autonomy under the Qing and, subsequently, under the Nationalists. In 1944, Xinjiang followed Inner Mongolia's example and declared its independence under the name of the East Turkestan Republic. Contacts were made with Chinese Communist guerrillas, and, in September 1949, the Nationalist forces there surrendered to the People's Liberation Army (PLA). In 1955, the Xinjiang-Uighur Autonomous Region (XUAR) was formally announced.

In the XUAR, ethnic minorities are in a majority in all but the capital city of Ulumuqi. Special provision is made for the five (of sixteen) prefects in Xinjiang where Uighurs are not in the majority: they are "autonomous districts," where Kazakhs or Kirghiz outnumber Uighurs. In the region as a whole, Party and government offices are distributed in rough proportion to the ethnic balance, though Han

Chinese almost always hold the top leadership positions. As in the IMAR, "autonomy" is mostly a fiction maintained for "historical reasons."

A key player in the development of the XUAR has been the Xinjiang Production and Construction Corps (XPCC). One of a number of Production and Construction Corps formed under the supervision of the PLA at the time of the founding of the People's Republic, the XPCC took primary responsibility for developing agriculture and, subsequently, new industries. All the PLA's Production and Construction Corps were disbanded in 1975, but the Xinjiang Corps was reestablished in 1982—this time under the supervision of the Ministry of Agriculture. The corps currently employs 2.4 million workers, nearly all of whom are Han; they and their dependents account for about 16 percent of Xinjiang's population, and the corps produces 20–25 percent of its total gross domestic product. It continues to focus on agriculture but is increasingly involved in building the industrial infrastructure. Xinjiang's gross domestic product in 1998 was $13 billion, of which, as is the case in the IMAR, roughly 64 percent derived from industry, 1 percent from agriculture, and the balance from "tertiary industry." Like the IMAR, Xinjiang served as a drain on national coffers, taking in $780 million in tax revenues and expending $1.75 billion in 1998.

Relations between the Uighur and Kazakh nationalities and the Han population in the XUAR have never achieved the level of mutual respect reported by visitors to the IMAR. And the Soviet Union took advantage of this dissent to stir up trouble. In the 1950s and again at the nadir of Sino-Soviet relations in the 1960s, Russians encouraged Uighurs and Kazakhs to immigrate to the Soviet Union. Close to a hundred thousand people did so—a decision that many of them have come to regret at a time, forty years later, when China's western territories are relatively affluent compared with Russia's southeastern territories.

In Inner Mongolia, Pan-Mongolism attracts few supporters, but the movement to establish an independent East Turkestan Republic attracts substantial support. In the 1980s, three groups were dedicated to this aim: the East Turkestan National Salvation Committee, the East Turkestan Popular Revolutionary Front, and the World Islamic Alliance. Twenty-two were killed in an uprising in Baren over the construction of a new mosque. A bomb blast in the summer of 1993 destroyed part of a hotel in Kashgar and killed three people. Four years later, ten were killed in demonstrations in the city of Yining, resulting in the executions of twelve people. A month later, three bomb attacks occurred in Beijing, hours after a memorial service for the deceased Deng Xiaoping, for which the "East Turkestan Freedom Organization" claimed responsibility; victims numbered close to a hundred. And early in 2000, when Uighur militants and Chinese security forces clashed in Aksu, several militants were killed, five were sentenced to death, and eight others were given long jail sentences. Beijing is particularly concerned about international involvement in these incidents. Chinese authorities cite evidence that Islamic militants in Saudi Arabia, Iran, Turkey, India, Pakistan, and Afghanistan have supplied weapons to Xinjiang separatists.

In an effort to address the issue of cross-border support for ethnic unrest in central Asia, representatives from Kazakhstan, Kyrgyzstan, and Tajikistan were invited to join Boris Yeltsin and Jiang Zemin in their 1996 summit meeting in Beijing. None of the three central Asian republics supports an independent East Turkestan, and all five states regard themselves as threatened by Islamic fundamentalists; they signed an agreement to cooperate in bringing stability to the area. Three years later, at a meeting in Bishkek, Kyrgyzstan, attended by Yeltsin and Jiang, the agreement was formalized in a treaty that established a "peace zone" along their common borders. Yet Islamic fundamentalists took and held hostages in a neighboring region of the republic while the summit meeting was in session.

Finally, there is Tibet, the least benign of our three cases. Like Inner Mongolia and unlike Xinjiang, Tibet is geographically isolated and has historically been cut off from the outside world. Like Xinjiang's and unlike Inner Mongolia's, most of Tibet's population—close to 90 percent—are non-Han. Unlike both the others, Tibet was the back door, as it were, through which Britain and the United States came to assault China. And most critically, it is virtually impossible to speak in neutral terms about Tibet. Those who think of it from the perspective of the Dalai Lama see no merit in China's position; those who sympathize with Beijing find no common cause with the Dalai Lama. The crux of the issue is the validity or invalidity of the Tibetans' claim that the territory was once independent and recognized internationally as being so.

Tibet is roughly a third the size of the United States, and there are also Tibetans living in portions of Sichuan, Qinghai, Gansu, and Yunnan Provinces. There are three major areas in the Tibet region: the northern plain, at seventeen thousand feet, the Tsangpo River valley in the south (the river is known as the Brahmaputra in India), at twelve thousand feet, and the forested slopes in eastern Tibet. Lhasa, somewhat surprisingly, lies at the same latitude as New Orleans. As a result of its latitude and altitude, summer days are often hot, nights are freezing, and there is little or no rainfall.

In its relative isolation, Tibet borrowed and transformed Buddhism into its own idiosyncratic religion. The Yellow Hat sect of this Buddhist offshoot was established in the fifteenth century and quickly spread to Mongolia, where the reigning prince bestowed the title "Dalai Lama" (All-embracing Leader) on the successors of the founder, Cong-ka-pa. The Manchus also welcomed Tibetan Buddhism; their admiration took architectural form in the Qing summer residence in Chengde, modeled after the Potala palace in Lhasa, and in the stunning Yonghegong (or Lama Temple) in downtown Beijing.

With the support of the Mongols, the Dalai Lama assumed temporal powers in Tibet at about the time of the founding of the Qing empire and established a tributary relationship with the Qing emperor in 1652. Qing armies intervened three times—in 1720, 1727, and 1750—reaffirming Chinese control over the territory.

Thirty years later, in 1780, the Panchen Lama, temporal ruler in western Tibet, received the first emissary from the British East India Company. This initial contact was thwarted when Gurkhas from

Nepal invaded Tibet, but the Qing once again reasserted authority in 1790 and closed off Tibet from all foreign contact. Britain, meanwhile, established its presence in the northern Indian hill states and, in a series of agreements in 1886–1893, acknowledged Chinese suzerainty over Tibetan foreign relations but assumed responsibility for trade between India and Tibet. When Russia, the other player in the "Great Game" for ascendancy in central Asia, made contact with the thirteenth Dalai Lama in an attempt to counter British interests, the British sent an armed mission into Lhasa under the command of Francis Younghusband. The result was a British protectorate over Tibet and recognition, in 1914, of its independence (accepted on the Chinese side only by the very short-lived government of Yuan Shikai in the wake of the 1911 revolution). This formula, reminiscent of that used by Russia in Mongolia and formally accepted by no other nation, has caused no end of international debate.

The People's Liberation Army invaded Tibet in 1950 and within a year subdued local resistance. Zhou Enlai skillfully negotiated with the Indian government to refrain from intervening on behalf of the Tibetans, and the British also refrained from intervening. The Chinese moved into Tibet with a soft hand at first, but by 1959, protests had expanded into armed rebellion. The PLA responded with force: many Tibetans were killed, and countless monasteries were destroyed. The Dalai Lama fled to a refuge in Dharamsala, India. The United States, meanwhile, flew Tibetan dissidents out of their country, trained them in Colorado, and repatriated them as guerrilla fighters, radio operators, and spies behind Chinese lines.

The 1960s was a difficult decade for the people of Tibet. The Chinese Party-state, emboldened by its successes in suppressing the Tibetan rebellion and in its border war with India in 1962, vigorously undertook the "socialist transformation" of Tibet. Collaboration with Tibet's upper classes, which had marked Chinese policy in the 1950s, was replaced by a vigorous effort to mobilize support among Tibet's working classes. Young men were discouraged from becoming monks, and, with the onset of the Cultural Revolution, most of the intact monasteries and temples were destroyed or defaced. Formal establishment of the Tibet Autonomous Region (TAR) in 1965 marked, paradoxically, the destruction of the last shred of Tibetan autonomy. China claimed it had accomplished the "liberation" of an impoverished, feudal society. International human-rights advocates claimed that China was engaged in a systematic effort at suppressing Tibetan religion and the human rights of the Tibetan people. Tibet was an international cause célèbre.

The TAR has a population of only 2.5 million people: smaller than the population of Chicago. According to official statistics, the Han percentage is four, but this calculation does not include the mounting number of migrant laborers who come to Tibet for work, nor does it count the PLA troops stationed there; the real number is probably four times that. Foreign critics accuse Beijing of a systematic effort at "Hanification" of Tibet by means of Han immigration, but the effects of this effort pale in comparison with the situation in the IMAR. Tibet's gross domestic product is a scant $1 billion, half of it from industrial production, less than 1 percent from agriculture, and the remainder from transportation, commerce, finance, and the like. To an even greater extent than neighboring autonomous regions, Tibet is dependent on central government funds: the regional government takes in $43 million in tax revenues and spends close to $550 million annually. Beijing argues that Tibet could not survive without support from the national coffers; Beijing's opponents argue that the support in no sense justifies the suppression of Tibetan rights.

Religion is a sensitive issue for the Chinese Party-state, and especially so in Tibet. The Chinese have argued that Tibetan Lamaism held thousands of young men as monks in a state of bondage equivalent to that of slavery or, at best, feudal serfdom. Beijing attacked the Panchen Lama for his opposition to its policies in the early 1960s and extended its attack to the Dalai Lama, then in exile in India, for "counterrevolutionary" resistance to the Party-state's authority. When the Panchen Lama died in 1989, both the Dalai Lama and China chose successors. Beijing's candidate was consecrated in ceremonies held in Xigazi in 1995, while the Dalai Lama's candidate (like his rival, a preschooler) is held under house arrest in Beijing. The official press described the situation as a "long-term, bitter, complex, you-die-I-live political battle with no possibility of compromise." This battle between Tibetan supporters of the Dalai Lama and the Chinese authorities has often taken the form of protest demonstrations. The most serious of them took place in the early spring of 1989, at which point the PLA was called in to restore order—a process that eventuated in the first declaration of martial law since the founding of the PRC.

The Dalai Lama, who lives in India with a growing flock of 100,000 followers, is an international figure whose work—and praise for it, notably the Nobel Peace Prize in 1989—attracts embarrassing attention to Chinese policy in Tibet. He would like to negotiate with Beijing to arrive at a formula for Tibet not dissimilar from those effected in Hong Kong and Macao and offered to Taiwan: "one country, two systems." A degree of genuine autonomy that would guarantee religious freedom and local political control would satisfy many Tibetans. Other Tibetans want total independence and international recognition of that independence. But one must ask how an independent Tibet would sustain itself, as one must ask under what circumstances the Chinese Party-state would feel confident enough of itself to grant genuine autonomy to a territory which it claims to have been "always Chinese," in which Han Chinese are such a small minority, and which is a strategic barrier between China and potentially hostile states to the south.

For the moment, the Dalai Lama, paradoxically, functions as a damper on ethnic separatism in Tibet. An international spokesperson with an enormous and attentive audience, his religious and secular influence moderates the impulses of those who want to be separatists. Xinjiang has no such moderating leader; Inner Mongolians seem not to need one. Nonetheless, ethnicity is, for the moment, a divisive, not a uniting, influence in China, and the Party-state is ill-equipped to deal with it.

X

THE CHALLENGE OF
ENVIRONMENTAL DEGRADATION

THE DARK SIDE of a high standard of living in the modern style is its adverse effect on the environment. With every improvement—greater mobility, a more varied diet, more living space, and more personal possessions—attendant costs must be borne by the environment. Given the huge size of China's population, the success of its rapid economic development in raising the living standard has posed a particularly ominous threat of environmental degradation. Coping with this threat is one of the most serious problems confronting China and, because China's environment is also our environment, the rest of the world as well.

The Chinese state in traditional times worked hard to preserve a delicate balance between human needs and natural resources. The central government took responsibility for mobilizing the labor needed to build and maintain a system of flood control and irrigation works, as well as a network of inland waterways. Generations of Chinese peasants perfected a system of farming that made maximal use of limited land and, by means of intensive recycling practices, preserved its fertility. There was very little profligacy in the Chinese people's use of natural resources.

That delicate balance has been destroyed in modern times, and for several reasons. The first of these was a very rapid growth in the Chinese population during the eighteenth century. As we have seen,

To counter these trends, China's interior provinces are actively courting foreign investors with bargain rates on real estate and labor and at the same time vociferously opposing any favoritism allowed to the coastal zones in the form of tax breaks for potential investors, arguing that only if they have comparable leeway can they compete effectively. In the meantime, they are learning to turn the successes of the coastal enclaves to their own advantage, becoming major investors themselves in enterprises and property in the coastal zones. Most recently, the central government has taken a hand once again in leveling the playing field. Over the last three years, Beijing has issued more than $30 billion in bonds for infrastructure projects to stimulate economic growth. The tranche of these bonds for the year 2000 was earmarked for the western provinces. At the same time, the governor of the China Development Bank announced that 60 percent of the bank's loans would go to projects in the central and western parts of the country.

Having grown accustomed to a greater degree of autonomy, the provinces now tend to resist any effort by the central government to recoup its control of local affairs. The center, for its part, believes that the major problems confronting the economy—deflation, the banking crisis, and the ailing state sector—can best be addressed at the national level. Many of the issues that pit regions against the center arise from this conflict of interests.

Bank credit is an example. The central government became concerned in mid-1993 that local governments were authorizing too many loans for highly speculative projects, limiting the amount of credit available for less lucrative but vitally needed infrastructure projects and, it was thought, contributing to the high inflation rate. Acting on this concern, the central bank ordered local banks to call in their most speculative loans. But six months later, Vice Premier Zhu Rongji, who had temporarily taken charge of the central bank, admitted that the order had been only modestly successful in freeing up local credit for worthwhile purposes.

Similarly, the central government wants to control and direct the

China's population remained stable at between 50 and 100 million people for nearly sixteen centuries; then, in the early years of the Qing dynasty in the late seventeenth century, it began to grow rapidly, multiplying by a factor of five within two hundred years. Although new crops and techniques increased agricultural productivity, the fivefold increase in population was accompanied by only a 25 percent increase in the amount of land under cultivation. The delicate balance of human needs and natural resources was destroyed.

A second factor contributing to the breakdown of this balance was industrialization. The Chinese had sat out the industrial revolution that swept Europe and the United States in the early nineteenth century, indeed were almost wholly ignorant of its products until Western powers used modern weaponry to force China to open its doors to trade. Weapons factories became the entering wedge of industrialization in China, and by the last years of the nineteenth century the Chinese government had reluctantly and belatedly decided to emulate the West with full-scale industrialization.

A third factor was that China's industrialization was achieved under socialist auspices. Capitalist industrialization can hardly be said to have proceeded without environmental damage, but as we have all seen in eastern Europe and Russia, socialist industrialization seems to have been especially pernicious in its effects on the environment. For one thing, with the land and its resources publicly owned, no one takes responsibility for the land or represents its interests. For another, water and energy are supplied to consumers at no cost or at a heavily subsidized cost, and there is no incentive to conserve their use. Worse, the deficiencies in the quantity and quality of land, air, and water are escalating rather than improving.

China has a serious shortage of arable land. As we have seen in Chapter 6, this shortage is daily exacerbated when land is taken out of cultivation and used for factories, roads, railroad rights-of-way, housing, and other accoutrements of rural industrialization and economic development. Scarce farmland is also lost as the unintended consequence of deforestation. Wood and plant stalks supply about four-fifths of the energy used for cooking and heating in the country-side, and this has resulted in the deforestation of nearly 300 million acres of land over the last forty years, which in turn adversely affects adjacent farmland. In the absence of forest windbreaks, some 16 million acres have been lost to desertification since 1949 and another 40 million acres are at risk. The cutting of trees also greatly increases water runoff, soil erosion, and siltation of riverbeds, raising the water level and augmenting the devastation caused by floods.

Air pollution is an especially serious problem in China: five of the world's ten most polluted cities are located in China. The air in 90 percent of China's cities does not meet Chinese government clean-air standards, which are not as stringent as Western ones. Beijing air is, on average, sixteen times more polluted than New York City air, and the city of Benxi, near Shenyang in Liaoning Province, periodically disappears from view on satellite maps because of the overlay of polluted air, the quality of which is second only to that of Milan, which has the dubious distinction of being the world's most polluted city.

The principal cause of air pollution in China is the burning of soft coal, which accounts for three-quarters of the energy used. Two-thirds of China's factories are contributing to air pollution in this way, and their outdated and inefficient equipment means they are using excessive quantities of the polluting fuel. China's industrial plant currently uses 5 times the amount of energy per dollar of gross national product (GNP) as Japan's and 2.5 times the United States'. But dust carried on prevailing winds from the desert regions of the northwest also contributes to urban air pollution, particularly in China's northern cities. Until recently, automobile exhaust was not a significant contributor to urban air pollution, but that is likely to change in the near future. There are currently only about 7 million automobiles on China's streets and roads—a tiny fraction of the 144 million automobiles registered in the United States—because the Chinese rely on bicycles and buses as their principal means of urban transportation. But in the fall of 1994, the government decided to make the automobile industry a primary force in the next stage of economic development, and an annual production target of 3 million new automobiles was set for 2000 (three-fifths of the current annual American production). Foreign manufacturers actively compete to participate in the joint ventures that will help China meet this target.

The decision to develop the automobile industry has sparked a lively debate in China. Government planners have published specifications for a small, fuel-efficient, and low-polluting "family car" of the future. But promoting such a car as the principal means of transportation carries with it a multitude of undesirable consequences. A quarter of a billion automobiles would pollute the air, require paving over still more acres of scarce farmland, exhaust the country's oil reserves, and render China's already congested cities unnavigable. Moreover, automobile engineers are skeptical that the features called for in the specifications can be achieved in a car that is supposed to cost no more than ten thousand dollars.

China is currently the world's fourth-largest source of greenhouse gases (producing about 700 million metric tons annually, or 10 percent of the total). In comparative terms, China produces 275 metric tons of carbon for each million dollars in gross domestic product, the United States produces 240, and Russia produces 502. China's rate of economic development translates into an increase of about 6 percent per year in energy consumption. At this rate, China will exceed the United States, which is currently the largest producer of greenhouse gases, by the early years of the twenty-first century and reach three times the current U.S. level of production by 2025.

Industrialization and a higher living standard are ordinarily accompanied by an increase in water consumption. Indeed, the consumption of tap water in China's cities has increased fivefold over the last twenty years. (Water consumption in Beijing amounts to some 500 billion gallons per year; the water table around the city has dropped nearly two hundred feet since the mid-1960s.) Because water is supplied free of charge to urban residents, there is no incentive to conserve it. Yet the water supply in China is neither adequate nor evenly distributed. Southern China, with about one-third of the arable land, has three-quarters of the water supply, while northern

China has a serious water deficit. More than half of China's cities currently have a water shortage.

Unless new sources of water are located or stringent conservation measures adopted, experts estimate that Beijing will be short by up to 250 billion gallons a year by 2010. A highly controversial solution to this problem is the proposed South to North Water Diversion Project, plans for which include an 850-mile aqueduct to move water from the Han River, in Hubei Province, to reservoirs near Beijing and Tianjin. Initially, it was estimated that the project would cost $5 billion and take six years to complete.

Not only is the water supply inadequate, but the quality of water is rapidly deteriorating. In 1995, factories and cities in China discharged 36.5 billion tons of sewage and industrial wastewater into waterways and coastal waters. Half of the waterways in China's seven major water systems are polluted, and 90 percent of the water flowing through its major cities is impotable.

This discouraging situation has not developed because of a lack of agencies, laws, or regulations. On the contrary, China has a reasonably complete set of environmental protection laws and regulations and a fully articulated structure of government offices devoted to environmental matters.

The problem of environmental pollution was first addressed at a national conference on the subject in 1973—five years before the economic reforms began. Six years later, the National People's Congress passed the Environmental Protection Law, and five years after that, in 1984, the National Environmental Protection Agency (NEPA) was formed. In 1998, NEPA was promoted to ministerial level under the State Council, becoming the State Environmental Protection Agency (SEPA). Revisions to the Environmental Protection Law, which were adopted by the National People's Congress in 1989, require environmental impact studies for all major construction projects and impose stiff fines for violating the pollution limits. Undeniably these conferences, new agencies, and new laws have had positive results. Among them is heightened public awareness. Many environmental groups have sprung up, and a stunning 98 percent of those surveyed in a government poll in 1998 called for stricter environmental regulation and increased government expenditure for environmental protection. China is currently spending close to 1 percent of GNP, or $10 billion, on environmental protection annually. This puts it within, if at the low end of, the international average expenditure as a percentage of GNP, which stands between 1 and 2 percent.

Research and training in environmental sciences have developed quickly at universities and research institutes, and these institutions are well connected with professional equivalents outside China. As is the case in other fields of academic endeavor, the hard science in these institutions is of reasonably high quality, while social science lags behind.

One specific result of this research effort is a new, clean-burning coal compound that is being introduced into China's cities to replace the highly polluting soft coal. There are other examples: in conjunction with its bid to host the summer Olympic games in 2000, the city of Beijing took steps to reduce air pollution by replacing coal with natural gas as a household and industrial fuel, cutting coal use to 15 percent of its earlier level and cutting particulate matter in the air by 50 percent; and both coal and water have been placed on the price-reform agenda, which will encourage conservation of their use.

Environmental issues are difficult to resolve in any political setting. Correcting one source of environmental degradation can often give rise to new and potentially more dangerous sources of pollution; action that benefits the environment in one region may have detrimental effects in a neighboring region. But environmental issues seem particularly difficult to resolve in the Chinese political system, where, as we have discussed, a clash of interests between the central government and regional authorities often ends in deadlock and inaction. The decision to build a dam on the Yangzi River at the site of the Three Gorges gives us a useful example.

The scenic Three Gorges is located on the Yangzi River between the cities of Chongqing and Wuhan. Damming the Yangzi at the Three Gorges was initially proposed by Sun Yat-sen in 1923, but revolution, war, and civil war intervened, and the idea was shelved. The project was revived again under the aegis of Mao Zedong in the mid-1950s, then buried in the chaos of the Cultural Revolution. In 1979, the project was revived yet again. As it has taken shape in our time, it has three objectives, each of which dictates a set of specifications and benefits a particular geographical region.

The first objective, to control flooding along the lower reaches of the Yangzi, is best served by a high dam, though it might be equally well accomplished by a series of smaller dams on the river's tributaries, and it benefits exclusively those living downriver from the dam. The second objective, to generate electrical power, a highly desirable clean alternative to coal, also points toward a high dam, since the higher the dam, the more hydroelectric power can be generated. Given China's electrical grid and the topography of the area upriver, most of the power generated at the dam will go to those living downriver from the Three Gorges. The third objective, to improve navigation by deepening the river channel behind the dam in order to allow ships of up to ten thousand tons of displacement to get upstream as far as Chongqing, would benefit exclusively the communities upriver from the dam. (In fact, there is some possibility that downstream navigation would become more difficult, given the reduction in flow.) Navigation enhancement also imposes some very specific restrictions on the design of the dam.

Obviously, several major issues, over which opinion was deeply divided, had to be resolved before work on the dam could begin. The first was the question whether to build a single dam or a series of smaller dams. Only a single, high dam would raise the water level and improve navigation, but hydroelectric power generation and flood control could both be accomplished with smaller, safer, less costly, and technologically simpler dams. A second, highly controversial issue was the height of the dam and its effect on the people now living in areas that would be inundated by the reservoir behind it. A 650-foot dam, with the capacity to produce twenty-five thousand megawatts of electrical power, would displace, by conservative estimates, more than 1.4 million people; a 450-foot dam would produce six thousand megawatts and displace about 250,000 people. A third set of issues concerned the cost and financing of the project. Estimates proved extraordinarily difficult, given the disagreements over objectives and varying sets of specifications. And it seemed almost impossible to do a cost-benefit analysis, since the cost bases for navigation, power generation, and flood damage differ. Moreover, the project is expected to take more than a decade to complete, during which time price reform will affect virtually every item in the budget, and future inflation rates are difficult to predict. So project costs are a moving target. These factors help to explain why pub lished estimates of the cost of the Three Gorges project vary by a factor of eight.

The current financing plan is based on an official budget of $25 billion, a figure that falls well below the median cost estimate. It calls for funding half the project from government revenues (a national tax on electrical power and profits from power generated at the Gezhouba Dam, downstream from the Three Gorges site). An additional 7.5 percent of the cost is to be covered by the sale of power produced at the dam once the first stage of the project is completed. The China Development Bank is to be tapped for loans covering a further 21 percent of the project cost, and an additional 4.5 percent is to come from loans extended by foreign providers of equipment. This still leaves a shortfall of nearly 20 percent of the money needed to cover a low estimate of the total cost. The World Bank has indicated its unwillingness to consider loan applications, which the Chinese have in any case been reluctant to seek, not wanting to deal with the required environmental impact studies.

Perhaps the most serious technological issue at stake in the dam project is finding a solution for the problem of siltation. Although silt carried by the Yangzi River is only a little more than a third of that carried by the Yellow River, it nonetheless amounts to some 500 million tons a year. Controlling the silt to protect the dam structure and to keep the upriver channel clear poses unprecedented technical problems; predicting the effect on the eroded downstream riverbed caused by a reduction in silt poses still more.

As originally conceived, the project had another seemingly insurmountable technological problem. Initial plans called for hydroelectric generators with a capacity of one thousand megawatts, but the largest generators produced in China have a capacity of three hundred megawatts, the largest outside China seven hundred megawatts. Generator-capacity technology has advanced at a rate of approximately one hundred megawatts a decade. At that rate, it will be well into the twenty-first century before big enough generators will be available for the Three Gorges.

It is no surprise that China's political system is so deeply divided—indeed, at loggerheads—over the Three Gorges project. There are not only sharp disagreements among several regions but apparently irreconcilable divisions among central government agencies. Within the Ministry of Water Resources and Electric Power, a recent merger of two ministries, the section responsible for water resources favors the dam, arguing that it is the most effective solution to the problem of flood control, while the section concerned with electrical power opposes the project on the grounds that a series of smaller dams is a less expensive, technologically more feasible, and more reliable way to increase the country's electric power supply. The Ministry of Communication and its Yangzi River Transport Bureau oppose the large dam on the grounds that its effect on the navigability of the river downstream of the dam is highly unpredictable and its very long construction period will disrupt existing river traffic. A third agency, the Yangzi River Planning Office, established in the mid-1950s to develop an overall plan for the Yangzi River basin, consistently advocated the high dam, primarily because of its positive effect on flood control.

Depending on the dimensions of the final plan, local governments along the Yangzi River differ substantially with respect to the costs they will bear and the benefits they will enjoy. The municipality of Chongqing is an enthusiastic booster of the project, because it hopes to be able to expand its port facilities to receive bigger ships. The city government has very specific dam heights in mind: a water level of 588 feet at the dam will raise the river such that ships of ten thousand tons can reach Chongqing; if the water level is lower than this, only smaller ships will reach the new port, and if it is higher, large ships will reach a largely flooded Chongqing.

The response of the provincial government of Sichuan was mixed. Expanding the port capacity of Chongqing will greatly assist Sichuan by strengthening its links to China's rapidly developing coastal provinces, but on the other hand, Sichuan will not benefit from flood control. Moreover, relatively little of the new power will benefit the province. Yet one of the greatest costs and most vexing problems—re-settling the people displaced by the reservoir—fell exclusively to Sichuan provincial authorities, a most unwelcome burden. This burden was substantially lightened when, in 1997, forty-three districts, cities, and counties were carved out of the province and turned over to Chongqing as it became a centrally administered city (like Beijing, Shanghai, and Tianjin). Seventy percent of the 1.3 million people displaced by the reservoir are among the 30 million new residents of Chongqing.

Similarly, the township and municipal governments in the areas to be flooded are divided in their views. Some towns along the river will be eliminated entirely; others must abandon riverfront property and rebuild above the new water level. Project funds are budgeted to compensate those displaced by the reservoir, a portion going to reset-tled people and a larger portion to the local governments responsible for building new homes and creating new job opportunities. The current allocation is 30 percent to individuals and 70 percent to local governments, which may well take this as a windfall. For example, the town of Wanxian, asked to draw up a relocation budget, came up with a figure of $2.9 billion. The central authorities were stunned, having budgeted only $3.5 billion for *all* relocation expenses. The current budget is in excess of $11 billion, but, like all public funds of large magnitude, it has been subject to misappropriation by corrupt officials, prompting, as we have seen, a stern warning from Zhu Rongji in mid-1999.

The governments of Hubei and Hunan Provinces are the most enthusiastic supporters of the Three Gorges project, for they are in a
win-win position, being the principal beneficiaries of flood control as
well as of increased power generation, and none of their residents
will be displaced by the reservoir. There is less enthusiasm downriver.
Jiangxi, Jiangsu, Anhui, and Shanghai will benefit from flood control
and power generation, but the river channel will erode in unpredictable ways with the newly silt-free water flowing over the dam;
farmland may flood, and river ports become inaccessible.

Given a virtual gridlock of conflicting interests, it is surprising that
the project was ever launched. But having been launched, it is highly
possible that the gridlock will keep it from being completed. That
construction started in June 1993 was largely because Premier Li
Peng adopted the project and exerted strong pressure to get it under
way. As minister of electric power in the early 1980s, he was on
record as having opposed it, but then he came to see it as a monu-
ment to his personal accomplishments. Using his authority as head of
government, he mobilized the various agencies supporting the
project, overrode the central agencies opposed to it, and engineered a
compromise in the project's scope that satisfied at least some of the
conflicting objectives.

Thus in March 1992, the National People's Congress considered a
proposal to build, at an estimated cost of $10 billion, a dam just over
600 feet in height with a reservoir level of 570 feet. The generating
capacity of the power plant would be eighteen thousand megawatts,
utilizing twenty-six seven-hundred-megawatt generators. The proposal estimated that 1.13 million people would be displaced by the
reservoir and that the project would take sixteen years to complete.
Responsibility for supervising the project was vested in a newly established Three Gorges Construction Committee chaired by Li Peng.
Although the proposition passed the legislature with an overwhelming majority, the level of opposition was unprecedented: of the 2,600-
odd delegates, 166 voted against the project and 664 abstained.

Although ground was broken in 1993 and the project has been
under way for seven years, many doubt it will be completed as

planned. The dam has its critics both inside China and abroad, the most vocal of them being the dissident Chinese journalist Dai Qing. Each cost estimate is significantly higher than the last. Financing has yet to be fully put in place. The technological problems have not yet been resolved. Local opposition takes the very effective form of foot-dragging, and corruption eats away at the funds for relocation of refugees. Environmental issues continue to plague the project. On the positive side of the ledger is that, at least over the short run, eighteen thousand megawatts of hydroelectric power will provide a clean-burning substitute for soft coal. But the negative side of the ledger also contains entries: many fish species are threatened with extinction because of the slower flow above the dam, and the upriver journey of river sturgeon to spawn will be thwarted. Archaeologists have reminded the Chinese government and the world that the site of the second "cradle" of Chinese civilization, as important as that in the Yellow River basin, will be inundated. So-called salvage archaeologists have been quick to take advantage of the situation, unearthing relics in the area and illegally disposing of them on the international art market. Finally, were this very large dam to fail for any reason, the downstream disaster is difficult to calculate.

The factor most damaging to the prospects for completing the project is not the environmental calculus but the fact that its leading proponent and former chairman of its Construction Committee, Li Peng, is now China's least popular politician. Zhu Rongji, who succeeded Li as premier, has manifested significantly less enthusiasm for the costly and problematic project.

Conflicts of interest over the Three Gorges Dam exemplify the broader problem that has, to date, kept China's environmental protection from being more effective: the conflict of priorities between environmental protection and economic development. When push comes to shove, the latter always takes precedence, as it does in many circumstances around the world.

First, there is insufficient funding for environmental concerns at the national level. Qu Geping, for many years head of the National

Environmental Protection Agency and currently chair of a National People's Congress committee on environmental protection, has argued that China has a double burden: not only to reduce the damage currently being done to the environment, but, like Russia and eastern Europe, to clean up the damage caused by past excesses and omissions. To accomplish both, he estimates that at least ten times the level of current expenditure is needed: instead of spending 1 percent of GNP, China should spend 10 percent, or $100 billion, a year—a figure corresponding to nearly 77 percent of the current total national expenditure budget.

As is clear in the case of the Three Gorges Dam, the conflict between economic development and environmental protection is worked out in the grid of China's political system, where local and national interests are often at odds. SEPA directives and regulations travel down the vertical paths of the grid and are thwarted at the horizontal local level, where the agency is represented by the provincial, municipal, or county Environmental Protection Bureaus (EPBs). These bureaus, like other central-government agencies at the local level, report not only to Beijing but also to the local government. When it is a question of developing the local economy by building a new factory, local authorities pressure the head of the local EPB to waive regulations so as to get the factory built as expeditiously and cheaply as possible.

The conflict of priorities is exacerbated by the fact that most of the central-government regulations take the form of unfunded mandates, and as a result, virtually the entire cost of compliance with them must be covered by local budgets. The local government that is in compliance thus suffers a double blow: construction is prevented or delayed on factories that might bring it income while poisoning the local air and water, and the local government not only loses the tax revenue the factories would have generated but also must pay for the EPB officials who stand in the way.

Newly built collective enterprises are by no means the only source of water and air pollution, of course. State-owned enterprises, many of them built when no thought was given to their detrimental ecological effects, are also serious polluters. And given the other fiscal problems plaguing China's state sector, they are in no position to cover the cost of upgrading their equipment.

There is yet another reason that rapid economic development always wins over environmental protection in China. In other countries, active and engaged grassroots movements have helped to build public consciousness about environmental concerns. Despite heightened public concern, there is still no such movement in China. The state is hypersensitive about groups that might become nuclei for political opposition, and this has made forming a "green movement" virtually impossible. But news of one grassroots protest movement reached the Western press in 1993. A township-owned chemical factory in remote Gansu Province was polluting a local stream so seriously that peasants wading in the stream to fish were getting blisters on their legs. When the factory operators and township authorities ignored the protests, the residents descended on the factory, drove its operators out, and shut it down. There are other examples like this one, and numerous local environmental groups have sprung up in recent years, but they are isolated from one another and show no signs yet of a national movement that will significantly affect the actions of local governments. Nor is Beijing likely to permit the emergence of such a movement, threatened as it is by any competition to the authority of the Party-state.

International pressure on China to do more with respect to the environment elicits a response heard elsewhere in the developing world. Concern for the environment, this argument runs, is a pastime taken up late in life by wealthy nations, which themselves achieved economic development with little or no attention to its environmental consequences. Given this, why should poorer countries be held to new and higher standards in their economic development than the developed nations were in years past? If the West believes that developing nations should be held to these new high standards, then it should help to pay for the very expensive process of meeting them. China held this position when, in agreeing to take part in the 1991

Montreal Protocols on reducing the release of chlorofluorocarbons, it made its participation contingent on being granted access to foreign aid and technology to assist in the reduction.

The fact is we all inhabit the same planet. Chinese people are the first to suffer from the poisoning of China's air and water, but ultimately we all suffer. The first line of responsibility for China's extraordinarily serious environmental problems is, of course, the Chinese state, but in the end the responsibility is international. Until the Chinese state has struck a balance between the conflicting priorities of economic development and environmental concern, however, international assistance is of little use.

XI

ONE BILLION PLUS:
CONTROLLING POPULATION GROWTH

FOR MOST CHINESE, China's population is the country's greatest problem and one that the Chinese government has acknowledged for more than twenty-five years. At the beginning of the reform period, the government initiated a series of programs and regulations designed to slow population growth. The one-child policy, as these are collectively known, is almost universally unpopular. In the cities, it is accepted as a necessary evil; in the countryside, it has met with widespread resistance. This resistance is triggered in part by a traditional preference for male children but also by the fact that the incentives and penalties of the one-child policy run directly counter to those of the household-responsibility system. The one-child policy tries to limit population growth by rewarding families with a single child and penalizing larger ones, but the household-responsibility system in effect rewards large families by giving them a high income, and in practice, the incentives to have a large family are significantly stronger than the penalties for exceeding the single-child limit.

The birth-control program is yet another good example of the problems in the power grid of China's political system. The central government has come up with a program it wants implemented everywhere, but it must rely on local authorities—indeed, government at the very lowest level of the political system—to enforce it. And, like pollution control, the birth-control program is an unfunded mandate. Because the program is both highly unpopular and unfunded, local governments have either modified, delayed, or thwarted it.

Alarmed by local noncompliance, evidence of which surfaces in each national census, the central government pressures the localities by imposing limits and quotas. Under the gun to meet these, local authorities resort to enforced abortions and sterilizations, practices that of course further alienate their constituencies, already disaffected by other grievances, and anger the central authorities, who denounce such draconian measures as illegitimate local violations of a legitimate central policy.

The birth-control program is in sharp contrast to the economic-reform program, the thrust of which is to remove the government from the daily lives of its citizens. The government makes fewer and fewer decisions for the Chinese people, who less and less often find the government looking over their shoulders to monitor their political correctness. But the birth-control program has inserted the government into their lives in an unprecedented way, involving it in their most intimate decisions. This imposition of political authority angers many people outside China, who regard the one-child policy as an invasion of the most private aspect of an individual's life and a violation of a fundamental human right. Many who hold this view are also unequivocally opposed to abortion. But with their own conception of national sovereignty, individual rights, and the overwhelming magnitude of their population problem, Chinese authorities find this criticism impossible to fathom.

During the year 2000, China's population passed 1.3 billion people. Were the Chinese population to continue to grow at its current rate, we could expect that each year about 18 million children will be born in China and about 6 million Chinese will die, for a net increase of about 12 million. With that net growth, the Chinese population will pass 1.4 billion by 2010 and 1.5 billion by about 2015. At that point, there will be three times as many people in China as there were at the founding of the People's Republic in 1949: the population will have trebled in sixty-five years. But China's efforts to slow the population growth rate are expected to succeed, such that the population will not reach 1.6 billion until 2050, at which point it will start to decline.

Demographers use three figures when discussing change in the size of a population. The first is the *birthrate*, usually expressed in births per thousand people in the population as a whole. China's birthrate in 1998 was 16.03 per thousand. The birthrate significantly differs for the urban and rural populations: the urban rate being 13.67, the rural rate being 17.05. The second figure is the *population growth rate*, the birthrate less the death rate. The death rate in 1998 having been 6.5 per thousand, the population growth rate was 9.53 per thousand. Expressing that figure in a percentage (as is most frequently done), the 1998 population growth rate was .953 percent. The third figure is the *fertility rate*, the average number of children born to women of childbearing age. China's fertility rate is currently 1.4.

Table 8
POPULATION GROWTH, UNITED STATES AND CHINA

	United States	China
Population 1998	270 million	1.25 billion
Birthrate	14.6/1,000	16.03/1,000
Mortality rate	8.65/1,000	6.5/1,000
Net migration rate	2.95/1,000	0/1,000
Population growth rate	.89%	.95%
Fertility rate	1.3	1.4
Life expectancy	76.7 years	71.2 years
Median age	35.2 years	26.6 years

(Sources: *China Statistical Yearbook 1999* and *World Almanac 2000*)

To bring its population problem under control, the Chinese government has set a target birthrate of thirteen per thousand, which the one-child policy, as it has been modified in practice over time, is designed to achieve. One obstacle is an unusually large number of women of childbearing age (between the ages of fifteen and forty-nine)—currently more than 300 million, or roughly 25 percent of China's total population.

Success in limiting births will exacerbate another social problem in China. With fewer young people, the median age will rise, accelerating the already rapid "graying" of China. In the 1990 census, the retired-age population numbered 117 million, or just over 10 percent of the population; it is estimated that by 2050 there will be more than 400 million retirees—more than 25 percent of the population. Whereas today there is one retired person for every four people of working age, by 2050 that ratio will be very close to one to one. (The problem in the United States is comparable, though the figures are somewhat smaller: our retired-age population is currently 12 percent of the total; that figure will grow to 20 percent by 2050.)

Attempts to limit China's population growth were slow in coming, largely because of Mao Zedong's views on the subject. It was his opinion that a large population was a national asset: he thought of every person added as two more hands whose work would contribute to national development and defense. For the first twenty years of the People's Republic, no effort was made to restrict births, and the birthrate was well over thirty per thousand (except during the years of recovery from the Great Leap Forward).

Zhou Enlai took a different view. He came to believe that controlling population growth was a prerequisite to economic development, and he was responsible for initiating China's first national program to limit births in 1971, the goal being to reduce the birthrate to twenty per thousand by 1980. In practice, Zhou's program amounted to a two-child policy. The campaign's slogan was "late, sparse, and few." Couples were encouraged to delay marrying until their late twenties, to space their children at least four years apart, and to limit themselves to two children. The campaign was a success. Although by no means every family was limiting itself to two children, the birthrate in 1980, at eighteen per thousand, had been reduced by a third in a ten-year period.

Despite this success, projections drawn up in 1978 suggested that the Chinese population would pass the 1 billion mark in 1980 and would reach 1.4 billion by 2000. Deng Xiaoping and his reformist colleagues shared Zhou's view that economic development could not proceed unless population growth were controlled, but they were alarmed by these projections and concluded that Zhou's gradualist approach to the population problem was insufficient. Out of their alarm was born the one-child policy.

The goals of the one-child policy are significantly closer to being realized in China's cities than in the countryside. There are a number of reasons for this success, some of them attributable to the policy, others having little to do with it. Urban couples are more removed from the influence of tradition and less likely to feel pressure from parents and relatives to produce large families and male heirs. Moreover, as we have seen, the cities are extraordinarily crowded and living space very limited, so city residents experience the problems of a large population every day, whereas those problems seem rather remote to people in the less crowded countryside. Urban couples are generally better educated, and worldwide there is a correlation between education level (particularly of women) and the decision to limit births. Finally, in most cases both members of an urban couple work outside the house, and because childbearing disrupts the woman's career, it is more likely to be delayed and limited. Child care is also more expensive and somewhat more difficult to arrange in the city than it is in the countryside, where grandparents are near at hand.

The one-child policy has proved much more difficult to implement in the countryside, where tradition is still strong and favors male children. The birth of a son is cause for celebration; the birth of a daughter is only a "small happiness." In part, this is simple gender bias: a son carries on the family line, a daughter does not. But in part, it is based on an economic reality: when a daughter is married, she leaves her parents' home and becomes a member of her husband's family, contributing to her in-laws' family exchequer, not to her parents', while a son is responsible for his parents as they retire and age.

In the absence of a public pension scheme, giving birth to a son means providing for one's retirement security.

As we have seen, the incentives of the household-responsibility system undermine efforts to enforce the one-child policy in the countryside because they reward large families: increasing the "hand-to-mouth ratio"—that is, the number of a household's able-bodied workers in relation to the number to be fed—gives one a direct increase in household income. At the moment, increased productivity is winning out over decreased fertility.

In the early years of American travel to China, after President Richard Nixon first went in 1972, a visit to a commune was obligatory on every tourist's itinerary. Directing the tour group into the production team's office, local officials would point with pride to a complicated chart on the office wall: a very public display of information on the menstrual cycles, birth-control practices, and pregnancy records of every woman in the team. When the tour guide translated the explanation, foreigners would be aghast—a reaction that, in turn, perplexed the officials—for the birth-control program, from its inception, made a public issue of what, to most foreigners, is a very private matter.

Yet the results of having done this are impressive. Today in China, information about contraception and contraceptive devices is widespread, and the Chinese government estimates that close to 85 percent of the sexually active population practices some form of contraception. Still, abortion is a common form of limiting fertility. Recent figures show that eleven million abortions are performed annually, or one for every two live births. This is higher than the rate in the United States, which is one for every three live births, but lower than that in Russia and parts of eastern Europe, where it is not uncommon to find rates of one abortion for each live birth.

To encourage compliance with the one-child policy, the government is prepared to offer an array of incentives. In Guangan County, in Sichuan Province, in the early 1990s, these included subsidies. Although the subsidy came to no more than a dollar a month, this constituted a 3 percent increase in the average household income there. There was also access to a pension plan, additional land in the household's farming contract, a reduction in the grain tax, and, finally, tuition assistance for a one-child family. This package seems well structured to appeal to the needs and interests of young rural couples, but in general, incentives packages like these are not enough to persuade the parents of a girl not to try once more for a boy.

When carrots fail, sticks are applied. Monetary fines are the most widespread form of penalty for noncompliance, the minimum fine being on average about four hundred dollars, or the equivalent of a year's income for the offending household. When the income exceeds four hundred dollars, the fine is usually 1.5 times the annual income, but even these substantial fines are often insufficient, since the income and family security a son will provide his parents over their lifetimes far exceed even the stiffest current fine. Many farming households consider noncompliance and payment of the fine a wise investment in the family's future. Fines can be as high as fifteen hundred dollars (six times the average per capita annual income of rural residents), and, as is the case in so many areas of Chinese life, they are the object of corrupt behavior on the part of local officials, who encourage multiple births and pocket the fines.

Frustrated by the failure of incentives and penalties to reduce reproduction, local officials often use coercion, especially when their superiors assign birth quotas and hold them personally responsible for meeting them. Coercion ordinarily begins with verbal harassment of noncomplying couples: women are urged to undergo sterilization, and pregnant ones are urged to have an abortion. Those who resist are threatened. One recent account describes the work of a tough-minded local family-planning official, identified as "Mrs. Liao," who marched into a remote rural community in south-central China, lined up the village women, singled out those with the most children, and told them that unless they reported to the local clinic for sterilization, their houses would be blown up. "Mrs. Liao" is not

alone: there is fairly widespread evidence of the destruction of personal property in retaliation against those who ignore the one-child
policy.

In extreme cases, women have been physically restrained and
forced to undergo abortions or sterilizations against their will, though
I have not found reliable evidence on which to base an estimate of
how frequently this occurs. There is reason to believe that it is not
common. Forcing a surgical procedure on an unwilling constituent
may satisfy a superior and avoid a fine, but the local official must live
with the consequences, and given conditions in most rural communities, the last thing he is interested in is further alienating his
constituents. Also, these atrocities attract unwelcome international attention, for forced abortions are repugnant not only to those for
whom abortion under any circumstances is wrong but also to
human-rights activists, even when they might favor abortion when
undertaken as a free choice.

In order to avoid alienating both the rural population and the
international community, China's population-planning authorities
have relaxed the one-child policy where resistance is greatest. In fact,
the policy has had loopholes from the outset. Ethnic minorities have
always been exempt, on the theory that it was important to preserve
their continuity and because the areas they inhabit are China's least
densely populated. Today the rural population is subject to a relaxed
policy that, in practice, permits one child where that child is a boy,
two children where the first child is a girl or handicapped, and no
third births. An exception is also made for families where both parents are themselves single children. In a 1994 survey of couples of
childbearing age, 63 percent had a single child. Somewhat more
than 25 percent had a second child, and only 10 percent had three or
more children. A new population control law formalizing the relaxed
policies is due out from the National People's Congress in 2003.

As with many unpopular policies, for every method of enforcement
the central and local governments have put in place, those determined to violate the policy have thought up a way of avoiding com-

pliance. The most straightforward of these is simply to pay the fine for over-quota births, treating the expenditure as an investment in the family's future.

Since the object, in the case of many families, is to produce a male heir, what is done in the unwelcome event of a "small happiness"—the conception or birth of a female? As sonograms have become more widely available, they have increasingly been used to identify the gender of fetuses. When a female is identified, many women choose to have an abortion. This use of sonograms has recently been outlawed, but enforcing this new law will be difficult. Sonogram equipment, now manufactured in China, is widely available, and there is money to be made in offering the service.

Once a female child is born, the simplest way of avoiding having her count against the family's quota of children is not to record her birth. The gradual relaxation of social control associated with the reforms and the possibility of going away from home to give birth have made it easier to conceal births from those charged with limiting their number. The widespread incidence of this practice was revealed in the 1990 census, generally regarded as the most thorough one ever conducted in China, when officials assured citizens that no retroactive penalties would be imposed on unregistered births. The census showed the Chinese population to stand at 1.13 billion, a figure that exceeded projections by some 13 million. Part of the discrepancy can be accounted for by statistical flaws in the projections, but most of it was due to the number of female children whose births had gone unrecorded.

Other methods of avoidance are more serious. Some parents decide to put girl babies up for adoption or, worse, to abandon them. The vast majority of children available for adoption in China or being raised in orphanages there are girls, or boys with handicaps. There are also stories of female infanticide, some involving medical practitioners. When girl babies' lives are terminated at birth, the deliveries are recorded as stillbirths. Other stories describe instances where infanticide is committed by parents or family members desperate to avoid having the child count against the family's one- or two-child limit, though the Chinese press emphasizes that infanticide is against the law in China and that cases are prosecuted wherever they are detected.

The cumulative effect of all these methods of avoidance is a marked skewing of the gender ratio among Chinese children. Whereas the worldwide ratio of male to female births is 106 males for every 100 females, the ratio in China rose to a disturbing 111 males for every 100 females in 1990; it currently stands at 108 to 100. Newspaper accounts describe the plight of unmarried Chinese men unable to find a spouse because of the shortage of unmarried women; the 1990 census showed three unmarried males for every two unmarried females. Among China's small but growing number of divorced people, the gender ratio is two males for each female. Some suggest that the one-child policy is responsible, but it is actually too recent to have had this effect. The gender ratio for the cohort now of marriageable age is very close to the worldwide norm.

When all other methods of avoidance fail, rural Chinese now have a new option that they are choosing with increasing frequency: they can leave home and migrate to a city. Although most floating workers are single males, there is also a significant number of couples who have found a way of avoiding the sharp eyes and draconian penalties of the redoubtable "Mrs. Liao" and her family-planning colleagues. Floating workers are in something of a limbo so far as China's system of social control is concerned, having severed ties with rural officials and not yet been picked up by urban ones, who are reluctant to legitimate their presence in the city. Many rural couples take advantage of this to pursue their quest for a son.

From the perspective of the central government, the one-child policy has the potential for solving China's most pressing problem. But from the perspective of local officials, the situation looks somewhat different. The one-child policy, even in its relaxed form, is highly unpopular among the rural population. To the extent that these officials align themselves with the central government and enforce the policy, they alienate themselves from their constituents; when they must resort to coercion, that alienation only deepens. And because they need to secure the compliance of their constituents on many issues besides birth control, they are reluctant to align themselves too closely with the central government's policy.

This is all the more true because they are less well qualified than their predecessors to enforce an unpopular policy. There was a substantial turnover of local officials in the 1980s, during the course of which older officeholders retired and were replaced by younger, less experienced ones, and the number of women holding public office in rural communities also declined. Some of the most effective family-planning workers at the local level had been older women, now retired, whose younger, male successors find it hard to take their place.

Economic reform in the countryside has also altered the function of local officials. Today they are significantly less pervasive a presence than were the production-team and brigade leaders they replaced. As the private realm has greatly expanded everywhere in China over the last twenty years, the government's ability to control individual behavior has declined.

Confronted with this decline in efficacy and seeking to ensure stringent enforcement at the local level, the central government has taken to making local officials personally responsible for the success of the family-planning program by docking salaries or fining them for over-quota births. Some officials respond positively to this pressure to resort to coercion, but others avoid the problem by making false statistical reports to their superiors.

A final problem is that the one-child policy is such an expensive unfunded mandate. Although the state claims that nearly $1 billion is spent annually on implementation of the birth-control program, virtually all that money comes from local governments, which, already pressed to meet other financial obligations, find themselves paradoxically funding the birth-control program exclusively from fines levied against those who violate it.

Family-planning policy in China since the early 1970s has been based on the premise that economic growth cannot occur until population growth has been brought under control. Some argue, however, that population growth can only be brought under control when economic growth has occurred. The experience of other developing countries has shown that two factors associated with economic development—urbanization and education—result in decreased fertility, and observers mark that this is true in China as well, that is, in Chinese cities. Along this line of reasoning, revisionists argue that the one-child policy has not significantly changed the population growth rate in China and that a more relaxed policy would have achieved about the same results and avoided the widespread anger and disaffection brought on by the attempt to enforce such a stringent program.

The one-child policy touches very sensitive nerves among foreign, particularly American, observers. Any policy that interferes with personal decisions regarding childbearing is for some a violation of human rights, for others not only a violation of human rights but also a sin. Still others find the one-child policy acceptable but are disturbed by enforcement measures that violate human rights. In the fall of 1994, the Chinese government released its newly drafted Maternal and Infantile Health Care Law, initially publicized as a "eugenics law," since it addressed the problem of the ten million people in China with birth defects that, in the words of the law, "could have been prevented." The new law called for sterilizing the mentally ill and aborting the fetuses of those suffering from hereditary diseases or abnormalities. The Chinese government seemed genuinely surprised and nonplussed by the storm of criticism from abroad, and its response was not to repeal the law but to avoid using the term "eugenics" when discussing it and to emphasize the provisions for ensuring informed consent on the part of those affected by it.

The Chinese claim that concern over reproductive rights, like certain environmental issues, is a luxury of the rich and less populous nations of the world and contend that the magnitude of China's population problem is such that honoring individual rights with respect to reproduction endangers the rights of the society as a whole. Extraordinary measures are necessary for China to continue to feed and clothe its population, they claim while deploring the excesses that they consider unintended consequences of their policy. It remains to be seen whether that policy will succeed in reducing the size of the rural Chinese family or whether, in trying to do so, it will dangerously undermine the already tenuous authority of local governments, in which case the state may be obliged to resort to the slower but in the long term equally effective strategies of urbanization and expanded educational opportunities.

XII

HUMAN RIGHTS
AND THE RULE OF LAW

FROM THE AMERICAN PERSPECTIVE, the single most significant obstacle to better U.S.-China relations is the Chinese government's systematic violation of its citizens' human rights, but almost as important is the absence of a fully articulated set of laws and, more fundamentally, of the concept of the rule of law. It is with human rights and our devotion to the rule of law that many of us are least willing to make concessions for cultural differences. We believe not only that our position on these issues is correct but that it is the *only* correct position and thus should be universally accepted.

Yet it is true that the cultural differences in this area are great. The American political system—and to a great degree the Western political tradition of the modern nation-state—is rooted in the concept of the rule of law, by which we mean that the law stands above individual officeholders as a neutral arbiter to which disputes are referred and on the basis of which they are resolved. All citizens are equal before the law, and everyone, regardless of position or status, is subject to it. But China's political system is rooted in the concept of the rule of men (in recent years expanded in a very limited way to include a few women), and the individual officeholder stands above the law and serves as the arbiter to whom disputes are referred. These diametrically opposed concepts derive from diametrically opposed ideas about the significance of the individual. The primacy of the individual, and his or her rights and freedoms, based on philosophical traditions that go from classical Greek thought through the European Enlightenment, is the firm basis of the American economy and political system, and our legal system is designed to protect it. But the concept on which Chinese culture is based is the primacy of the family and the society, and the emphasis in that tradition is on individual obligations, not rights or freedoms. The individual has obligations to the family, and the family has obligations to society. The ruler's task is to ensure that these obligations are fulfilled.

There is a school of Chinese philosophy that supports the necessity of a fully articulated legal system. Han Fei, whose ideas were taken up by the first Qin emperor in the third century B.C., asserted the principle that people are inherently evil; therefore, good behavior could be elicited only by means of carefully drafted laws backed by generous rewards and stringent punishments. Emperor Qin Shi used these ideas, later known under the name of "legalism," during his brief but repressive rule, the most important accomplishment of which was the first unification of the Chinese state. But because of his brutality, legalism was discredited, and subsequent rulers looked to the very different views of Confucius as the basis for their state ideology.

Confucius, who predated Han Fei by two centuries, began with an opposite presumption about human nature. Believing that human nature is fundamentally good, he argued that good behavior was most effectively elicited by means of the ruler's example. Confucius's concept of a web of human relationships, which we examined in Chapter 2, involved mutual responsibilities: the subordinate was obliged to obey, the superior to provide a moral example, and if all went well, laws, rewards, and penalties would be superfluous.

In describing the cycle of dynastic growth and decline, I have touched on the so-called right to rebel. There were, in fact, circumstances under which the obligation to obey was suspended: when the ruler failed to provide the moral example that it was his obligation to embody, an official had a duty to remonstrate, but this was not a kind of embryonic freedom of speech, for the emphasis was on not the official's freedom to disagree but his *obligation* to disagree. Carrying out this obligation might prove fatal, but the obligation stood nonetheless. Moreover, the right to rebel was only granted ex post facto to the successful rebel. The unsuccessful rebel was guilty of treason.

The system that emerged under the Confucian order was not devoid of written law. Although there was little in the way of written civil law, there were criminal and administrative codes, regulations for the conduct of criminal investigations and the administration of justice. Nonetheless, the performance of the ruler or official, not the written code, was the critical element in the successful functioning of the political system.

Scholars have noted analogies between the political system constructed by the Chinese Communist Party under Mao Zedong and the Confucian political system that preceded it: Marxism-Leninism and the Confucian canon, the Party cadre and the scholar-official, the core leader and the emperor. Yet the legal system as it operated under Mao Zedong only faintly resembled its Confucian antecedent. Like the Confucian past, there was no rule of law under Mao, but unlike the Confucian past, there was essentially no law at all under Mao.

When the Chinese Communists did make some effort to introduce new legal codes, as in many other areas of life in China in the 1950s, the Soviet Union was their model. The legal system was made up of three institutions: the Ministry of Public Security, which was responsible for police work; a "procuracy" at each level of government, which investigated and prosecuted crimes and reported to the Supreme People's Procuracy; and courts at each level of government, headed by the Supreme People's Court, which heard and decided cases and set punishments.

Despite this formal apparatus, the major political movements of the 1950s and 1960s—in which millions of landlords, bureaucrats, dissenters, intellectuals, and Party officials were stripped of status, wealth, and power and sentenced to long periods of hard labor or even to death—took place without reference either to laws or to the system, which focused most of its attention on criminal cases. Civil disputes were most often resolved within the units where the conflicting parties worked, disputes between work units by the administrative agency to which both reported or, more informally, by Party members within the contending units.

Mao believed in ideological principles, not laws. Ideological principles gave rise to a "line" of correct thinking, which in turn was translated into specific policies, each of which had implementing regulations. The regulations tended to be vague and subject to broad interpretation. And even ideological principles were subject to change. Late in life, Mao began to manipulate his ideology to serve his own purposes. At that point, the only reliable guide to action became the chairman's gnomic "latest instruction."

Mao rejected the idea that the law is universally applicable, borrowing from Marx and Engels the idea that law is a tool that one social class uses to oppress another: in years past, the landlord class had used Chinese law to oppress the peasantry; in a capitalist society, the bourgeoisie used the law to oppress the proletariat; but in socialist China, the law would be used to overthrow and suppress the landlords and bourgeoisie.

By the late 1950s, these enemy classes had effectively been eliminated or rendered powerless—though not through the force of law—at which point Mao's concept of class became more fluid. He abandoned the categories "proletariat" and "bourgeoisie"—categories that had plausible roots in the workplace—and instead began to use the broad categories "the people" and "enemies of the people." The people were those who followed the current line; enemies were those who opposed it. One set of rules (which he chose to call "democracy") was to apply among the people, who, he said, constituted the vast majority of the population; another (which he termed "dictatorship") applied to the small minority that made up the enemies of the people.

In the years leading up to and during the Cultural Revolution, Mao resumed the use of class labels, talking of a renewed class struggle, but this time the line between "bourgeoisie" and "proletariat" was just as fluid as the line between "the people" and their "enemies." In both instances, the defining criteria were attitudes toward ideological principles, not economic or social relationships.

Three elements of this largely lawless system remain in post-Mao China. The first is the crime of counterrevolution, which, until its abandonment in 1997, served as the basis for the prosecution of political crimes. In practice, the ambiguous term "counterrevolution" was up to the Party to define, and the definition could also be changed ex post facto. The demonstrations in Tiananmen Square in 1976 that marked the beginning of the end of the reign of the Gang of Four were initially branded counterrevolutionary, and participants were prosecuted accordingly. After the Gang of Four fell, a "reversal of verdicts" came, and first the 1976 demonstrators, and subsequently a host of those persecuted during the Cultural Revolution, were rehabilitated on the basis of a new set of definitions of "revolution" and "counterrevolution." Today there is talk of another "reversal of verdicts," this time to clear the names of those who demonstrated in Tiananmen Square in 1989.

In the mid-1990s, a few cautious voices went so far as to suggest that it was time to eliminate once and for all the crime of counterrevolution from the statute books. And, at its meeting in March 1997, the National People's Congress approved legislation eliminating counterrevolution as a crime and substituting for it the crime of endangering state security. While the new language is more up-to-date, it retains its ominous ambiguity.

A second carryover from the Maoist era is the concept of thought reform. Hundreds of thousands of people branded as counterrevolutionaries were executed, and many millions more were subjected to what, in its most extreme form, was "brainwashing"; its much more common form was "reform through labor" or "reform through education." The principle behind the concept was that counterrevolution was a mistaken pattern of thought that could be changed, most effectively by indoctrination and persuasion, accompanied by a stiff regimen of physical labor. In extreme cases, persuasion was accompanied by isolation and torture.

The third surviving Maoist element also present in its Confucian antecedent, was the absence of a presumption of innocence. The criminal who was brought to trial was presumed guilty, which wherever possible should have been established by means of a confession. Because any profession of innocence was likely to be taken as a mistake with counterrevolutionary implications, defendants who refused to confess to the crime of which they were accused were often subjected to all the tools of thought reform I have described. Once brought to trial, the defendant was routinely granted access to a defense lawyer, whose function was not to establish the defendant's innocence but to offer evidence in mitigation at the time of sentencing. As noted earlier, the 1997 revisions to the criminal procedures law are a step in the direction of establishing the presumption of innocence and giving defense lawyers an active role in criminal trials.

The initial impetus to establish a system of laws during the reform era arose from China's rapidly expanding interaction with the world economy. Foreign firms that wanted to invest in or trade with China were reluctant to do so without laws in place that would regulate these transactions and protect all parties' interests. So the first new laws defined the terms on the basis of which joint ventures would be formed and trade conducted. Since then, the reforms themselves have created new circumstances that require regulation and adjudication, in response to which many new laws have been written and adopted by the National People's Congress.

China's legal profession has grown at an extraordinary rate. Starting from a base of about 3,000 lawyers at the beginning of the reform era, the government set as a goal a legal profession numbering 150,000 by the end of the century. Law schools and law departments have proliferated, though their number is insufficient to meet the need. In fact, there were about 100,000 lawyers in China as the millennium began (roughly half of them with formal training), or one lawyer for every twelve thousand people. (The comparable figures in the United States are 885,000 lawyers, or one lawyer for every three hundred people.) But even more important than their expanding numbers is the emerging sense of independent professionalism among Chinese lawyers, who, in the past, saw themselves as no more than minor government bureaucrats.

Legal reform proceeded smoothly and without interruption during the 1980s. Unlike other aspects of reform that periodically threatened to undermine the Party's monopoly of political power, legal reform was a nonthreatening way to create the appearance of moving toward a more modern, less arbitrary political system. But the goal was always to create a *system of laws*, never to establish the *rule of law*, a distinction that became fully evident at the end of the decade in the Party's handling of the Tiananmen demonstration in 1989. A small group of retired leaders, feeling that their backs were to the wall, set aside laws, regulations, procedures, and regularly appointed officials in order arbitrarily to impose their disastrously misguided solution.

The need for a genuine rule of law in China has become more urgent as political corruption has increased over the last decade. As we have seen, corruption is pervasive throughout China's political system, and periodic efforts to attack it founder because those assigned to the task are themselves the worst offenders. The problem appears unsolvable until the law takes the place of the arbitrary official.

The events in Tiananmen Square on the night of 3 June 1989 served as a wake-up call for many thoughtful people in China. They also brought about a radical shift in American public opinion about China. Ever since Richard Nixon's visit to China in 1972, Americans seemed to suspend judgment on the subject of Chinese politics, and many of those who called attention to the violation of human rights in the Soviet Union and Eastern Europe appeared to ignore comparable violations in the People's Republic of China. But this dual standard suffered a fatal blow when tanks rumbled down the streets of Beijing.

Serious misunderstandings arise when Americans and Chinese sit down to talk about human rights. There are not only very different assumptions that the two sides bring to the table but also very different definitions of the term "human rights" and what it encompasses. Where Americans emphasize China's failure to guarantee political and civil rights, the Chinese emphasize the American failure to acknowledge China's accomplishments in guaranteeing its citizens' economic and social rights.

A comprehensive definition of human rights would include economic, social, political, and civil categories. *Economic* rights protect the individual's access to sustenance and participation in the workforce. *Social* rights guarantee access to goods and services provided by the state, such as education, social security, and health care. *Political* rights guarantee the individual's ability to participate in the political process. *Civil* rights protect the individual from illegitimate interference by other individuals or by the state. And it is true that an assessment of the protection of human rights in all four of these categories reveals both positive and negative results in China. Paradoxically, economic reforms have expanded human rights in some areas but restricted them in others.

The Chinese point with pride to the accomplishments of the Chinese state in extending the right of sustenance to the entire population. They claim that with the exception of the period immediately following the Great Leap Forward, when many starved to death and hunger was widespread in much of the country, China has managed to avoid the devastating famines of the past. Output of food has increased, the distribution system has improved, and public-works projects have reduced the destructive effects of natural disasters. Yet economic reform has both advanced the right to sustenance and jeopardized its future: it enhanced agricultural productivity but failed to limit population growth and reduced the amount of land under cultivation.

Prior to the initiation of economic reforms, China's planned economy provided universal employment, and though many people in the rural and urban sectors were underemployed, they were all guaranteed right of access to the workforce. The creation of a labor market and a gradual loosening of controls over the flow of workers from job to job, place to place, and even sector to sector have given China's workers new freedom, but employment is no longer universal. Rural production-team leaders are no longer at their posts finding some kind of work for everyone. Now that the fiscal crisis in the state sector is being seriously addressed, many workers once guaranteed jobs are finding themselves unemployed. If current trends persist, unemployment rates among women will be significantly higher than those among men.

With respect to social rights, the achievements of the Chinese government during its first fifty years in power are impressive. In 1949, less than 50 percent of China's elementary-school-age children were enrolled in school; fifty years later, 97 percent were enrolled. Access to medical care has also substantially improved. In 1949, there was one doctor for every 1,500 people and one hospital bed for every 7,000 people; by 1999, the figures had increased to one doctor for every 650 people and one hospital bed for every 380 people. Similarly, in 1999 about one in every five members of the workforce had access to some form of state-provided retirement plan.

The economic reforms have had mixed effects on the state's ability to guarantee these social rights, particularly to rural citizens. The household-responsibility system has led to an increase in the number of children leaving school before graduation, since the system's incentives encourage parents to make their children work in the fields or local factories as soon as they are old enough.

Public health officials took justifiable pride in China's rural health care delivery system. "Barefoot doctors"—young workers with only rudimentary medical training—were deployed in brigades and teams throughout the commune system to give basic care in a well-organized referral system of commune clinics and county hospitals. But barefoot doctors have all but disappeared from the Chinese countryside. Disparaged for their lack of formal training, substantially underpaid, and attracted by more lucrative employment opportunities, a large number of them left their posts. It has been hard to replace them, and there are consequent gaps in the once quite complete rural system.

As for social security, the shrinking of the state sector has reduced the proportion of workers with access to state-funded pensions. A new system funded directly by the government rather than by individual state-owned enterprises, with workers matching the government funds with a percentage of their wages, is beginning to be implemented. Until this system is fully operative, the vast majority of Chinese workers will have no access to regular income upon retirement.

The record with respect to political rights is somewhat different. Here, although the right to participate in politics is widespread, that participation is, generally speaking, devoid of significance. Elections are regularly held for executive and legislative posts but, until recently, never with more than a single candidate for each post, a candidate selected and vetted by the Party. A little-publicized component of the political reforms of the 1980s, the democratization of local politics, has eventuated in having several candidates run for certain offices, and it is by no means always the Party-endorsed candidate who wins. So the reforms have made political participation somewhat more meaningful, if only locally.

Civil rights are the subject that Americans debate about most, and the debate is sometimes difficult for Chinese to understand. Asked whether their lives are subject to more or less government interference than they were fifteen years ago, the majority of Chinese would likely respond that they are significantly freer. They can speak freely and critically about political issues, read and hear a reasonably broad range of information and opinions, and make decisions about their places of residence, careers, and leisure that were formerly made for them. But this expansion of civil rights is less the intended consequence of Party or government policy than the unintended consequence of the weakening of Party and government influence. An exception are the debates within the Party-state about expanding freedom of information. In this debate, it is assumed by both sides that unorthodox ideas are imported, not domestic, commodities. A campaign against "spiritual pollution" was launched in 1983, and there have been sporadic rumblings since about "bourgeois liberalism." Arguing against the conservatives who advocate closing off China from undesirable foreign influences, Deng and his like-minded colleagues used an analogy: to allow fresh air into a room, one must open the windows; along with the fresh air, flies and mosquitoes may come in, but that is not enough to justify closing the windows.

As the debate has gone on, however, technology has intervened. The fax machine, the satellite dish, and on-line information services have exponentially increased the information, ideas, and images available to the Chinese public. The proliferation of these new sources of information far outstrips the government's ability to monitor and control them. In fact, when a regulation was passed banning personal ownership of satellite dishes, it was revealed that the single largest supplier of the dishes was military-owned factories, and the regulation remains on the books, unenforced. Eight million Chinese had access to the Internet in early 2000, and the number was doubling every six months. It is a skewed population, however: 85 percent are male, 67 percent are in their twenties, and two-thirds have incomes in the top decile.

American human-rights organizations and the U.S. Congress have been interested less in the rapid expansion of civil rights for the majority of Chinese people than in the very serious violation of a small minority's civil rights, the individuals who have been imprisoned or sentenced to reform through labor for their dissident political or religious views. As many as twenty million people, it is estimated, are incarcerated in Chinese prisons and labor reform camps, but I have seen no reliable estimate of the fraction who are imprisoned for political crimes. The Chinese government says that it is holding two thousand political prisoners, but that number does not include those in labor reform camps. Those who have survived prolonged incarceration in the labor reform camps say that prisoners are often treated with extraordinary harshness, deprived of regular contact with their families and friends, and only under very unusual circumstances released and allowed to return to their normal lives when their sentences expire

Wei Jingsheng, the most highly publicized political prisoner in China, was jailed in 1979 for his views on the need to democratize the Chinese political system. He was released in September 1993, six months before his fifteen-year sentence expired, in what many took to be a transparent ploy to help China secure the 2000 summer Olympics. Six months thereafter, he was rearrested and imprisoned, accused this time of illicit contact with foreign visitors and reporters. Three years later, on the eve of Jiang Zemin's trip to Washington, he was released and exiled to the United States, on the grounds that his health had deteriorated and that he required specialized medical attention. Wei experienced particularly harsh treatment for at least two reasons: first, he was a worker, not an intellectual or a student, and the government considers disaffected workers a greater threat to political stability than it does disaffected intellectuals or students; second, what he wrote and said seems to have aroused the personal animosity of Deng Xiaoping. As a result, his case was always dealt with at the very highest levels of the government, and favorable treatment was accorded him only with the greatest reluctance.

Other prominent political prisoners whose cases have been closely followed by the international community were imprisoned because of their roles in the student demonstrations of 1989. Although most of the student leaders were successfully spirited out of China after the suppression of the movement (most through Hong Kong), some were arrested, tried, and jailed. One of them, Wang Dan, was imprisoned for four years, released in 1993, and then re-imprisoned in 1995. Like Wei Jingsheng, he was released for a second time on the eve of a state visit—this one President Bill Clinton's visit to China in 1998—and he was sent to the United States for medical treatment. The most senior official to be arrested, tried, and imprisoned for his actions in connection with Tiananmen was Bao Tong, an aide to Zhao Ziyang, who was dismissed from his position as premier for having sympathized with the student demonstrators. Released in 1997, Bao Tong has disregarded the government's insistence that he refrain from airing his political opinions. He has often publicly demanded a re-assessment of the Tiananmen episode and a stop to its characterization as a "counterrevolutionary incident," a demand in which he has been joined by his former boss, among others, who was only very recently released from house arrest in Beijing. On the tenth anniversary of Tiananmen, more than 150 people remained in prison for their actions in 1989, and a handful more were arrested, tried, and sentenced for their attempts to mark the anniversary.

International human-rights organizations have been very effective in compiling information on China's prisoners of conscience, tracking their cases, and putting pressure on the government to improve their treatment in prison, to give them medical attention when needed, and even, in some cases, to release them prior to the expiration of their sentences. Based in part on the information gathered by these organizations, the U.S. government has espoused particular cases, too, sometimes with positive results, in other instances less successfully.

There are several points on which it is worth reflecting as we consider what Americans can do to bring about an improvement in China's human-rights record. The first has to do with our assumptions about the universality of our views on law and human rights, our notion that they are appropriate standards for all societies to adopt, regardless of their possible disjunction with other traditions and cultures. The second point is often raised in Chinese rejoinders to American complaints about their human-rights violations. In looking at conditions in another country, Americans often measure real conditions abroad against an idealized vision of conditions at home, and thus seem blind to violations of human rights in their own society at the same time that they ferret out evidence of violations elsewhere.

A third point to bear in mind is that in asking China's leaders to allow dissidents freedom of movement and expression, we are asking them to do the very thing they are least likely now to do willingly.

China's leaders understand the Party's weaknesses and are well aware of the many sources of dissatisfaction within Chinese society. As they often say, political instability threatens the nation's continued economic development; more, it threatens the leaders' own power, position, and perquisites. Under these circumstances, they would regard giving free rein to dissidents as an act of national betrayal and political suicide.

The importance Chinese attach to the question of sovereignty is a fourth point worth touching on. The Chinese interpret the history of their interaction with the outside world during the nineteenth century as a long series of painful episodes of national humiliation in which foreign powers constantly trampled on China's sovereignty. "Ours will no longer be a nation subject to insult and humiliation. We have stood up" were the words Mao chose to mark the founding of the People's Republic of China in 1949. Over a half century, the Chinese government has been especially sensitive to incursions on its sovereignty, and it regards foreign comment on its handling of the civil and political rights of its citizens as a serious infringement. The position is not irrational: imagine the reactions of the American government were the Chinese to make continued American investment in joint ventures contingent on Congress's strengthening affirmative action programs, for example.

Another point has to do with tactics. We often seem to forget that when we deal with Chinese officialdom we need to do so in a way that minimizes the potential for their losing face. This is problematic, for very often U.S. government actions are effective in the American political context only if they are carried out in a high-profile and public manner. Two examples—the one successful, the other much less so—serve to illustrate this point. The American embassy in Beijing served as a safe haven for the well-known dissident astrophysicist Fang Lizhi and his wife for several months when they sought refuge there in the immediate aftermath of the Tiananmen massacre. Through quiet, protracted, and skillful negotiations, James Lilley, then American ambassador, secured permission from the Chinese authorities for Fang and his wife to leave China unharmed. Lilley

was successful because he gave the authorities a face-saving strata-
gem: Fang had suffered a mild heart irregularity, and when told of
this, the authorities could describe his release for treatment abroad as
a humanitarian gesture on their part, not a caving in to foreign pressure. But considerably less successful, because carried out in the
glare of full press coverage, were former Secretary of State Warren
Christopher's efforts to raise human-rights issues during his visit to
Beijing in March 1994. The Chinese foreign minister could not afford to appear as though he had given ground to the United States—
particularly because the entire National People's Congress was then
assembled in Beijing. Christopher, likewise, had to take a tough position in order to reassure those in the United States who were arguing
against renewal of China's most-favored-nation (MFN) status. No
progress was made during the visit.

The most consistently successful efforts on behalf of Chinese religious and political dissidents were private, not public. They were the
work of an American, John Kamm, who, for several years while he
was based in Hong Kong, took up with the Chinese authorities the
causes of dozens of dissidents on a case-by-case basis. He was effective because he understood the importance of working slowly and
quietly with his Chinese interlocutors to get them to agree without
their losing face.

The final point has to do with linking human rights with access to
the American market. Frustrated by a lack of leverage in dealing with
the Chinese government, members of Congress seized on China's
MFN status as one of the few tools available to secure compliance
with demands related to human rights, and the administration responded with an argument about the number of American jobs that
would be lost were China to retaliate by cutting back its imports from
the United States. Each year the administration proposed renewing
MFN for China, and after extensive debate, Congress approved it.
After thirteen years of negotiations, a U.S.-China trade agreement
was signed in 1999 that paved the way for China's entry into the
World Trade Organization. One provision of this agreement has the
United States granting China permanent "normal trade relations" (a

new and more accurate term than "most favored nation"). This was a difficult decision for Congress to make, because it deprived it of the annual opportunity to assess China's human-rights practices, but the approval was coupled with new laws creating a commission that would undertake an annual assessment of human rights in China.

It is my view that using trade sanctions to promote greater attention to human rights in China is inevitably counterproductive. Trade sanctions cannot be crafted in such a way as to hurt those in the Party-state responsible for the violation of the civil rights of dissidents and cannot avoid penalizing the very sectors of Chinese society that are most receptive to the ideas we want to promote. Sanctions will also reduce contact with the outside world, through which some Chinese have begun to become familiar with the rights of citizens in other countries and, armed with this new knowledge, to press their own government to guarantee them the same rights. Restricting that contact will reverse this process and delay the political liberalization that is already under way and that has significantly expanded the freedoms enjoyed by most Chinese citizens.

XIII
INTELLECTUAL FREEDOM
AND CHINESE EDUCATION

IN AMERICAN CULTURE, the term "intellectual" carries several connotations along with its standard meaning of someone who devotes himself to the life of the mind, who thinks about thinking. The other connotations are frequently uncomplimentary. Intellectuals are seen as iconoclasts. They question orthodoxy. They are assumed to be liberals—in the political sense, but more often in the sense of seeing both sides of an issue and being reluctant to come down firmly on one side or the other, spending a lot of time saying "on the one hand . . . on the other hand. . . ." Finally, "intellectual" may often be a term of disapproval. Americans have a long tradition of anti-intellectualism, intellectual historians point out. Pointy-headed intellectuals are absentminded and hopelessly impractical, isolating themselves in ivory towers rather than offering practical solutions to real-world problems.

Yet American culture takes intellectual *freedom* very seriously indeed, the freedom that individuals—not just intellectuals—have to think, say, write, publish, and teach whatever they choose. American law offers safeguards for intellectual freedom as well as for what is called "intellectual property." Moreover, American schools and universities with their tenure systems protect teachers and professors from political reprisals against what they publish or what they teach in the classroom.

Chinese intellectuals are aware of this Western—indeed peculiarly American—concept of the intellectual but know it to be very different from the concept of the intellectual in the Chinese tradition: an individual who had mastered a particular canon. Mastery was confirmed by passing an examination set by the imperial government, and, once credentialed, the intellectual might contribute to the canon by modifying it incrementally with interpretations or commentaries. But it was not his role to be openly critical or iconoclastic. Tradition and authority were to be respected, not assaulted. The goal of intellectual life was not to retreat from the world and engage in reflection but to enter public life, ideally in an official position. Public service was the intellectual's obligation. Once in office, he was obliged to serve as a moral and ethical example to those whom he governed and to hold not only himself but also his colleagues, his superiors, and even his emperor to the highest standards of conduct and to criticize them when they failed to uphold these standards. Carrying out this latter obligation might cost him his job or even his life, but even under these circumstances, the obligation held.

Chinese intellectuals first became acquainted with the American concept of intellectual life in the late nineteenth century. American missionary organizations set up schools and colleges in China in which many young Chinese students were educated; some of them came to the United States, continued in colleges and universities here, and then returned to China.

The moment most frequently associated with the abandonment of the old image of the Chinese intellectual and the adoption of a new, Westernized image is the May Fourth Movement in 1919, when a protest against Japanese incursions on Chinese sovereignty at the end of World War I gave rise to a movement that marked the emergence of a new nationalism in China and the acceptance by many young Chinese intellectuals of the obligation to take a politically active and iconoclastic stance against traditional culture. Mao Zedong was a part of the May Fourth generation, but he also separated himself from its intellectuals; though for a brief period as a young man he lived and worked on the fringes of their group at Beijing University, he was never fully accepted by them, presumably because they took

him for something of a hick. When they began to explore the ideas of
Marx and Lenin, Mao became committed to these ideas far more fer-
vently and faithfully than they.

He came to hold a highly contradictory view of intellectuals, perhaps because he had been bruised by their not accepting him, perhaps because he scorned their liberal tendency to equivocate in
commitment to a new political orthodoxy. Whatever the reason, despite the fact that Mao *was* an intellectual—he read, he wrote, he
thought, he occasionally composed poetry—he was deeply mistrustful of intellectuals and made them the target of political attack on
several occasions, the anti-Rightist campaign in the late 1950s and
the Cultural Revolution in the mid-1960s being the most sweeping
among them.

The notion of intellectual freedom—that special protection must
be given to a person's right to expound his own point of view—was totally foreign to Mao's thinking. Mao's quite different goal was to develop a new intellectual community that would be, in his words,
"both red and expert." He was looking for people who were absolutely dependable in their political orthodoxy but at the same time
scientifically and technologically adept.

Chinese official attitudes toward intellectuals have changed since
Mao's death. Deng Xiaoping's own record in this respect was far from
admirable. He was deeply involved in the campaigns of the late
1950s during which many Chinese intellectuals were imprisoned or
denigrated, yet he and some of his like-minded colleagues assigned a
high priority to China's becoming fully modern and realized that this
could not happen without the active cooperation of China's intellectuals. In part because he thought they had too favorable an attitude
toward the intellectual community, Mao tarred them all with the
same brush, and Deng and his colleagues suffered the same terrible
fate as intellectuals did during the Cultural Revolution.

Shortly after Deng returned to power in 1977, he lent his support to a remarkable burst of public expression of dissident views.
Democracy Wall, near the center of Beijing, became a place where a
vigorous debate on China's recent past and its future course was per-

mitted. It was here that Wei Jingsheng posted a manifesto critical of Deng for having failed to add democracy to his "four modernizations" (of agriculture, industry, science and technology, and the armed forces) as the critically needed "fifth modernization." But this support for intellectual freedom was highly instrumental and very short-lived. Deng used the dissidents and their views to help him displace Hua Guofeng, Mao's designated successor, but once that was accomplished and his position was secure, he first moved the wall to a distant part of the capital and then closed it down entirely. Wei Jingsheng was arrested on a technical charge of having given state secrets to a foreign reporter and sentenced to jail.

Intellectuals in China today have recovered a measure of the status they lost during the Maoist era and are respected because of the contribution they can make to their country's effort to modernize. They are allowed a measure of latitude with respect to the ideas they propound, but this absolutely does not extend into the realm of political ideas. Intellectuals have not recaptured the preeminent position their forebears enjoyed in traditional society, for in today's China that position is already occupied—by the entrepreneur.

China's schools have a total enrollment of nearly 300 million students. Schooling begins with prekindergarten nursery schools, widely available in China's cities, less so in the countryside. Elementary school begins with six-year-olds in kindergarten and extends through six grades. Neighborhood schools are the rule, though most cities have "key schools," where some or all of the places are filled by competitive examination. Elementary education is close to universal.

Secondary education begins with lower middle schools, grades seven through nine, admission into which is by examination. About four out of five elementary-school students continue on to lower middle school. Students are assigned to a class of about fifty, which stays together for all their courses during the three years. Admission to upper middle schools, grades ten through twelve, is again based on examinations; depending on these and on their preferences, students are assigned to either academic or vocational high schools. Two out of five lower-middle-school students go on to upper middle school on average, though the figure is much higher in the cities than in the countryside.

Table 9

SCHOOL ENROLLMENT IN CHINA AND THE UNITED STATES

	China	United States
Percent enrolled in primary school	99	99
Percent enrolled in middle school	93	98
Percent enrolled in high school	20	90
Percent enrolled in college or university	3	40
Number enrolled in graduate school	200,000	2.1 million

(Sources: *China Statistical Yearbook 1999* and *World Almanac 2000*)

Expanding the availability of China's postsecondary education has been a priority since the economic reforms began. Nonetheless, there are fewer than four million places in colleges and universities for the close to seventy million young people of college age. Most of the colleges and universities are four-year institutions, with students admitted on the basis of a national competitive examination taken the summer after their high-school graduation. Entering students are assigned a major field of study and take courses only in the relevant department; professional education in law, business, and medicine is offered at this level. Beginning in 1982, university departments were also accredited to admit graduate students. There are now just under 200,000 students enrolled in graduate programs leading to an M.A. or a Ph.D.

Given the wide range of available adult-education opportunities, one in six adults is enrolled in part-time schooling, correspondence courses, or television classes, a quarter of them in elementary literacy programs, most of the rest in secondary-school courses. Only a small number of college-level courses are available.

Expenditure for education is 15 percent of total government spending in both China and the United States. But as a fraction of gross national product, China's expenditures are less than half those of the United States and below those of many developing countries.

Table 10

EDUCATIONAL FINANCING IN CHINA AND THE UNITED STATES

	China	United States
Amount spent on education, 1998	$15 billion	$510 billion
Average percentage increase, 1988–1998	15	5
Average percentage increase after inflation, 1988–1998	6	1
As percentage of total government expenditures	15	15
As percentage of 1998 GNP	2	6
Per student, 1998	$48	$7,800

(Sources: *China Statistical Yearbook* 1999 and *World Almanac* 2000)

Primary and secondary schools are tuition-free for urban residents, being financed by the municipal governments or, in some instances, by large state-owned enterprises. Parents must pay only for books and school supplies. Schools in the countryside charge tuition, because their school budgets are met principally through tuition receipts, with only supplementary funds coming from local governments.

Universities are operated by the central government and by provincial and municipal governments. Funding for national key schools comes directly from the budget of the Ministry of Education, for other colleges and universities from the government that operates them. Government funding no longer fully supports the operating costs of postsecondary institutions, which have been encouraged to devise other income-producing strategies.

Until 1992, university education was given at no cost to the student; since then students have been charged a tuition that varies by school and discipline, the average today being approximately $250 a year. Tuition is lower in those disciplines to which the government is interested in attracting students; teachers colleges, for example, charge nothing at all. Scholarships are given out on a system based on financial need and academic achievement. Universities generate additional income by admitting students who failed the national qualifying examination but whose families will pay a special high tuition for their postsecondary education.

In addition to the usual forms of academic funding, most colleges and universities have established collective enterprises, which run the gamut from small factories to consulting companies, and some schools lease out space on their already overcrowded campuses for shops and restaurants.

The most recent education act passed by the National People's Congress allows for the establishment of private schools at all levels. A few are now in operation, most of them built with funds contributed by overseas Chinese. High tuitions are charged at these schools—figures as high as three thousand dollars per academic year are not uncommon.

The substantial American influence on education in China is in part due to the many Americans who taught in and ran missionary schools there. It is also the result of the work of John Dewey, the American educator and pragmatic philosopher who spent two years lecturing in China in the early 1920s and supervised the work of Chinese graduate students who became influential educators in their own country. Despite this extensive influence, one of the fundamental principles of American education—the community-based school system—was never adopted in China. Looking to Japanese and later Russian examples, Chinese educators advocated the adoption of a uniform curriculum for the entire country.

The current version of that national curriculum is fairly restrictive at the primary and secondary levels, allowing for very little local innovation. It stresses basic skills and gives short shrift to the arts and humanities. Arts training for gifted students is available in after-school programs or in special schools. English-language instruction is now almost universal in lower middle schools, and at the primary level for students at the best urban schools. Methods of instruction rely heavily on rote memorization and in-class recitation. Cross-cultural studies have shown that these methods produce, as might be expected, students with excellent memory skills but weak creative and analytical skills.

The curriculum at universities and colleges, also set by the national government, allows for more local flexibility. Because students take courses only in their major department, a college education in China is highly specialized, and the idea of a liberal arts education, or even of imposing requirements designed to expose the student to a wider range of subject matter, is absent. Mastery of an accepted body of knowledge, not the development of critical intellectual skills, is the goal of most of China's university educators.

Many positive changes have been made in Chinese education since the reform period began. During the Maoist years, primary and secondary instruction was heavily larded with political lessons: ideological maxims figured prominently in language texts; problems in mathematics required students to quantify and calculate the landlord's exploitation of his peasants, say. Periods of physical labor were integrated with periods of study at all levels, with a view to ensuring that intellectual lessons were not divorced from the realities of the workplace.

With the education reforms came a depoliticization of instructional materials and the end of almost all the work-study programs. Reformers believed that the earlier efforts to universalize primary education and expand the number of middle schools, notably in the countryside, had gone too rapidly and that the quality of instruction had deteriorated. They consolidated some schools, closed others, dismissed inadequately prepared teachers, and expanded and professionalized teacher-training programs. They also increased the number of vocational secondary schools. At the outset of the reform period, only one in twelve high schools offered a vocational curriculum, while the other eleven, with their equivalent of a college preparatory curriculum, were doing a disservice to their students, only a handful of whom could be accommodated in universities.

Building new vocational high schools and introducing a vocational curriculum in existing high schools have nearly equalized the number of vocational and academic high schools today.

Postsecondary education was the level hardest hit by the Cultural Revolution, during which schools at all levels were closed down. University enrollment peaked at close to a million students in 1960, but ten years later only forty-eight thousand students were enrolled, so expanding university education was a first priority in the reform period. In 1977, there were 625,000 spaces in colleges and universities for a college-age population of close to 70 million; in the two decades since, spaces in colleges and universities have quintupled, and postsecondary adult-education programs have trebled, for a total capacity of close to 5 million students today. Despite this, only 3 percent of college-age young people are enrolled in school.

As colleges and universities reopened in the later stages of the Cultural Revolution, admission was based almost exclusively on a kind of affirmative-action program for the politically correct. Class background and political attitude alone counted in making admissions decisions. Schools became populated by students who, in the words of one college instructor, "would have been happier somewhere else." One of the very first acts of the reform period was to reinstitute the national college entrance examination as of 1977 and to open it to a broad age range. As currently administered, the entrance examination is offered once each year, in the July following a student's high-school graduation. Those who fail can take it again, but not after they reach the age of twenty-two.

Because of Mao's mistrust of intellectuals, worker-peasant-soldier instructors were introduced into college classrooms during the 1970s. Their experience and background were considered fitting for monitors of the academic faculty, to ensure that the faculty presented ideologically correct material and to supplement excessively abstract lessons with real-world information. When political priorities changed, though it proved easy to change the composition of the student body, it was very difficult to change the faculty. Like all government employees, faculty members, including the political monitors, were virtually impossible to fire. Even today, one encounters departments in Chinese universities where faculty members outnumber the students and where a handful of qualified instructors carry the full course load while their less competent colleagues have no teaching responsibilities. Paying these nonfunctional faculty members drains the already straitened university budgets.

During the Cultural Revolution, China was almost completely cut off from contact with the outside world. This had a deleterious effect on the academic community, whose members not only could not do research in China but were allowed virtually no communication with their colleagues abroad. Libraries received neither books nor journals from abroad. Scientists lost touch with what their colleagues were doing in laboratories outside China.

The academic community immediately took advantage of the open policy that accompanied the reforms. Scholars were encouraged to travel abroad, "sister school" relationships were established with foreign colleges and universities, professors and teachers were invited to China for short- and long-term teaching assignments, and Chinese students enrolled in American graduate and professional schools, even a few as undergraduates. Asked during his 1979 visit to the United States whether he was worried about a brain drain, Deng was nonchalant. He would send twice as many students and scholars to the United States as were needed in China, he said. Then, when only half of them came home, China would still be adequately served. To date more than 300,000 Chinese have studied abroad, about half of them in the United States, where they currently constitute the largest national group among the international students at colleges and universities.

The most pressing issue facing China's schools is inadequate funding. With expenditures on education totaling only 2 percent of gross national product, China lags behind the world average of 5 percent, and many developing countries outspend it on their schools.

More money for primary and secondary education would help to attract and keep teachers. Because teachers' pay and prestige are very low, it is hard now to attract anyone into the profession, much less highly qualified people. University applicants who find themselves in a teachers college will do almost anything to avoid the fate of a classroom career: entire graduating classes of teachers colleges have failed to report to their assigned schools, going into the infinitely more promising private sector instead. To counteract this, some teachers colleges have withheld the diplomas of their graduating seniors, handing them over only after they actually show up and begin their first teaching assignments.

Universities, too, suffer from a shortage of funds. The austerity of university budgets restricts the scholarship funds available for those to whom the newly instituted tuitions are an insurmountable obstacle. But the most important shortfall is in adequate space. Although they have expanded rapidly, China's colleges and universities can still turn out only 750,000 graduates each year, which means that less than 3 percent of the Chinese population has a college education (as compared with 22 percent in the United States), a wholly inadequate number to support the development to which China aspires.

Like their primary- and secondary-school colleagues, university teachers suffer from low pay and low status. Efforts have been made to ameliorate this situation, especially to encourage foreign-educated intellectuals to return to classrooms and laboratories in China, but many faculty have to take a second job to make ends meet. This has an immediate adverse effect on the quality of research and instruction. Similarly, the time and energy that faculty and administrators spend devising new moneymaking schemes to augment inadequate budgets are time and energy not spent on educational tasks.

A second issue facing China's educators is the high dropout rate from rural schools and the consequent high rate of illiteracy, especially among young women. The reasons are economic: it costs money to send a child to school, and while the child is enrolled, the family does not get what the child would earn in the workforce. Rural people in China do not see that investment in education will yield a return. In addition, as we have seen, an unintended consequence of the economic-incentive structure in the household-responsibility system is to encourage parents to end their children's education early; the economic rewards for doing so seem both more immediate and more tangible than those that accrue when the child is educated through a high-school diploma, since a high-school education is not yet considered useful preparation for work on the farm or in the local factory. Government-supported, tuition-free rural schools would encourage families to keep their children in school, and as the rural economy develops and higher skills are required, perceptions about the value of a high-school education may change. But eliminating the financial gain from putting teenagers into the workforce instead of the classroom is difficult to do.

Table 11

GENDER DIFFERENCES IN EDUCATIONAL ATTAINMENT IN CHINA

	Percentage of total population age six and over	Percentage of male population	Percentage of female population
Illiterate	14	8	20
Primary school	40	39	40
Middle school	32	38	29
High school	11	12	9
College or university	3	3	2

(Source: *China Statistical Yearbook 1999*)

Access to education is very limited for those with physical or learning disabilities. This is particularly true at the higher levels, from which the physically disabled are generally excluded. Because it is presumed that the limited number of spaces at the college level should be reserved for the able and fit, applicants are screened by physical as well as academic examinations.

A third issue facing Chinese educators is the spread of excessive competition and examination-based education. The root of the problem is the paucity of spaces in comparison with the size of the applicant pool, which makes college entrance extraordinarily competitive, a tone that has spread downward through the whole system. It was the national college entrance examination that gave rise to a system of entrance examinations at every level. The result of this hierarchy of examinations is to make students intensely competitive in the classrooms and to limit what is taught there to the material students will need to master in order to clear their next academic hurdle. The pressure on students is intense. Fourteen-hour high-school days are not unknown, and this has led Education Ministry officials to put forward a new set of regulations to reduce pressure on students. Beginning in the 2000–2001 school year, there are to be no mandatory classes during evenings, weekends, and vacations, no written homework for first- and second-graders, no tests for primary-school students except in Chinese language and math, and no entrance examinations at the middle-school level.

All this competition and pressure adversely affects students' motivation once they are at college. As in other highly competitive systems—Japan's is an example—students know that a bright future is guaranteed them regardless of their performance in the classroom. But many university students in China find the quality of their college experience far below the high expectations generated by the competition that they have successfully survived. Classes are large, the curriculum is unimaginative, and the level of instruction is often disappointingly low. Moreover, housing and food are generally far worse than in their own homes. Students are housed eight to a room that is barely adequate for two in an American dormitory. Three times a day, they carry bowls to a canteen too small to have tables and chairs and must consume their unpalatable food on the run.

The dissatisfactions generated by campus life give rise to academic apathy and periodic outbursts of student protest. It was very concrete complaints about university life, not abstract demands for democracy, that brought students onto the streets of China's cities in the protest demonstrations that began in the mid-1980s and culminated at Tiananmen Square in June 1989.

Finally, although Deng seemed sanguine in 1979 about the possibility of so many Chinese young people staying abroad after finishing their education, the problem is in fact much more serious than he was willing to allow. Since 1979, some 300,000 Chinese students and scholars have gone abroad for further education, and of that number, only about 75,000 have returned. In the mid-1980s, incentives were put in place to encourage them to do so, but these were only modestly successful, and the problem was seriously aggravated by the Tiananmen massacre, after which many Chinese studying abroad took public stands against their government that made it dangerous for them to return. Foreign governments relaxed immigration regulations to take account of their situation. Although many Chinese intellectuals living abroad have gone home in recent years, they are attracted by business opportunities, not by academic careers. The brain drain has been slowed, but Chinese colleges and universities have yet to feel the effect.

It is as good a time to be an intellectual in China as it has been since the People's Republic was founded fifty years ago, for, despite occasional conservative rumblings that are largely ignored, the country is enjoying greater intellectual freedom than at any time since the May Fourth Movement of 1919. But unfortunately, just when the restrictions on intellectual life have been somewhat relaxed, many intellectuals find themselves wishing they were entrepreneurs.

To say that intellectual freedom has increased is not to say that the Chinese are free from all restrictions with respect to what they write, say, or teach; public expression of unorthodox political ideas is still unacceptable. Yet dissident intellectuals concern the regime less than dissident workers or dissident unemployed, and the most serious repressions have been exerted against those like Wei Jingsheng and Han Dongfang—workers who the government believes can organize fellow workers in opposition to Party and government authority. This assessment of relative threats to the regime seems well founded. Chinese intellectuals have inherited a disdain for, and thus an inability to collaborate with, the country's working population, and although their protests in 1989 were joined by workers and even government officials in eighty cities, the students and intellectuals who initiated the movement were reluctant to ally themselves with workers and actively resisted taking their movement to the rural workforce.

Dissident intellectuals everywhere have a morbid tendency to fragment their efforts, and this is true in China. Those who occupied Tiananmen Square impressed observers with their ability to organize themselves, to distribute food, information, and medical care, and to use telephone, fax, and the foreign and domestic press to spread word of their protests to other cities in China and to the outside world. And after the massacre, a spontaneous and highly effective underground railroad sprang into being along which numerous dissidents were spirited out of harm's way. But on the other hand, neither the dissidents who escaped China nor those who remained could organize an opposition to the Chinese Communist Party. A significant amount of money was collected in America and Europe in support of their work, conferences were held, and publications distributed. Nonetheless, individuals and groups found their differences greater than their common ground, as was manifested at a colloquium at Harvard University marking the tenth anniversary of the massacre when public presentations by prominent dissidents gave way to private bickering.

If Chinese intellectuals could outgrow their fractious tendencies and their disdain for the working classes, they might be able to join hands with the huge numbers of other people in China who have reason for discontent. Were this to occur, the regime would be obliged to take them very seriously indeed.

XIV

ARTISTIC FREEDOM AND
CHINA'S CONTEMPORARY CULTURE

IN CHINA TODAY, artists, like intellectuals, are enjoying more latitude than they have experienced for a half century. The dead hands
of political didacticism and socialist puritanism do not rest as heavily
on the arts as they did, though there are still boundaries that artists
cannot cross. The cultural scene is vibrant, diverse, and cosmopolitan, as Chinese artists take advantage of their newfound liberties to
produce works that are beautiful or bizarre, crass or transcendent, es-
oteric or merely sensational.

Traditional Chinese culture was in many respects as rigid as its socialist successor. As iconoclasm was frowned on in the intellectual
world, so it was also in the arts. Aspiring artists were trained to study
models of calligraphy and painting and then to duplicate them flaw-
lessly; only after they had mastered this skill was subtle innovation or
refinement of the tradition deemed appropriate. Forms and styles in
art changed very slowly, and looking at the tradition as a whole, one
is impressed more with its continuities than with its changes.

Among the many ideas it borrowed from its Russian mentors, the
Chinese Communist Party brought socialist realism to the arts in
China. Many artists and writers were attracted to the Communists'
base area in Yan'an, in the northwest, during the 1930s; they looked
to the Communists as an honest and patriotic alternative to the
corrupt and ineffectual Nationalist Party and supported the anti-

Japanese war effort under Communist leadership. In 1942 at a "forum" on art and literature, Mao introduced some of these men and women to the Party's political line on the arts—a line that remained in force until his death thirty-five years later.

According to Mao, art and literature exist to persuade and to teach—appreciation of art for its own sake is unacceptable—and the central ideological lesson to be conveyed is the superiority of the worker and peasant who serve the revolution through their labor. Art, literature, and the performing arts should depict exemplary figures to serve as either models or counter-models for the rest of society. The audience for the arts, in Mao's view, is made up of working people; and because they are simple, uneducated, and uncultivated, art must be uncomplicated and straightforward. Heroes and heroines should be glorified, villains debased. Acting styles in theater and film should be broad and melodramatic. Mao singled out for criticism what he called "middle characters," who simply complicate the message—those who have doubts, good characters who have flaws, and villains with redeeming features.

Taking their cues from these instructions, painters painted larger-than-life, perfectly modeled, ruddy-complexioned workers strategically posed in front of factories and power plants. Writers wrote novels and short stories in which oppressive landlords are shamed into subjection by honest, good-hearted, and hardworking peasants. Playwrights composed plays about corrupt, degenerate Nationalist Party members who sell their country to sadistic Japanese agents, only to be defeated in the end by burly Communist patriots. Music, dance, and film followed suit. Given that the work of foreign artists met virtually none of Mao's criteria, contact with the international art world was severed early on.

The Cultural Revolution aimed to draw the strings of the straitjacket even more tightly. A lingering fondness for traditional Chinese culture was to be eliminated by encouraging young people to break, tear, or deface any remnants of the tradition that had survived. The Yan'an rules for art and literature were scrapped and new regulations drawn up. Writers and artists were now suspect and not considered trustworthy to convey the ideological lessons of the day. It was no longer enough that art and literature be *for* working people, they must be *by* working people as well.

In much the way that Mao had found himself on the fringes of the Beijing intellectual community in the May Fourth era, his third wife, Jiang Qing, an actress in B-grade Shanghai films, had found herself on the fringes of the Yan'an artistic community in the 1940s. And it was Jiang Qing who took on an unofficial position as commissar of arts when the Cultural Revolution began. Her mission was to ensure that the rigid didacticism of the 1940s was reasserted, with a glorified Mao as the focal point of every work of art. She brought the performing arts to heel, insisting that every theater, dance company, and film studio restrict itself to productions of five model works based on inspirational tales from the revolution. Jiang Qing's control of the cultural world remained firm until, as a member of the infamous Gang of Four, she suffered her downfall in 1976.

Since the end of the Cultural Revolution and the beginning of the reform period, diverse currents have influenced China's culture, both popular and high. By far the most important among these has been the influence of Western art forms, with which Chinese artists have become reacquainted after long isolation. But a revisiting of the Chinese artistic tradition has also been important and has been both inspired and facilitated by extensive new archaeological finds over the last thirty years and their exhibition in impressive new museums that use advanced preservation and display techniques, many of them introduced with advice and assistance from abroad. A third current, which is felt particularly in popular culture, comes from the Chinese diaspora. Popular culture on Taiwan and in Hong Kong exerts a powerful influence on music, television, and pulp fiction on the mainland, and the influence of the overseas Chinese community elsewhere is beginning to be felt. A fourth, somewhat unexpected current can be seen in a new use of the styles and forms of socialist realism. The plodding images of the recent past are put to diverse, often surprising uses, sometimes whimsical, sometimes critical.

China's two premier music conservatories—in Beijing and Shanghai—had extensive experience training students in performing, composing, and instrument making in both the Chinese and Western classical traditions. But during the Cultural Revolution, the faculty at these conservatories were humiliated, beaten, and confined, a plight movingly depicted in Isaac Stern's film *From Mao to Mozart*, released in the United States in the early 1980s. The movie describes the violinist's first visit to the conservatories, and it introduced Western audiences to several extraordinarily talented young performers, many of whom have later had successful careers on the international concert stage.

Musicians have figured prominently among the Chinese scholars at American schools since the 1980s. All the major American conservatories have enrolled large numbers of Chinese students, and their Chinese graduates are beginning to appear regularly in opera companies, orchestras, and recital series. The well-known cellist Yo-Yo Ma (born in Paris and trained in the United States) has been active in introducing young Chinese musicians to concert audiences in the United States.

And there is a small but appreciative audience in China for Western classical music. Beijing and Shanghai both support symphony orchestras and chamber groups of high quality. Shanghai boasts a state-of-the-art concert space in its Grand Theater. Most recently, plans for a new National Theater in Beijing designed by the French architect Paul Andreu were unveiled—first abroad, later in China. The theater is controversial because of its striking "floating bubble" design, because the design was that of a foreign architect, and because of its $350 million price tag. Now under construction behind the Great Hall of the People on Tiananmen Square, the facility will include a twenty-five-hundred-seat opera theater, a two-thousand-seat music hall, a twelve-hundred-seat theater, and a smaller experimental theater.

Chinese classical music has also been revived in recent years, though not with quite the same gusto. China's major conservatories offer training on Chinese instruments and in the Chinese repertoire, but concert and recital opportunities are more limited than are those for Western music. The Beijing and other opera companies are once again offering the rigorous training required to perform the highly stylized, complex classics of traditional Chinese opera, but few young people are taking the time to acquire it. Chinese opera audiences are most often made up of at least as many curious foreign tourists as appreciative local aficionados.

In a somewhat bizarre contretemps in 1998 that involved the Chinese tradition, Sino-American dramaturgy, and American impresarios, a twenty-two-hour-long Shanghai Kunju Opera Company production of the 1598 Chinese opera *Peony Pavilion* was scheduled to travel to New York for the Lincoln Center Festival. Directed by Chen Shizheng, a Beijing-born performing artist living in New York City, the production ran afoul of the doughty director of the Shanghai Bureau of Culture, Ma Bomin. Chen's intent was to return to the opera's sixteenth-century sources and, in his words, "bring alive its deeper meaning." Ms. Ma, a former Beijing opera singer, denounced the production as "feudal, superstitious, and pornographic." She impounded the sets and costumes and arranged to have the passports of the cast members withheld. Beverly Sills, then chair of the Lincoln Center board, reacted sharply: "I'm insulted that this woman considers herself an ex–opera singer. Us divas don't work like that." A year later Chen mounted a successful American production of the opera, this time with a mixed cast of Chinese performers from Beijing and the United States, which subsequently toured to Paris and Caen.

Chinese composers have been liberated from the political constraints of socialist realism, but much of their creative work is being done outside China. Jin Xiang's opera *Savage Land*, based on a play by the popular modern Chinese playwright Cao Yu, was well received in a Kennedy Center production in 1993. Tan Dun, a composer currently living in New York City, is experimenting with syntheses of traditional Chinese sounds and contemporary Western musical forms; his symphony *Heaven, Earth, and Man* was composed for and premiered during the return of Hong Kong to Chinese sovereignty in 1997, and his opera *Marco Polo* premiered in New York City in the same year. The voluntary exile of these composers has to do less with political constraints—though the official press occasionally rumbles about "inaccessible" music—than with the lack of financial support and appreciative audiences at home. But then, of course, one could say the same of composers of contemporary classical music everywhere.

No such problems exist for the composers and performers of popular music, whose audiences and the revenues they generate are vast. Some critics deplore what they consider a baneful and ubiquitous influence of American popular music: if Chinese popular music is subject to this influence, much of it comes indirectly, via Hong Kong and Taiwan. In any case, the popular songs and MTV videos produced in China give an initial impression of being politically engaged and dissident. But in fact the lyrics and general tone are marked by an apolitical—or, perhaps better, post-political—cynicism, well expressed in the title of a hit song by the Taiwanese female vocalist Su Rui: "Follow Your Feelings."

Rock musicians are subject to more political constraint because their audiences number in the tens of thousands. Crowds of that magnitude, particularly when young, are inevitably disturbing to the peace of mind of municipal authorities. One of China's best-known rock stars, Cui Jian, who was peripherally involved in the events leading up to the Tiananmen massacre, has often had difficulty booking space and securing permits for his concerts, though he claims his music is "cultural," not political.

Some years ago, the pop music scene was invaded by a bizarre phenomenon. An enterprising musician resurrected the fervid if tedious songs of the Cultural Revolution—"The East Is Red," "Socialism Is Good," "Without the Communist Party, No New China"—and repackaged them in new arrangements backed by a synthesizer's soft-rock beat. The cassettes were wildly successful. The fad was over before the authorities had decided whether this was homage or sacrilege.

Performing-arts companies were among the first of China's state-owned enterprises to be introduced to market reform. The introduction was brutal: their state subsidies were cut from 100 percent of their operating budgets to 30 percent. Despite their unique character, these companies malfunction just like factories in the state sector. They are responsible not only for paying a large, tenured staff but also for giving them housing and health care and for meeting the pension payments of their retirees. The reduction in state subsidies could not have come at a worse time, for the audience for theater, opera, ballet, and dance, which had been steadily shrinking, declined sharply at the beginning of the reform period, as Chinese bought television sets in record numbers and the film industry increased production. Although theater companies continue to exist in China's major cities, they are having a difficult time remaining solvent. To supplement box-office receipts, they engage in every imaginable form of for-profit activity: they run restaurants and karaoke bars; they dub translations for foreign films; they make television commercials and feature films; and then, time permitting, they produce plays.

One can still find "politically correct" potboilers on the Chinese stage—plays about the economic development of the new Pudong region of Shanghai, for example. One director suggests that a potboiler or two each season pleases the local cultural bureau and gives the company leeway for the contemporary dramas in which they and their audiences are really interested.

Two hits from the 1990s give a sense of what serious playwrights are creating for the Chinese stage. The Beijing Art Theater mounted a highly successful production of Guo Shixing's Bird Men in 1994. Set in a Beijing park, the play depicts the conversations of three men who meet periodically to engage in a unique urban pastime for Chinese men: walking their caged birds. Miss Stay-at-Home, produced by the Shanghai Art Theater, focuses on what, for Chinese audiences, is the fascinating experience of those who go abroad, in this case from the perspective of those left behind. A man and woman meet and, discovering that each has a spouse working in the United States, keep each other company and fall in love. Both plays featured a naturalistic acting style that contrasts sharply with the overdrawn manners of earlier Chinese stage and film actors that are still encountered today. The Shanghai production was innovative in its use of an unusual cabaret format. Both productions attracted large audiences over extended runs.

The best publicized of a number of joint productions with foreign directors, plays, and actors was Arthur Miller's 1983 Beijing production of *Death of a Salesman*. A highly popular and significantly more complex joint production took place in Beijing in 1996 when the China National Beijing Opera and the New York Greek Drama Company collaborated in mounting Euripides' *Bacchae*, with spoken parts in Chinese, singing in Greek. The production was directed by Chen Shizheng, whose next project was the initially ill-starred *Peony Pavilion*.

A great many novels and short stories are published in China today, but, as in every country, lowbrow fiction attracts the largest readership by far. Among the most successful writers of popular novels is Wang Shuo, who writes in a highly colloquial, breezy style—atypical of most contemporary Chinese fiction—and critics compare him to Jacqueline Susann and Danielle Steel. Like their works, Wang's books appear regularly and reach a wide audience of devoted readers. But reading his work in a very different way, other critics compare it to the cynical satires of Evelyn Waugh.

Jealous of the financial success of writers like Wang Shuo, Jia Pingwa, a serious novelist, turned his hand to writing lucrative trash. His novel *Fei Du* (The abandoned capital) was a *succès fou*. It was described by one reviewer as a "steamy sex fest," but much of the steam it generates depends heavily on the reader's imagination. Periodically, when the action becomes most intense, the author resorts to a novel device for titillating his reader: "Here the author has omitted

368 characters," the text reads. In its official version, the novel sold well over a half-million copies; several industrious printers sold at least another million pirated copies.

Following in the lucrative footsteps of Wang Shuo and Jia Pingwa, twenty-something author Zhou Weihui published her fifth novel, *Shanghai Baby*, in 1999. The novel graphically describes the adventures of its heroine, Coco, who falls in love simultaneously with a tall, attractive, but drug-addicted and impotent man named Tian Tian (who later dies of a heroin overdose) and a married German (who subsequently returns to Germany). "One is for love, the other for lust," the author explains. After the novel's sales exceeded an estimated 100,000 copies in six printings and several pirated editions, government-controlled media denounced the author as "decadent, debauched, and a slave of foreign culture." Her publisher dutifully responded by recalling and destroying all the books remaining in stock, observing tersely, "It's an ideological matter." Unbowed, Ms. Zhou continued work on her sixth novel, *Evil Pearl*.

A fourth example of contemporary popular fiction relies, as does *Miss Stay-at-Home*, on the interest generated by people who live abroad. *Beijing Man in New York*, which originally appeared in serial form in the *Beijing Evening News*, is an extended soap-opera-like treatment of the complicated lives of Chinese transplanted to New York City that capitalized on the sudden popularity of television soaps—some imported, some domestic. One of the most popular domestic soap operas, a fifty-five-episode series called *Kewang* (Yearning), attracted a huge following, despite stilted acting and a plotline so filled with "family values" that it won the endorsement of the Ministry of Culture.

Three trends mark the rapid changes occurring in the visual arts in China. First, some artists have returned to traditional images and media but reworked them. The restrictions against innovation having been set aside, traditional forms are radically modified by these contemporary hands. A second trend looks to modern Western art. Since contact with European and American artists and their work has been restored, some Chinese have carefully perused the stages of Western art over the last half century to find out what they have missed, while others move directly to contemporary media and forms. As with music, theater, and film, these contemporary and foreign styles of art are known to only a very small public in China. It is mainly abroad that these artists find viewers and a market, and many have become expatriates for that reason. A third trend is a revisiting of the socialist realist tradition. Artists take the larger-than-life images of the past and, in paintings reminiscent of American pop art, of Andy Warhol or Roy Lichtenstein, juxtapose them incongruously with icons of the commercial world today, thus expressing the disjunction between current lifestyles and those of the very recent past.

Like the Cultural Revolution songs reset to a rock beat, these last paintings coincided with a broad wave of Mao nostalgia that swept across China's popular culture in 1993, just as the Party-state was grappling with the sensitive issue of how to mark the centenary of the chairman's birth. Mao badges were pulled out of the bottoms of drawers and worn and sold on city streets; plastic-encased Mao amulets were hung from rearview mirrors in automobiles, buses, and taxis; and a Cultural Revolution theme restaurant opened in Beijing that was supposed to recapture the chaotic ambience and bad cooking of the 1960s. In one light, the phenomenon was simply a fad. But for some, superstition also played a part. If asked why they were displaying the Mao amulet in their taxis, drivers would cite accidents in which only those who had no amulets were injured. Others—many serious artists among them—used Mao's image as a vehicle for political protest under a perfect cover: it was hard to object to the display of the image, and who could really tell whether it was intended to honor or to mock?

Many people in China have a genuine nostalgia for the Mao era, and it has lingered long after the fad has passed. It will be a long while before the men in power in China will feel able to undertake a thoroughgoing public reassessment of the former chairman, since to do so would jeopardize the very foundations on which the power of the Party rests. As a result, much about Mao's professional and personal life is not known in China. (The partial reassessment that took place shortly after the fall of the Gang of Four in 1976 concluded that Mao was "60 percent correct and 40 percent incorrect," meaning, really, that he was 100 percent correct for the first 60 percent of his career and 100 percent incorrect for the last 40 percent.) But for all the privations people suffered during the Mao period, they thought it had its virtues, at least in retrospect. Rather like older Americans who look back on an earlier, simpler, clearer, and better time, some Chinese look to the 1950s and 1960s in China as a time when, they think, values were crystal clear, the government was honest, and life was predictable. All that is appealing today, when self-enrichment is the chief value, the government is corrupt, and change is ubiquitous.

Thanks to the bridge across languages provided by subtitles, Chinese film is the popular cultural vehicle most accessible to audiences outside China. Paradoxically, the movies that have been most successful in capturing international awards and attracting international audiences are least successful in the Chinese market and least acceptable to the Chinese authorities.

In 1998, China's thirty-one film studios produced more than eighty officially approved feature films, the vast majority of which were historical epics revisiting great moments in the Chinese Communist revolution and glorifying its heroes and accomplishments. They play to large audiences, though not as large as they were when television was duller and less accessible. The leading film school in China, the Beijing Film Academy, was closed down during the Cultural Revolution but reopened in 1977. The students of film direction in the fifth class to graduate after its reopening, who left the school in 1982, are referred to as the Fifth Generation of Chinese filmmakers, and it is their work that is best known to moviegoers outside China: Zhang Yimou, Chen Kaige, and Tian Zhuangzhuang.

Some Fifth Generation films veil their criticisms of the recent past by the use of symbols; others are more direct. Zhang Yimou's *Ju Dou* and *Raise the Red Lantern*—both set in the early years of the twenti-

eth century, both featuring a spectacular use of color and imagery—
are critical of the old order. In *Ju Dou*, the heroine is married against
her will to the much older owner of a cloth-dyeing factory, and she
falls in love with his young assistant. In *Raise the Red Lantern*, the
heroine is forced to become one of several concubines in the house
of a wealthy landowner. Although the oppressors in both cases are
part of the old order that the Communist regime overthrew in 1949,
both films can be read as commentaries on contemporary Chinese
society.

Setting a film in the more recent past is a dangerous game for Chinese filmmakers. Chen Kaige's *Farewell My Concubine* portrays two
actors who join a Beijing opera troupe as young apprentices in the
1930s, follows their lives through the end of the Cultural Revolution,
and concludes with the suicide of one of them. The film was unacceptable to the authorities not so much because of its characters (one
of whom is homosexual) as because the suicide takes place after the
"bad old days" are over and the current period of reform has begun.

Much more mundane lives are explored in Zhang Yimou's *To
Live* and Tian Zhuangzhuang's *Blue Kite*. *To Live* portrays a young
man who, having lost his family fortune at the gambling tables of the
old society, becomes a puppeteer and lives with his young family on
the margins of the new society. The central character in *Blue Kite* is
a boy born in 1953, just as word of Stalin's death is being broadcast in
his parents' neighborhood. The two films depict most powerfully the
lives of Chinese city dwellers in the 1950s and 1960s. In both cases,
families are buffeted by events and movements over which they have
no control, while being only dimly aware of their substance. Because
neither film distinguishes clearly between the officially accepted
"good" era that ended in 1958 and the "bad" period that extended
from the Great Leap Forward through the Cultural Revolution, they
were banned from screens in China.

But Fifth Generation films—those that have not been banned—
are not especially popular with Chinese audiences, who find them
too slow, rather obscure in their symbolism, and occasionally too critical. Most recent films by Fifth Generation directors are foreign

co-productions and rely on screening abroad to recoup their investments.

Exceptions to the critical stance assumed by Fifth Generation filmmakers are Zhang Yimou's more recent films, *The Story of Qiu Ju* and *Not One Less*. Frustrated by the fact that his films have not been accessible to audiences in China, he has decided to work within the parameters set by government censors. In the first of these two films, the heroine's husband, a farmer, is injured when he is kicked in the groin by a village official. The film depicts her numerous trips to seek redress from officials at ever-higher levels of the rural bureaucracy. Apart from the violent act that sets the plot in motion, government and Party officials are treated rather sympathetically in the film. *Not One Less* treats a number of the issues and themes we have been exploring in earlier chapters. Its heroine, a thirteen-year-old villager, is pressed into service as a long-term substitute in a rural elementary school. Told she will receive a bonus if there are no dropouts during her tenure, she goes to extraordinary lengths to retrieve one of her fifth-graders, who leaves the village for a distant city to seek work that will provide an income for his widowed mother. Although, like *Qiu Ju*, the film has its unsympathetic characters, they are by no means all associated with the Party-state, and they are treated with an ironic edge. (From a technical standpoint, these two films are particularly intriguing because of Zhang Yimou's highly successful use of nonactors, many of them playing on film the roles they play in their daily lives.)

A group of younger filmmakers—sometimes called the Sixth Generation—tend to express the cynical nihilism of the youth culture: Zhuang Yuan's films, *Beijing Bastards*, *Square*, and *Sons*, and Wu Wenguang's *Bumming in Beijing* and *My Time in the Red Guards* have all been banned.

Chinese filmmakers in Hong Kong and on Taiwan make films that are very different from the mainland ones. Hong Kong movie people are a wild lot, churning out a hundred or more movies a year, most of them martial-arts action films. One of the more interesting Hong Kong filmmakers is Tsui Hark (Xu Ke), who combines the conventions of kung fu films with those of farce and Beijing opera to retell modern Chinese history. And Fruit Chan Kuo's 1997 film, *Made in Hong Kong*, is very reminiscent of Sixth Generation films in Beijing. By contrast, Taiwanese films are rather staid, except for those of Ang Lee, who was trained in the United States and whose films attract an unexpectedly large American audience. Ang Lee concentrates on family relationships, and his humor is situational rather than visual. His *Wedding Banquet*, though produced by a government-owned film company, was hardly the usual Taiwanese fare: its hero is a young, gay Taiwanese professional in New York City. When it won a prize at the Berlin Film Festival, the Taiwan government warmly acknowledged Ang Lee and the film, despite its unorthodox plotline. Taiwan's reaction contrasts sharply with the mainland authorities' stiff-lipped response to the Cannes Film Festival's award of the Palme d'Or to Chen Kaige's *Farewell My Concubine*.

As I have said, the political straitjacket in which Chinese arts are confined loosened in the 1990s, but the arbitrariness of what is acceptable and what is forbidden makes for an incongruous, often unpredictable cultural mélange. The government censors' puritanism appears to have been relaxed, and the sex, violence, and nihilism of contemporary popular music, film, and literature are largely ignored. For example, only when sales of Jia Pingwa's *Fei Du* approached a million copies did the Party-state get around to banning it. Zhou Weihui encountered the same belated official disapproval. It is also acceptable to be critical of the past, notably if the criticism is directed against events prior to 1949 or during the excesses of the Cultural Revolution.

What triggers censors' attention and disapproval is any criticism of the Party-state and its policies prior to 1957 and after 1977. They are particularly sensitive to any mention of the events at Tiananmen Square in 1989. Foreign books and foreign films are almost always a cause of concern. Until very recently, Chinese distributors imported few films, and publishers translated few foreign books. With the important exception of *The Sound of Music*—which seems to have been seen at least once by every living person in mainland China—most available foreign films are cheap B-grade movies: the criteria for what gets imported concern cost more than salaciousness or political incorrectness. As Chinese audiences become better informed about international culture, the demand for foreign films rises, and it is to satisfy this demand that the burgeoning industry of pirated video cassettes has sprung up, to the distress of all those in other nations who have agreed to protect intellectual property rights.

As standards of acceptability have relaxed, many of the government and Party control mechanisms of the arts have fallen into disarray, though in certain areas they still function. For example, virtually all performance spaces are owned by the state, and all major performing-arts companies depend on state funds for at least part of their budget. Local bureaus representing the Ministry of Culture must review and approve the repertoire of all performing-arts companies and all art exhibits. Most gallery and museum space is state-owned and managed, and exhibitions are subject to government monitoring. The major film studios are government-owned; their films are screened and, if necessary, censored before public release.

The situation is very different with respect to the printed word and television. Prior to the reforms, Party officials reviewed virtually everything before it was published; that they no longer do so is partly the result of rapid growth in the publishing industry. Official statistics for 1978 and 1998 show a fivefold increase in the number of newspapers during that time, an eightfold increase in the number of books, and a ninefold increase in the number of magazines, and these figures do not include the burgeoning unofficial publications. The government used to control book publishing by issuing book numbers to state-owned publishing houses, without which no book could be published. Publishers have taken to selling their unused book numbers, at a profit of course, to private publishers and printers who turn out great quantities of books, many of which the authorities find unacceptable.

Like the publishing industry, television has become more difficult to control. Television stations now number more than eight hundred, and the number is growing 15 percent per year. The number of television sets has doubled over the last decade and now stands at close to 300 million. The government owns all television stations and monitors the content of their broadcasts, but with the proliferation of stations, most of them locally managed, the diversity of programming has increased significantly. The old, stultifying diet of official news and didactic documentaries has given way to soaps, MTV, and even talk shows (with a built-in fourteen-second delay to allow for screening callers' comments before they hit the airwaves). In addition, satellite dishes and cable connections bring a range of foreign programs to Chinese viewers.

Television coverage of the events in Tiananmen Square in 1989 is an interesting case in point. The extensive international coverage of these events was the result of a coincidence. Foreign reporters, cameramen, and satellite hookups were all in place for the visit of Mikhail Gorbachev to Beijing in May. His visit was given a share of coverage, but most of the reporters were riveted by the demonstrators and their hunger strike, and so these images reached television viewers all over the world.

The extensive Chinese television coverage of the early stages of the demonstrations and occupation of the square was generally sympathetic to the demonstrators. Students and workers in cities across China learned of the events in Beijing through the official media, and they acted on what they saw, heard, and read by going out into their own city streets. Only after the declaration of martial law in late May was domestic television coverage reined in and closely scrutinized. Even then, television reporters were able to signal their opinions by means of dress, body language, and facial expression. And once official television ceased to be an effective means of communication between demonstrators and their out-of-town sympathizers, the fax machine took its place.

The images of what actually occurred on the streets of Beijing on 3 and 4 June were seen by viewers outside China and by the few Chinese who had access to foreign television broadcasts in hotels and offices, while the events were described and analyzed on Voice of America and the British Broadcasting Corporation's shortwave radio transmissions. But Chinese television did not cover the events, and the Party-state could make up its own story, which, devised with carefully edited footage, told of student demonstrators as perpetrators of violence and innocent soldiers as victims of their aggression. Broadcast over and over again in the aftermath of the massacre, this account persuaded many in China that the students had erred, that the People's Liberation Army had saved the day, and that the foreign press was manufacturing other versions to smear the reputation of the Chinese army, state, and Party.

This recasting of news would be difficult or impossible to bring off today, given the proliferation of uncontrolled and uncontrollable media within China and between the Chinese people and the outside world—satellite dishes and cable connections, fax machines, and, of greatest significance, international on-line information services. Realizing the potential dangers of free access to the information superhighway, the Chinese government issued new regulations on Internet use in 1996. Modeled after laws in effect in Singapore, the new measures aimed to provide censored access. The Ministry of Posts and Telecommunications began by monitoring three access ports— in Beijing, Shanghai, and Jinan. While it might have been possible for the government to monitor the Internet at its 1996 level of fifty to a hundred thousand users, with the number of users in excess of ten million and doubling every six months, and with "hackers" becoming daily more adept at circumventing restrictions, effective control of access to the Internet has proven beyond the technical capability of the Party-state. Information is pouring into China far faster than the censors can repair the leaks in the roof and the walls of the once-solid isolation booth.

It is certainly no easier to assess China's contemporary culture than it would be to assess the state of the arts in our own country. For every Chinese critic who waxes enthusiastic, there is another who deplores what has been lost. One group of critics finds *Fei Du* a new Chinese classic in the tradition of *The Dream of the Red Chamber*, while another dismisses it as the limited sexual fantasies of a small-town literary wanna-be. There are architects who laud the glass-and-steel structures that now dominate Beijing, and others who deplore the loss of the courtyard houses these new buildings displaced. Foreign critics praise the works of Chinese painters, and wealthy patrons collect their works, but the Chinese public avoids them. What is one person's gold is dross for another.

One can say, however, that for better or worse the cultural scene is the part of Chinese society that most closely approximates the non-Chinese world. There is a freedom to explore and experiment, to enjoy or reject, that never existed in China before and that does not yet exist in other parts of Chinese society even today.

XV

HONG KONG AND MACAO:
THE SPECIAL ADMINISTRATIVE REGIONS

HOW THE CHINESE GOVERNMENT handles the administration of Hong Kong as a newly minted special administrative region is a matter of great moment. This vibrant financial center, which supplies just under half of China's external direct investment, could become a stagnant urban backwater if badly handled. On the other hand, effectively administering Hong Kong could not only enhance its economic future but also demonstrate to the people of Taiwan the viability of the "one country, two systems" formula. A failure to maintain Hong Kong's political, economic, and social systems intact will only confirm the expectations of Taiwan's many skeptics.

The quiet, Mediterranean-like enclave of Macao, until 1999 Europe's oldest colonial holding in Asia, is another matter. China's second special administrative region has an economy heavily dependent on gambling revenues and a social structure plagued with organized crime. Whereas the British government surrendered Hong Kong to Chinese sovereignty with considerable resistance and great regret, the Portuguese government seemed relieved as it received its folded flag on 20 December 1999. China's success or failure in administering the Macao Special Administrative Region will have few consequences outside the region itself.

The British Crown Colony of Hong Kong was formed on the basis of three treaties between Britain and the Qing dynasty government of

China. The Treaty of Nanjing was signed in 1842 at the conclusion of the First Opium War, fought when the Chinese imperial government tried to exclude British opium from China. By its terms, the Chinese government ceded in perpetuity the island of Hong Kong to Great Britain. Foreign Secretary Lord Palmerston was not pleased with the work of his envoy, Charles Elliot, who negotiated the treaty, and described Hong Kong (accurately, it happens) as "a barren island with hardly a house upon it." Eighteen years later, at the conclusion of the Arrow War in 1860, the First Convention of Beijing ceded more territory to Britain, including Stonecutter's Island and the peninsula of Kowloon as far north as present-day Boundary Street. Hong Kong's territory today includes a third parcel of land several times the size of the earlier ceded land: the New Territories, the subject of the Second Convention of Beijing, signed on 1 July 1898. The terms of this agreement were different: rather than ceding the land outright, China leased this additional land to the British government for ninety-nine years, a lease that expired on 30 June 1997.

Taken together, the three parcels—a large peninsula at the mouth of the Pearl River on the South China Sea and a number of islands surrounding the peninsula—amount to about 419 square miles, making it roughly one-third the size of Rhode Island.

The colony got off to a slow start. Ten years after it was first established as a base for British naval and military operations in East Asia, fewer than two thousand foreigners and a little more than thirty thousand Chinese lived there. As a commercial center, it was eclipsed by Guangzhou, and, by the early twentieth century, Shanghai had outpaced it as a manufacturing and financial center.

On the eve of World War II, Hong Kong's population stood at close to a million. When the Japanese occupied Hong Kong in 1941, the foreign population was imprisoned, and many Hong Kong Chinese fled for Macao, which remained neutral under Portuguese control. By the end of the war, only about 600,000 people were living in Hong Kong, but the number grew swiftly, as civil war between Nationalist and Communist forces swept southward through the Chinese mainland, and quadrupled in less than five years. Many of

Hong Kong's new residents were businessmen and their families from Guangzhou and Shanghai, who, fleeing from the prospect of life under Communist rule, brought their skills and capital to Hong Kong.

After the founding of the People's Republic in 1949, Chinese citizens continued to enter Hong Kong, a few legally and many, many more illegally. Most came from neighboring Guangdong Province, and many risked their lives in making their escape. A large proportion of Hong Kong's current population of about seven million are people who chose not to be citizens of the People's Republic of China (PRC).

The economy of Hong Kong has undergone several transformations over the last fifty years. Through the 1950s, its principal economic raison d'être was commerce—as a free port and as China's main economic window to the outside world—and then in the 1960s it began to industrialize. The process began with the manufacture of low-end consumer goods and gradually shifted into appliances and electronics. In the early 1970s, when Hong Kong's labor and real-estate costs rose, manufacturers moved to other East Asian countries that were cheaper, and the Hong Kong economy shifted to money and banking; the city became, after Tokyo, East Asia's second financial center.

Following the inauguration of reforms in China and its opening up to the world economy, Hong Kong's focus shifted once again to manufacturing. This time, however, although the companies are owned and managed by Hong Kong residents, the factories are located across the border in Guangdong Province, in the newly opened special economic zone of Shenzhen or elsewhere. Today, between two and three million people in Guangdong are employed in Hong Kong–owned businesses and factories.

When Prime Minister Margaret Thatcher, flush from the British victory over Argentina in the Falkland Islands in 1982, visited Beijing, she had been urged to raise the issue of the future of Hong Kong with her hosts. Hong Kong businessmen, concerned over the status of their holdings once the lease on the New Territories expired in 1997, wanted to know whether the Chinese intended to renew the lease.

The existing arrangement had always worked to the benefit of the Communist government. When local leftist zealots had attempted to take advantage of the chaos of the Cultural Revolution to overthrow the Hong Kong government, Mao and his colleagues had reined them in to preserve the symbiotic relationship. By 1982, Hong Kong had come to provide 40 percent of China's foreign exchange and had become China's largest trading partner. Hong Kong firms were investing in joint ventures in Shenzhen and Guangdong and gave every indication they would continue to do so. Hong Kong issues were occasionally discussed by the Foreign Ministry and the British ambassador in Beijing, but day-to-day relations between China and the Hong Kong government were carried on by the former's unofficial emissary in the territory, the head of Xinhua, the New China News Agency.

Thatcher did indeed raise the issue of Hong Kong during her meeting with Deng Xiaoping. She reminded him rather starchily that the British always honored their treaties and expected other nations to do the same. Making her remarks in this setting and framing them as she did, Thatcher simultaneously touched two raw nerves: China's view of its sovereignty and the matter of "face." Questioning China's right to govern its own territory was bad enough, but she did this in a public way such that failure to respond would entail China's loss of face. Deng reminded Thatcher that the treaties to which she referred were signed under duress by a Chinese government no longer in power. He said that Hong Kong, being Chinese territory, must be returned to Chinese sovereignty and that he hoped he lived long enough to visit the city after that occurred. He came within five months of realizing his hope.

Had Thatcher made her point in different terms and another setting, the Chinese might have considered renewing the New Territories lease. But that was now out of the question, and the British concluded that the ceded territories alone—Hong Kong Island, Stonecutter's Island, and the tip of Kowloon—did not constitute an economically viable entity. Some arrangement for the transfer of sovereignty to China would have to be negotiated.

The negotiations, involving seventeen sessions over three years, resulted in the Joint Declaration on the Question of Hong Kong, signed in December 1984. The declaration set up the Sino-British Joint Liaison Group, responsible for ongoing negotiations with respect to questions that might arise between the two sides during what the British called the "run-up" to 1997. Two other bodies were constituted at the same time: the Basic Law Drafting Committee, made up of Hong Kong and PRC citizens, to draw up a constitution under which Hong Kong would be governed after 1997 as the Hong Kong Special Administrative Region (SAR); and the Basic Law Consultative Committee, made up of Hong Kong citizens and charged with assessing Hong Kong public opinion with respect to the provisions of the Basic Law.

Several aspects of these negotiations—not all of them perfectly clear at the time—came to be very significant as the transfer of sovereignty approached. One was a conflict over the premises of negotiations. The Chinese position was based on an offer the government had first extended to Taiwan in 1981 and then to Hong Kong in 1983: to leave their economic and political systems intact for fifty years after the transfer of sovereignty. The Chinese understood this to mean that no change would be made to Hong Kong's economic and political systems *as they existed at the time of the signing of the agreement in 1984*, while Britain presumed that it could legitimately make alterations in Hong Kong's governance, as it saw fit, prior to the transfer of sovereignty in 1997 and that China's offer meant Beijing would make no change to the economic and political systems of Hong Kong *as they existed at the time of the transfer of sovereignty in 1997.*

During the negotiations, both sides used the "through train" as a metaphor for the transition. Visitors to China in the 1970s will recall the ritual of boarding a train at the Kowloon station to go to mainland China and traveling on it to Lowu, a town on the border. One got off the train at Lowu, walked across a bridge spanning the border, and, after going through customs formalities, boarded the Chinese train on the other side at the Shenzhen station. For frequent travelers, it was a great moment when a through train was inaugurated that allowed passengers to board in Kowloon, cross the border on the train, and disembark in Guangzhou. In the context of the negotiations, the through train meant that every effort would be made by both sides to ensure that the political system in the time just before the transfer of sovereignty would fit as closely as possible with the political system to be inaugurated after it. If the track were properly laid and the train properly built, the shift of sovereignty would require no one to disembark.

One final aspect of the negotiations proved significant: the people of Hong Kong were not represented in them, though the British had pressed at the outset for three-way negotiations among representatives of the governments of China, Britain, and Hong Kong. The Chinese rejected the idea, insisting on bilateral negotiations between Britain and China, with the Hong Kong governor seated as an observer, since the Hong Kong government, they argued, reported ultimately to the British government, and the people of Hong Kong, being Chinese, were adequately represented by the Chinese government. But if the people of Hong Kong had been represented by their own delegates, they would certainly have made a strong case for maintaining the status quo. Polls taken in Hong Kong in the early 1980s showed that an overwhelming majority favored a continuing British presence in the territory and opposed a transfer of sovereignty to China—not surprising, given the substantial number of Hong Kong citizens who had fled Communist rule in China.

These views began to change, however, in the years immediately following the signing of the Joint Declaration. Hong Kong residents observed the rapid reform and growth in the Chinese economy and its extensive new links to the world economy. Many of them took advantage of this to establish business ties across the border. By 1989, more than two thousand factories in Guangdong were wholly or partially owned by Hong Kong interests. Adding in subcontracting agreements between Hong Kong and Guangdong firms, it was estimated that Hong Kong–related enterprises accounted for more than a million jobs in southern China. As Hong Kong business interests became linked with those of China, people began to have a personal stake in a smooth working relationship among Beijing, London, and Hong Kong. And as political reforms began to alter somewhat the character of the Chinese government, making it seem slightly less repugnant, widespread skepticism about the future was superseded by cautious optimism.

The massacre in Beijing in June 1989 was a major turning point, however, not only in public attitudes in Hong Kong but also in the relations among Beijing, Hong Kong, and London. The news from Beijing on 4 June had a devastating effect on public confidence in Hong Kong, anger and fear politicizing a large segment of a population famous for its lack of interest in politics. Millions of Hong Kong residents poured into the city streets to express their outrage. Thousands contributed in various ways to support the democracy movement and to aid its fugitives by means of a hastily constructed underground railroad to safe havens in Europe and the United States.

Several political groups were founded in Hong Kong in 1989 that have subsequently evolved into formal political parties. Martin Lee and Szeto Wah are the two most prominent among the many individuals who stepped forward at this time, motivated by concern that without an effective political voice, Hong Kong citizens faced as precarious a future as did the advocates of good government in China itself.

A comparable shift of attitude occurred in Beijing. The image of Hong Kong as an apolitical golden goose faded, and in its place Chinese authorities saw a hotbed of pro-democratic dissent and a potential threat to their own stability. The situation seemed dangerously out of control when not only the editor of a PRC-supported newspaper in Hong Kong but even Beijing's chief spokesman in the colony, Xu Jiatun, spoke out against their government's actions.

The British position shifted as well: Britain joined the many other nations that responded to the Beijing massacre with economic and political sanctions. The future of Hong Kong looked significantly less secure than it had during the negotiation of the Joint Declaration. With London's concurrence, the Hong Kong government announced a $17 billion proposal to develop a new airport and expand harbor facilities, a measure designed to stimulate the economy, hard hit by the sudden interruption in China's economic interaction with the outside world, and to bolster the confidence of the Hong Kong population in Britain's intention to take positive actions on its behalf in the time remaining under British sovereignty. Realizing that to do its best for Hong Kong it must be in dialogue with China, London resumed its conversations with Beijing, moving to a successful negotiation of an agreement on the new airport in mid-1991.

At the same time, the Hong Kong government pushed forward with plans, initiated in 1984 and refined on the basis of a study conducted in 1987, to democratize the territory's political system. It proposed to enlarge the functions of elected local councils and to expand the number of elected positions on the fifty-seven-member Legislative Council. Beijing agreed to these proposals in early 1990, and the election for seats on the Legislative Council was held in September 1991: this election marked the debut of political parties in Hong Kong. The United Democrats, under Martin Lee and Szeto Wah, took sixteen of the eighteen contested seats; the other two went to the Liberal Democratic Federation, a pro-business alliance; the pro-China Hong Kong Democratic Federation failed to capture a single seat. Despite the flurry of interest generated by the election, in a now all too familiar pattern, voter turnout was very low—only 32 percent of those eligible to participate. Observers describe the Hong Kong electorate as "interested spectators" who have an active interest in political issues and keep themselves well informed but are reluctant to participate.

At this point, the differences in understanding the terms of the Joint Declaration began to emerge, for Beijing took a dim view of these developments in Hong Kong. The Chinese side, registering its disapproval, reminded Hong Kong and London that it had committed itself to preserving the political and economic status quo as of 1984. The British side, noting that it retained sovereignty over Hong

Kong through 1997, reaffirmed its right to do to the form of government of the territory what it saw fit. The Chinese therefore stalled in
negotiations over every issue that arose between the two sides, the
most important being capitalization for the new airport.

Christopher Patten, appointed governor of Hong Kong in May 1992,
replaced David Wilson, who had served in the post since 1987. Wilson, like many of his predecessors, had been well prepared for his job
and knew the Chinese, but after Tiananmen, understanding and sensitivity were regarded by Westerners as inappropriate, and Wilson was
deemed too ready to yield to the Chinese when negotiating the many
disputed issues that were obstacles to a good relationship. Patten, by
contrast, was neither a Sinophile nor a Sinologue but a highly successful politician who had been head of the Conservative Party and
had recently suffered an embarrassing electoral defeat in his bid to
retain a seat in Parliament.

Patten's mandate was to take a strong stand with the Chinese and
to proceed at full speed with democratizing the Hong Kong government. With this mandate, the through-train metaphor was dropped
and in its place came talk of making Hong Kong "indigestible"—as
democratic as possible in the time remaining so that when the Chinese took control in 1997, undoing the changes would cause them
the maximum possible international embarrassment. It was a mandate unlikely to endear Patten to his Chinese collocutors. He began
his term with a series of extensive conversations with people in Hong
Kong, probing for their views on whether and how the government
should be restructured in the five years remaining. Five months after
taking office, he presented proposals for political reform to the Legislative Council, based, he said, on the opinions he had gathered;
they called for an accelerated expansion of representative government that would double the size of the electorate, make local governing bodies elective rather than appointive, increase the number of
elected seats on the Legislative Council, and shift the balance of
power from the governor and his Executive Council to the now fully
representative Legislative Council.

The Chinese response to Patten's proposals was unrelentingly negative. Although Patten claimed to have hewed very closely to the letter of the newly adopted Basic Law, Beijing took the position that the proposals were fundamentally at odds with it. Were the Legislative Council and reconstituted government to adopt the Patten proposals, they said, the authority of that government would be terminated when sovereignty was transferred.

Reaction to the proposals in Hong Kong was mixed. Initially they were supported by a strong majority, but two factors caused that support to diminish: First, the proposals were out of sync with the electorate's reluctance to participate. The political activism stirred up by reactions to the Beijing massacre was relatively short-lived, and although sizable crowds turned out to mark the anniversary of the event each year, for most of the rest of the year the Hong Kong public was more comfortable being an interested spectator than an active political participant. Second, the Hong Kong business community, reacting to Beijing's opposition, was cool; with more and more Hong Kong firms dependent on links with the mainland, China found it easier to disengage the business community from support for democratization.

Before putting his proposals to a vote in the Legislative Council, Patten agreed to discuss them with China. After seventeen rounds of negotiations and no progress, he submitted his proposals to the Legislative Council in two batches, one in December 1993, the other in July 1994. The first, and relatively noncontroversial, batch passed easily; the second, and more difficult, one survived a hostile amendment by a single vote and then passed thirty-two to twenty-four.

There were adverse and perhaps unanticipated consequences of the decision by the British and Hong Kong governments to abandon the idea of a through train. Although Sino-British relations had improved enough by mid-1995 to allow for talks on issues critical to Hong Kong's future, the Chinese position hardened with its formation of what they called a "second kitchen"—a legislature chosen by the four-hundred-member Selection Committee, which, in its wisdom, selected fifty of its own number to fill all but ten of the seats in the new body. This made the Hong Kong government all the more a lame-duck one and, in the eyes of some observers, rendered the territory ungovernable for the remainder of the run-up.

The Chinese policy of ignoring the Hong Kong government was strengthened by their enormous amount of ill will toward Patten. The Chinese press called him virtually every uncomplimentary name their style sheets permit (including what Patten said was his favorite: a "tango dancer"), and for years the Chinese turned their backs on him on every possible public occasion. He was not included on the schedule of Chinese officials visiting the territory, and Chinese officials did not receive him in Beijing. This tactic effectively dissuaded Hong Kong citizens from viewing their government as efficacious.

The Chinese also tried, somewhat less successfully, to discredit Hong Kong's democratic parties. Beijing made it abundantly clear that participation in the post-1997 government by Martin Lee, Szeto Wah, or any of the other prominent and outspoken members of Hong Kong's democratic parties was unacceptable. They denounced the September 1995 elections for seats on the Legislative Council carried out under Patten's new electoral rules and gave notice that the council seated by this election would be dismissed on 1 July 1997. Paradoxically, they also campaigned actively in that same election for a slate of pro-Beijing candidates, who, in the event, were soundly defeated at the polls. Voter participation, at 35 percent, was neither much lower nor much higher than in past elections.

The dispute over the election gave rise to questions about the legality of the Beijing-appointed Provisional Council. A decision adopted by the National People's Congress (NPC) in 1990 stipulated that if the composition of the Legislative Council in June 1997 conformed with the Basic Law, it would remain in office after the transfer of sovereignty. Patten consistently argued that he had carefully crafted his electoral reforms to conform to the law, and he challenged the Chinese to show where they did not conform. Without giving details, China declared that the reforms violated the Basic Law and proceeded to create its "second kitchen." Tung Chee-hwa, coming to Beijing's support soon after he was named chief executive by the selection committee in 1996, disappointed those in Hong Kong who had hoped that he would uphold the results of the territory's eleventh-hour democratization. For their part, some members of the former council threatened to mount a legal challenge to the legitimacy of the new body. Thus, whether they meant to or not, all parties involved helped to undermine the new Hong Kong government's authority.

Educated in Britain, Tung Chee-hwa had worked for General Electric in Boston and San Francisco before returning to Hong Kong in 1969 to join his father's Orient Overseas shipping company. Prior to his selection, questions had been raised over the fact that in 1986 he received what the press referred to as a $120 million "bailout" from Chinese investors to save his ailing firm. Some found it unlikely that in light of this favor, he would be able to hold his own against the importunings of the Beijing government. He has also described himself as an admirer of Singapore's Lee Kuan Yew and the "Asian values" he espouses, which has aroused concern among Hong Kong's democratic opposition, with whom he has little patience.

Two factors have made Hong Kong the successful financial center it is: the free flow of information and a careful adherence to the rule of law. Because neither of these is a characteristic of the People's Republic of China, both seemed in jeopardy as the transfer of sovereignty approached.

One of the most serious legal issues to arise at that time was the post-1997 composition of the Hong Kong Court of Final Appeal. The original plan was for seven justices, three from the Hong Kong legal community, three from a panel of British Commonwealth judges with experience in common law, and a chief justice. The Chinese proposed that there be only one non–Hong Kong justice, drawn from either an international or a local panel. After extensive, unsuccessful negotiations, the British agreed to this—but the Legislative Council rejected it. The Chinese subsequently conceded that more than one justice could be drawn from an international panel but adopted a

very vague definition of the court's jurisdiction that leaves many cases
to be decided by the National People's Congress. Reluctantly, and after much campaigning by the Hong Kong government, the Legislative Council ratified this proposal. Nonetheless, serious doubts had
been raised, within Hong Kong and in the international business
community, about the future integrity of Hong Kong's legal system.

The Hong Kong government belatedly adopted a Bill of Rights in
1991, intended to supplement protections provided in the Basic Law,
but China denounced this as a violation of the Basic Law, and at its
March 1997 meeting, the National People's Congress invalidated it,
as well as some two dozen other laws and regulations. Here again,
Tung Chee-hwa disturbed many in Hong Kong with his unhesitating
endorsement of the NPC's action. Without these changes, he said,
Hong Kong risked becoming an "indulgent Western society."

The constitution of the People's Republic of China guarantees
Chinese citizens freedom of the press, yet whenever the press oversteps the boundary of discourse deemed appropriate by the Party, it is
brought back into line. For example, in 1989 the authorities shut
down the privately owned *World Economic Herald* in Shanghai when
it continued to print favorable comments about the demands of the
demonstrators in Tiananmen Square.

Hong Kong's Basic Law also guarantees freedom of the press and
publication, and citizens are expected to believe that the phrase
means something more substantial than it does in the Chinese constitution. But their confidence was not strengthened by the case of
Yang Xi, a reporter from the Hong Kong newspaper *Ming Pao* who
was arrested in 1994 while reporting in China and sentenced to
twelve years' imprisonment for stealing and publishing state secrets—the secrets in question being a change in the People's Bank of
China interest rate, which Yang reported on before it was officially
announced. Yet the media in Hong Kong are numerous, vibrant, and
diverse, with nearly seventy daily newspapers and as many as six hundred periodicals, three television stations, two privately owned and
one managed by the government, and two privately owned radio stations. People in the communications business in Hong Kong are

skeptical about the extent of their freedoms under the Basic Law, and
some are hedging their bets, usually with voluntary self-censorship.

Such self-censorship is often a business decision. In 1993, the
British Broadcasting Corporation (BBC) produced a documentary
marking the centenary of the birth of Mao Zedong. Because it was
more critical of aspects of Mao's life than the Chinese Communist
Party permits, the Chinese government demanded that it not be
shown in Hong Kong. Rupert Murdoch's Star TV pulled it from its
broadcast schedule, claiming there had been insufficient time to ac-
commodate it; subsequently, Murdoch removed BBC programming
entirely from the cable service he was in the process of selling to
mainland China.

In other cases, the decision to self-censor is less obviously business-
driven. A number of Hong Kong Chinese-language newspapers, for
example, have eliminated their editorial pages; owners and editors
presumably believe that in the minefield of Sino-British contention,
there is no telling what might offend Chinese sensibilities and what
might detonate in the future. Expressing no opinion at all is the safest
course, and the loss of the editorial page has not significantly affected
circulation.

On the eve of the transfer of sovereignty, it was hard for many to
imagine that the Chinese government, as currently configured,
would allow Hong Kong's free flow of information, so vital to its financial life, to continue uninterrupted.

In the first moments after midnight on 1 July 1997, in a solemn ceremony presided over by Prince Charles and Jiang Zemin, Britain
relinquished and China resumed sovereignty over Hong Kong, ending 155 years of British colonial rule. In many ways, the immediate
aftermath of the transfer resembled the immediate aftermath of the
turn of the millennium two and a half years later: despite widespread
expectations to the contrary, very little actually changed. In truth, the
Asian financial crisis that began two months later had a much more
detrimental effect on Hong Kong than did the transfer of sovereignty.
By the end of 1998, the Hang Seng index of Hong Kong stocks had

fallen by half since its peak in the summer of 1997, property values were down by as much as 60 percent, tourism—a mainstay of the Hong Kong economy in the past—was off by 25 percent, unemployment reached 6.1 percent, and gross domestic product was down 5.1 percent for the year. To stabilize its currency, the Hong Kong government resorted to the unprecedented step in September of pumping $15 billion into stocks and futures, boosting the Hang Seng index by 18 percent but shocking those who look to the territory as the last bastion of laissez-faire capitalism.

The trend to integrate the Hong Kong economy with that of Guangdong Province has accelerated. Today, about three-quarters of Guangdong's exports go to or through Hong Kong. More than five thousand factories in Guangdong are Hong Kong–owned. Double that number of factories operate as subcontractors for Hong Kong firms. In all, between two and three million people in Guangdong are employed by Hong Kong–affiliated enterprises, well in excess of twice the number of blue-collar workers in Hong Kong itself.

The Hong Kong economy began its recovery from the Asian financial crisis very quickly; at the end of 1999 quarterly growth figures were at a respectable 4.5 percent, and per capita gross domestic product was about thirty thousand dollars, the third highest in Asia (after Japan and Singapore). Its close relationship with the mainland economy, which was insulated in many respects from the financial crisis, helped contain the effects of the crisis in Hong Kong. Over 70 percent of Guangdong's external direct investment comes from Hong Kong, most of it from Hong Kong investors but some of it Chinese capital channeled through Hong Kong investment companies in order to take advantage of special privileges accorded external investors. Hong Kong is also the point through which most of the legal trade and investment between Taiwan and the mainland passes. By Taiwanese law, all economic activity with mainland China must take place through a third party, and in the majority of cases, Hong Kong is that third party. Taiwan's investment in mainland China totals some $46 billion in committed funds, about half of which is currently in use, and the two-way trade is estimated at $24 billion.

The gross domestic product of the now closely integrated economies of Taiwan, Hong Kong, and the mainland provinces of Guangdong and Fujian (where most Taiwanese and Hong Kong investments are situated) amounts to more than $600 billion, or close to two-thirds of the total gross national product of China as a whole.

The economic interdependence between Hong Kong and the southern provinces will have important political consequences in the years ahead. As noted above, one consequence has been to mute some voices in Hong Kong that might otherwise be critical of Beijing. It is also safe to assume that the southern provinces, recognizing their dependence on a strong and viable Hong Kong economy, will continue to serve as advocates and allies of the Hong Kong SAR in its relations with Beijing.

As promised, Tung Chee-hwa disbanded the elected Legislative Council (Legco) upon taking office on 1 July 1997, replacing it with the Provisional Council appointed in 1996. The question of the legal standing of the Provisional Council was resolved, oddly, during a criminal trial over the theft of a wristwatch: a three-judge panel ruled that the SAR courts were powerless to question Beijing's decision to disband the elected legislature. In September, the Provisional Council approved plans for the 1998 election by which it would be replaced. The new sixty-member body would have twenty members elected by a system of proportional representation, thirty members elected by "functional constituencies"—professional and trade associations—and ten members appointed by an eight-hundred-person selection committee.

Defying their reputation as hopelessly apolitical, and ignoring a daylong driving rainstorm, 53.2 percent of the 2.7 million eligible voters participated in the election the following May, exceeding the previous record participation of 39 percent in Hong Kong's first direct elections in 1991. More than seventy percent of the vote went to democratic politicians ousted with the appointment of the Provisional Council. Martin Lee, the most prominent among Hong Kong's pro-democracy politicians, took his seat in the new Legco and promptly called for speeding up the timetable leading to the direct

election of all Legco members and the chief executive. Tung Chee-
hwa rejected the suggestion, claiming that the Hong Kong public
needs time to learn about democracy. Following his schedule, in
elections held in September 2000, twenty-four seats in Legco were
open to direct election; that number will increase to thirty in elections scheduled for 2004. Procedures for the 2008 election are to be
decided on in 2007.

The issue of overpopulation has come to the forefront in the years
since the transfer of sovereignty. Hong Kong's population will soon
exceed seven million, up nearly 20 percent since 1990. Paradoxically,
before 1997 it was not overpopulation but rather a population drain
that was of concern. Many Hong Kong residents who lacked confidence in the future of the territory emigrated in the decade preceding the transfer of sovereignty. Before the negotiations, Hong Kong
lost an average of 20,000 residents per year, but this was not a net
loss: an equal or greater number moved into the territory each year.
Between 1985 and 1997, however, the number leaving Hong Kong
increased to a yearly average of 65,000, while the current rate of legal
immigration from the mainland is 150 per day, for an annual total of
more than 50,000. There is no accurate count of illegal immigration,
but arrests of illegal immigrants are running just short of 100 per day.
  During the 1980s, the British government revised its policy with
respect to residents in its overseas territories: a new British overseas
passport entitled the bearer to visit Britain but not to take up residence there. A few Hong Kong residents were able to get regular
British passports, but the vast majority could only obtain these new
overseas passports, which do not qualify them as British subjects.
Given this situation, many Hong Kong people who could do so decided to seek citizenship elsewhere—the United States, Canada, Australia, or New Zealand. Other countries took advantage of the
situation by offering Hong Kong residents citizenship in exchange for
a pledge to invest. Those who argued that Hong Kong citizens were
being abandoned to an uncertain fate by the retreating colonial
power brought pressure to bear on the British government after 1989,

in response to which London offered to make available fifty thousand passports good for residence in Britain; up to 200,000 people, including dependents traveling on these passports, could be accommodated by this offer.

Most very wealthy people in Hong Kong have held foreign passports for years. Unlike the boat people who left Vietnam after the fall of their government, these "yacht people," as they are sometimes sarcastically called, have no difficulty establishing residence outside Hong Kong when and if they choose to do so. But most members of Hong Kong's working class could not afford to emigrate even if they had the papers to do so. Hence the middle class was disproportionately represented among those who left in advance of the transfer of sovereignty. The mid-levels of most professions were seriously affected by a brain drain. And these well-trained and experienced emigrants from Hong Kong were replaced by immigrants, most of them from the mainland and nearly all of them less well trained and experienced.

A potential population flood triggered the new SAR government's first major and highly controversial test of its autonomy under the "one country, two systems" formula. At issue was a court case in the spring of 1999 involving four PRC citizens whose parents are citizens of Hong Kong and who sought Hong Kong citizenship (a provision of the Basic Law governing the SAR states that children of Hong Kong citizens born outside Hong Kong have the rights of Hong Kong citizens). The Hong Kong Court of Final Appeal had ruled in their favor at the end of January, but Beijing immediately protested, calling the decision "a mistake [that] should be rectified." Beijing's position was that the NPC, not the Hong Kong court, has the sole authority to interpret the Basic Law. The Court reviewed the case in February and upheld its decision while at the same time noting that it "cannot question the authority" of the NPC.

The Hong Kong government sided with Beijing against the Court. Citing a figure of 1.67 million Chinese citizens who are children of Hong Kong parents and who could in theory take up residence in Hong Kong if the Court's decision stood, the government petitioned the NPC to reverse the Court's decision. It did so in late June. In December, the Court acknowledged the final authority of the NPC to interpret the Basic Law and reversed its decision. Although the reversal met with the approval of most Hong Kong residents, opponents criticized it as setting a dangerous precedent with respect to the independence of the Hong Kong judicial system.

The civil rights record of the SAR government has been better than many expected it would be. With the transfer of sovereignty, certain civil liberties were curtailed: Hong Kong residents are now required to seek police permission before engaging in street demonstrations, and protests advocating independence for Taiwan or Tibet are forbidden. But the media remain freer from constraints than their mainland colleagues. In 1998, Xu Simin, an outspoken pro-China Hong Kong delegate to the Chinese People's Political Consultative Conference (CPPCC) meeting in Beijing, denounced the Hong Kong government-run radio and television network as a "remnant of colonialism" and called for Beijing's intervention. Initial reaction in Hong Kong was to denounce the CPPCC for favoring interference in the internal affairs of the region, but when both Jiang Zemin and CPPCC head Li Ruihuan warned Xu and his fellow delegates against commenting on SAR affairs in national government bodies, opposition changed to admiration for Beijing's "hands-off" approach.

A number of organizations clearly hostile to the interests of the Chinese Party-state continue to operate in Hong Kong with few, if any, restrictions. For example, the Information Center of Human Rights and the Democratic Movement in China, the most comprehensive source of information on dissidents and their activities, complains only that Chinese authorities thwart their efforts from time to time by jamming their beepers.

Every year protest demonstrations in Hong Kong mark the anniversary of the Tiananmen massacre; indeed, seventy thousand people turned out for the candlelight vigil marking the tenth anniversary in 1999. While there are no restrictions on participation, members of Hong Kong's Democratic Party have complained that they are unable to acquire visas to travel in the mainland and say that when they asked for Tung Chee-hwa's intervention to remove their names from Beijing's blacklist, he responded that they would receive more favorable treatment if they would "put the Tiananmen protests behind them."

On the eve of the transfer of sovereignty, Tung's approval rating in Hong Kong opinion polls stood at 57 percent, whereas that of the much vilified retiring governor, Christopher Patten, stood at 79 percent. Two months later, the transition successfully completed, Tung's approval rating had climbed twenty points. After three years in office, his reputation, in the words of one foreign observer, is that of "a genial if sometimes clumsy caretaker" who is careful to take his cues from Beijing. His first term expires in 2002, and it is not yet clear whether he will run for a second term. Some see Leung Chun-ying, appointed in 1999 as head of the Executive Council, as Beijing's choice to succeed Tung.

Hong Kong's negative image in Beijing is almost exclusively due to popular reaction in Hong Kong to the suppression of China's democracy movement. Patten's proposals to democratize the Hong Kong government and the rise of political parties opposed to the terms of the transfer of sovereignty both occurred after that suppression. Were the Beijing government to cease categorizing the Tiananmen demonstration as a counterrevolutionary rebellion, democracy in Hong Kong might seem less threatening.

Frustrated by glitches and difficulties in an otherwise remarkably well functioning city, Hong Kong people sometimes complain that "Hong Kong is becoming more like China every day." But the reverse of that sarcastic comment is also true: China, particularly its southern provinces, is becoming more like Hong Kong every day. The more that marketization and liberalization spread through the Chinese system, the brighter is Hong Kong's future.

Even the darkest scenario for China's future—the weakening of central control and the breakup of the country into regional satrapies—is not the worst news for the future of Hong Kong. If the central Chinese government cannot impose its will on cities like Shanghai and Guangzhou, which have been under its close control for nearly a half century, why should we assume that it can do so with the Hong Kong SAR?

The key to Hong Kong's future lies in the quality of the people chosen to lead it after 1997. Optimists point to the truth that Hong Kong people have survived and thrived against what appeared to be insurmountable odds in the past: the settling of the unpromising island in the nineteenth century; the rebuilding of the colony after World War II; the dark days of the Cultural Revolution, when it seemed that sovereignty would be transferred under circumstances of violence, anarchy, and chaos. They believe it can happen again, and they may be right.

On 20 December 1999, sovereignty over the former Portuguese colony Macao passed to the People's Republic of China under a plan modeled after the Hong Kong transfer. The occasion was marked by ceremonies at the stroke of midnight presided over by Portugal's president Jorge Sampaio and China's president Jiang Zemin. With the transfer, Macao became China's second SAR, enjoying, like Hong Kong, substantial autonomy except in foreign and military affairs.

Macao, first colonized in 1557, has a population of 430,000 and occupies some seven square miles of territory: a small peninsula and a series of islands on the southern coast of China's Guangdong Province, thirty-six miles across the Pearl River estuary from Hong Kong. Twice in the recent past Portugal tried unsuccessfully to return the colony to China—once during the tumultuous first months of the Cultural Revolution in 1966, and again after a leftist revolution in Portugal in 1974. Terms of the transfer were successfully negotiated in 1987 and formalized in the Joint Declaration signed by the Portuguese and Chinese governments; the National People's Congress passed the Basic Law under which Macao is governed in 1993. But Portugal handled the issue of Macao residents' nationality very differently from how Britain treated residents of Hong Kong: all Macao's residents were given the option of immigrating to Portugal with Portuguese citizenship; few, in fact, took advantage of the offer.

The new head of government in Macao is Edmund Ho, a middle-aged banker whose appointment was announced by Beijing in May 1999. Ho's first priority is controlling crime; the former colony is notorious as a haven for criminal gangs. A garrison of eleven hundred People's Liberation Army soldiers is now stationed in Macao, the first seven hundred troops having arrived the day after the transfer of sovereignty. The garrison had been a point of contention before the transfer, with the Portuguese asserting that its stationing in Macao violated the terms of the Joint Declaration, but many Macanese welcomed the arrival of the troops as a further contribution to the restoration of civil order.

Macao's economy has a gross domestic product of just under $6 billion and exports manufactured goods, including clothing, textiles, and furniture; a very significant portion of its tax revenue derives from tourism and gambling. For many years, Macao has attracted visitors from Hong Kong (and, more recently, from nearby Shenzhen and Guangzhou) to its hotels, bars, and casinos. To facilitate the tourist trade, it opened an international airport in 1995.

The transfer of sovereignty struck observers as significantly more relaxed than that in Hong Kong. The Portuguese were not sorry to relinquish control, and most Macanese were not sorry to see them go. "As a local, I'd have to say the Portuguese haven't done a good job," said one businessman. "But in fairness," he continued, "they had their own problems and couldn't pay attention to a little spot of land on the other side of the world." The transfer marked the end of what was once a vast European colonial empire in East Asia.

XVI

DEMOCRATIZATION ON TAIWAN: MODEL OR RIVAL?

TAIWAN, AN ISLAND of about four thousand square miles that lies about 120 miles off the coast of Fujian Province, in the East China Sea, is nominally a province of China, though the government on the island calls itself the Republic of China and, until very recently, claimed sovereignty over all of China. In addition to ruling the island of Taiwan, that government exercises sovereignty over three other tiny islands: Penghu, located in the Taiwan Strait about forty miles off the coast of Taiwan; Matsu, just a few miles off the coast of the mainland near the city of Fuzhou; and Jinmen (Quemoy), located even closer to shore near the city of Xiamen.

Taiwan, a little smaller than the state of Connecticut, has a population of twenty-two million, seven times that of Connecticut. The people of Taiwan enjoy a per capita gross national product of about fourteen thousand dollars, which is fourth in Asia after Japan, Singapore, and Hong Kong and about eighteen times the figure for mainland China. Its economy, now the world's nineteenth largest, is growing about 6 percent per year; inflation stands at about 5 percent.

The question of the relationship between the government on Taiwan and the government of the People's Republic of China, unresolved for more than fifty years, is a source of friction in both governments' relations with the United States. In the spring of 1996,

and again as the millennium began, it became a potential flash point
that had many of China's East Asian neighbors concerned.

Those who believe that Taiwan should be unified with the mainland
begin their argument by asserting that "Taiwan has always been an
integral part of China." Despite the frequency with which this is repeated, the statement is a myth, not a fact. Only during the decade
1885–1895 and in the three years immediately after the end of World
War II was Taiwan governed as a province of China. At all other
times, Taiwan has been largely independent of the control of a mainland Chinese government.

Prior to the seventeenth century, there was virtually no contact between Taiwan and the mainland. Sparsely inhabited by a population
of Malay-Polynesian ethnic origin, the island was "discovered" during
the sixteenth and seventeenth centuries by Portuguese explorers, who
named it Formosa. Dutch settlers, who arrived on the island at about
the same time as the Portuguese, set up fortified bases, and meanwhile Japanese pirates had begun to use it as a base for coastal operations.

With the collapse of the Ming dynasty in 1644, loyalists to the
fallen house, pursued by Manchu forces, retreated across the Taiwan
Strait. Forty years later Qing dynasty forces finally brought Taiwan
under their control, and it was placed under the administration of the
governor of Fujian, where it remained for two hundred years. That
control of the island population was something less than wholly effective is attested to by a Taiwanese saying: "Small rebellions every
three years, big ones every five." Only in 1885 did Taiwan gain its
own provincial administration—and that was short-lived. Ten years
later, following China's defeat in the Sino-Japanese War of 1894–
1895, Taiwan was ceded in perpetuity to Japan. It remained under
Japanese control for the next fifty years, administered as an agricultural colony, its principal crop being sugarcane. Japanese was
adopted as its official language and was taught in the schools. Gradually, if reluctantly, Taiwan culture began to grow away from that of
mainland China under the influence of its Japanese rulers.

At the Cairo Conference in December 1943, the Allied powers agreed that Taiwan would be returned to Chinese sovereignty after the defeat of Japan. The Nationalist forces received the surrender of Japan on the island, and Taiwan began once again to be administered as a province of China, this time under the Nationalist government based in Nanjing. But on 28 February 1947, less than two years later, the local population rose up against the Nationalist forces occupying the island. The Nationalist government brutally suppressed this uprising, with the loss of many lives, and declared martial law, which was not lifted for forty years.

In much the same fashion as the Ming loyalists who, pursued by Manchus, had fled to Taiwan in 1644, Nationalist loyalists, pursued by the Red Army, fled to Taiwan in 1949—about two million of them—and set up residence on the island. The population of Taiwan today includes the result of these two retreats. Descendants of the seventeenth-century influx, often referred to as "Taiwanese," make up about 85 percent of the population; the survivors and descendants of the twentieth-century influx, called "mainlanders," make up the remaining 15 percent. A very small number of the aboriginal population remain, amounting to less than 1 percent of the total.

A kind of modus vivendi was established on Taiwan in the years following the arrival of the mainlanders. Politics, the professions, and the armed forces were controlled by mainlanders; the economy was dominated by the Taiwanese. The political system, a highly authoritarian one based on a constitution adopted by the Nationalist forces when their Republic of China was still located on the mainland, began with a National Assembly and a legislature composed of representatives elected on the mainland in 1947.

The United States did not at first intend to protect Nationalist forces on Taiwan against attack from the Communist regime on the mainland, though the United States did not recognize the government in Beijing, instead tacitly supporting the Nationalists' claim to be the rightful government of China. The outbreak of war on the Korean peninsula altered that policy militarily, and the U.S. Seventh Fleet was ordered to begin patrolling the Taiwan Strait; a mutual de-

fense treaty was signed. During the 1950s, the United States contributed some $2 billion in economic and military aid to Taiwan's
postwar economic recovery and became deeply involved in the relationship between Taiwan and the mainland. Despite its best efforts to
extricate itself, it remains deeply involved today.

Reunification with Taiwan, peaceful if possible, by force if necessary,
is currently motivated in the first instance by economic interest. It
could be argued, in fact, that China would stand to lose economically as a result of reunification. Rather, as with many other issues
concerning the outside world, Beijing is driven by its conception of
national sovereignty and its determination to gain face and avoid losing it.

Were economic logic to govern Beijing's position on Taiwan, it
would dictate maintaining the status quo. Taiwan is now the fourth
largest supplier of external direct investment to China, and there is a
substantial two-way trade between them. It is unlikely that economic
interaction could improve with reunification; indeed, there is a
strong likelihood that it would deteriorate. As with Hong Kong, even
if the Chinese government wanted to keep its promise to leave the
capitalist system on Taiwan intact for fifty years after reunification,
the likelihood that it could do so is very slim. Authorities in Beijing
have no experience in allowing a capitalist system to function without excessive regulation, and the situation on Taiwan, like that in
Hong Kong, is far too sensitive for the authorities to let well enough
alone.

But why is the Chinese concept of national sovereignty at stake?
The senior leaders in Beijing believe their own myths: they *believe*
that Taiwan has always been an integral part of China and that national sovereignty will be incomplete until they control the province.
At one time, it seemed only a handful of the oldest leaders in China
took this hard-line position, and it was hoped that once they departed
the political stage, younger successors would adopt a more flexible
view, but the armed forces have weighed in decisively on the side of

early reunification, and the politicians who depend on the support of the People's Liberation Army (PLA) find that they cannot be flexible with respect to Taiwan. Moreover, the Party-state's revival of Chinese nationalism in recent years has significantly increased the number of Chinese people for whom Taiwan is a hot-button issue.

Loss of face is a concern with respect to Taiwan in several ways. First is the long-standing rivalry between Chinese Communists and Nationalists: for the older generation in China, the revolution will be complete and face regained only when Taiwan is "liberated" from Nationalist hands. But there is also a link between reunification with Taiwan and regaining sovereignty over Hong Kong, since the "one country, two systems" arrangement negotiated with Britain for the future of Hong Kong is seen as a model for a future relationship with Taiwan. Taiwan also involves a potential loss or gain of face vis-à-vis the United States. Given recent history, Beijing refuses to believe that the United States can be a neutral party in the resolution of this issue, and its leaders are confirmed in their views by the public statements of many influential Americans who feel strongly that it would be wrong for the United States to be neutral: were the Chinese government to retreat from its policy on reunification, then, it would be seen as a serious loss of face vis-à-vis the Americans.

Yet Beijing's unequivocal and public policy on Taiwan, reaffirmed so strongly in recent years, has only escalated the intensity of the conflict. Beijing believes that Lee Teng-hui, the former president of the government on Taiwan, was moving in the direction of independence. To discourage him from taking those steps, and at the same time to discourage Taiwan's voters from reelecting him in March 1996, the PLA engaged in provocative military exercises, with live shells and missiles fired into the East China Sea near the coast of Taiwan. Four years later, the situation deteriorated still further from Beijing's perspective with the election of Chen Shui-bian as Lee's successor. Chen ran as the candidate of the Democratic Progressive Party (DPP), whose platform's principal plank for many years had been Taiwan independence. Although Beijing refrained from engag-

ing in military action (perhaps having learned that it was counterproductive), it reasserted its intention to respond to a declaration of independence with military force. Under these circumstances, to effect
reunification on mainland terms is to gain face, to accept any other
arrangement is to lose face.

With this saber-rattling, the Chinese government is close to coming full circle. Thwarted in its initial effort in 1949 to cross the Taiwan Strait in pursuit of the defeated Nationalist forces, it set as a goal
the eventual liberation of the island by force. China acted on this
policy in 1954 and again in 1958, but it overestimated the support it
would receive from its Soviet allies, and underestimated American
support for the Nationalists. When, in 1971, Mao decided to effect a
rapprochement with the United States—a move designed to intimidate the now wary Soviet Union—the policy toward Taiwan became
that of promoting "peaceful reunification." In response, the American government "acknowledged" (the Chinese translation of the
Shanghai Communiqué on this subject read "recognized") that "all
Chinese on either side of the Taiwan Strait maintain that there is but
one China and that Taiwan is a part of China." The use of force was
never renounced entirely but was now seen as a backup, not a first
step.

This new policy (and, by implication, the Shanghai Communiqué
itself) was based on a second enduring myth about Taiwan, which
has it that the vast majority of the people of Taiwan—as contrasted
with the tiny handful of their reactionary leaders—harbor a deep desire to be governed as a part of the People's Republic of China.
Countless opinion polls taken on Taiwan suggest that the reverse is
the case: it is only a tiny handful, not the vast majority, who favor reunification. But this has done nothing to dispel the myth.

In 1978, Deng reiterated Mao's policy of peaceful reunification
with Taiwan and the priority assigned to it: quoting Mao, he said it
didn't really matter "if it took a hundred years for Taiwan to return to
the embrace of the motherland." But evidently not all Deng's elder
colleagues agreed with this relaxed timetable. Theirs was, after all,

the generation for whom Taiwan symbolized a revolution uncompleted. By 1980, Deng had begun talking about a decade instead of a century, and he said that he wanted to live to see the day when reunification had been achieved.

In 1981, Ye Jianying, a senior military officer with impeccable revolutionary credentials, was made the spokesman for a new proposal on Taiwan. His Nine Points document is the locus classicus for the concept of "one country, two systems." (It is worth noting that this was issued a full year before Margaret Thatcher's visit to Beijing, which precipitated the process of recouping sovereignty over Hong Kong.) The Nine Points called for the establishment of a special administrative region for Taiwan, within which its present political and economic system would remain intact for fifty years. Details were to be worked out in direct negotiations—not between the government in Beijing and the government on Taiwan but between the Chinese Communist Party and the Nationalist Party. This latter provision, delegitimizing the government of the Republic of China, ignored the interests of the island's Taiwanese majority, who were then ill-represented in the Nationalist power structure. Ye Jianying's Nine Points also contained a critical caveat: were Taiwan to resist reunification, and particularly were it to declare independence, China reserved the right to use force to bring about reunification.

Chiang Kai-shek, who had led the Nationalists through their conflict with the Chinese Communists and the Japanese, had died three years before Mao and was eventually succeeded by his son, Chiang Ching-kuo, who now responded unequivocally to the Nine Points with a policy of Three Noes: Taiwan would engage in no official contact, would have no negotiations, and would make no concessions.

It was against this background that Beijing turned its attention to Hong Kong. The successful execution of the plan for recouping sovereignty over Hong Kong could serve as a model for the more critical and difficult case of Taiwan. Moreover, Taiwan had extensive business interests in Hong Kong, and a Hong Kong controlled by Beijing put the Taiwan authorities in a bind: they would either have to aban-

don their Hong Kong business interests or have to give up the Three
Noes and come to the negotiating table. Hong Kong was thus both a
model for Taiwan and a goad.

Until Taiwan president Lee Teng-hui's controversial visit to Cornell
University in the summer of 1995, the American media had totally
ignored one of the most stunning political transformations of the
postwar period: although the Nationalists remained in power on Taiwan, the political system they controlled had been, during the previous decade, transformed from a highly authoritarian one-party state
to a vibrant multiparty democracy. Chinese culture and democracy,
said to be the oil and water of political practice, were a viable mixture
after all.

The rough-and-tumble of Taiwan politics, with its vociferous and
often disrespectful opposition, has given rise to frequent fistfights in
the legislature and occasional violent street demonstrations. It is a political style that belies several common assumptions about Chinese
culture, such as its preference for harmony over chaos and its rever-
ence for the elderly, and it elicits disdain from the starched and
buttoned-down Singaporean Chinese. No doubt it also sends chills
down elderly Communist spines in Beijing.

Among the forces that led to this startling change, three stand out.
The first is the person of Chiang Ching-kuo himself. Stricken with
leukemia in the 1980s and given only a few years to live, he devoted
himself to accomplishing two goals: democratizing Taiwan's political
system and opening up contact with the mainland.

Chiang took the first step toward liberalizing his government in
1985, when he selected a Taiwanese rather than a mainlander as his
vice presidential running mate: Lee Teng-hui, an American-educated
agronomist who had made his career in Nationalist Party politics.
The second step came the following year. Opposition parties had
been outlawed on Taiwan, and opposition politicians campaigned as
individuals (collectively known as *dangwai*, meaning outside the [Na-
tionalist] Party). In 1986, when the *dangwai* politicians organized

themselves into a new opposition party, the DPP, and campaigned on a party ticket, Chiang Ching-kuo decided not to prosecute them and not to disband their party but, rather, to repeal the law that banned opposition parties. A year later he lifted the martial law that had been in effect on Taiwan since 1947. With this move, political rights—guaranteed in the constitution but suspended by martial law—were restored to the citizens of Taiwan. His fourth, and final, step was taken in October 1987, when he lifted the ban on traveling to mainland China. Initial visits were made under the guise of being merely *tanqin*—visits to relatives—but soon the regulations were very liberally interpreted, and many Taiwanese went to China to observe, to sightsee, and ultimately to begin to do business. Chiang died the following year, having accomplished his goals and having put his legacy in place.

The second force that helped to transform Taiwan's political system was the courage and persistence of the *dangwai* politicians who, against all odds, brought about this political awakening. Harassed, beaten, imprisoned, and exiled by the authoritarian Nationalist government, they had persevered in their determination to be heard. Although Chiang's decisions were critically important, it is unlikely that he would have made them or that they alone would have had the effect they eventually did were it not for the boldness of the opposition.

Finally, a third force was the mainland government's calculated guess that the impending change of sovereignty in Hong Kong would help to make Taiwan more flexible about the reunification issue. When the Joint Declaration on Hong Kong was released in 1984 and the Taiwan government's initial reaction was to say that, given its terms, the policy of no contact would apply to Hong Kong as well after 1997, Taiwan businessmen immediately responded that this was not acceptable. Contact with Hong Kong was critical to their businesses and thus to the economic health of Taiwan. The government would have to come up with a new and more flexible policy. Beijing's goad had proved successful.

Liberalizing the political system on Taiwan involved four related processes: bringing the Taiwanese majority into full political participation, legalizing a political opposition, reconstituting the government, and opening relations with the mainland.

Lee Teng-hui's election by the National Assembly as Chiang's vice president had been the culmination of a long, slow "Taiwanization" of the Nationalist Party and government. The informal division of labor between the Taiwanese majority and the mainlander minority in 1949 had largely excluded Taiwanese from politics, but over the years, Taiwanese were actively recruited for Nationalist Party membership and gradually rose to positions of leadership. Chiang's selection of Lee was taken by his mainlander senior colleagues to be no more than a symbolic gesture, but to their surprise, Lee not only succeeded to the presidency upon Chiang's death but also was appointed head of the Nationalist Party. Very shortly thereafter, he was elected by the National Assembly to his own term as president, though mainlanders brought all their forces to bear against this happening, even enlisting the support of the elderly but determined Madame Chiang Kai-shek, who returned to Taiwan from her home in New York to lobby in favor of a mainlander. Their failure marked the real completion of the process of Taiwanization. Today more than three-quarters of the Nationalist Party are Taiwanese, and they hold virtually all the leading positions in the Party and, until the election of March 2000, the government.

In office, Lee kept to the policies of his predecessor. In legislative elections in 1991, the DPP adopted a platform plank that called for Taiwanese independence: advocating independence violates Taiwan law, and some demanded that the president arrest the leaders of the DPP and strip the Party of its legal status. He refused to do so.

Reconstituting the government on Taiwan was more difficult. The legitimacy of the government's claim to sovereignty over all of China rested on the fact that the legislature and the National Assembly were initially made up of representatives of all of China's provinces, elected to office prior to the Nationalists' departure from the mainland. Almost fifty years later, though, these representatives were aged, ill, and infirm; supplementary elections held to increase the number of representatives from Taiwan were only a partial solution to the problem.

Shortly after he took office as president, Lee inaugurated discussions about reconstitution, and the government began a series of steps to alter the political system to conform to contemporary reality. A new, smaller National Assembly was elected in 1991. The following year, elderly legislators were forced to retire, and elections were held for the posts they vacated. In 1993 and 1994, local elections were held for once-appointed mayors and other officials. In December 1994, mayoral elections were held in Taiwan's two largest cities, Taipei and Kaohsiung, and a gubernatorial election was held for the province of Taiwan. The final stage of the process was the March 1996 election, in which the president was directly elected for the first time.

Through this process, the DPP gradually strengthened its position, and a number of new political parties emerged. When the DPP campaigned on a platform of Taiwanese independence, it tended to lose support but otherwise garnered about a third of the vote. As Table 12 makes clear, its support was mostly in the cities; it did not fare well in small-town and rural elections. The New Party, which formed in 1993 as a splinter of the Nationalist Party, has campaigned on an anticorruption and pro-reunification platform. In the December 1994 elections, Nationalist candidates were elected to office as governor of Taiwan and mayor of the large southern city of Kaohsiung. The DPP candidate, Chen Shui-bian, won the election for the mayor of Taipei, in which position he sat ex officio in the cabinet of the national government—the first opposition politician to do so.

In 1991, though the Three Noes policy was technically still in force, President Lee put forward a proposal for a three-stage process of reunification with the mainland. The first stage had already begun, with the informal contacts initiated by Chiang Ching-kuo in 1987. According to Lee's plan, this stage would feature a policy he called "flexible diplomacy" to break the international isolation imposed on Taiwan by China's insistence that any government recognizing Beijing sever its ties with Taiwan.

Table 12

RESULTS OF RECENT ELECTIONS ON TAIWAN

(IN PERCENTAGES OF VOTES CAST)

Date	Election	Nationalist Party	Democratic Progressive Party	New Party	Others
12/89	Legislative Yuan	59	30		11
12/91	National Assembly	71	24		5
12/92	Legislative Yuan	53	31		16
11/93	Medium-sized cities	48	41	3	8
2/94	Small cities	69	7	5	19
12/94	Large cities	52	39	8	1
12/95	Legislative Yuan	46	33	13	8
3/96	President	54	21	15	10
11/97	County and small cities	42	43	1	14
1/98	County and city councils	49	16	NA	NA
1/98	Townships	55	19	NA	NA
12/98	Legislative Yuan	46	30	7	17
12/98	Large cities	51	46	NA	3
3/00	President	24	39	NA	37

(Sources: Asian Wall Street Journal and Far Eastern Economic Review)

Stage two in Lee's reunification plan would move the two sides from informal to formal state-to-state communications. This stage would require that China continue its economic reforms, renounce the use of force as a means of effecting reunification, and accept the government on Taiwan on an equal standing and as entitled to recognition in the world community. In the third, and final, stage, the two sides would engage in "long-term consultation and unification."

Informal contacts between the two sides have resulted in substantial economic ties between Taiwan and China. Every year, more than a million Taiwan citizens visit China; Taiwan investors have put more than $25 billion into some thirty thousand enterprises (most of them in Guangdong and Fujian Provinces); and whole industries on Taiwan—such as shoe manufacturing—have moved their plants to China in search of inexpensive real estate and labor. Though direct trade with and investment in China are prohibited under Taiwan law—goods and capital must pass through a third party, in most instances in Hong Kong, as we have seen—this two-way trade exceeded $24 billion in 1999.

In 1993, Prime Minister Lien Chan of Taiwan proposed moving to the second stage of Lee Teng-hui's reunification process, though the preconditions laid down earlier had not been met. Still, some form of legal protection was needed for Taiwan's substantial mainland investments. A first step in this direction occurred at a meeting in Singapore in April 1993 between the heads of unofficial organizations set up by the two governments. Taiwan's Strait Exchange Foundation (SEF) and China's Association for Relations Across the Taiwan Strait (ARATS) followed up this initial Singapore meeting with subsequent meetings in Beijing and Taipei.

The talks were interrupted twice: once by Taiwan, after a group of Taiwan tourists were robbed and murdered on a pleasure boat in Qiandao Lake in Zhejiang Province and the Taiwanese complained that the Chinese had engaged in a clumsy attempt to cover up the crime; and then once by Beijing, in protest against Lee Teng-hui's June 1995 visit to the United States. The two sides differ on what should be included on the agenda, in any case. The SEF has authority to discuss only economic and social matters; ARATS's mandate calls for it to introduce political issues. To date, the two sides have negotiated an agreement on the return of hijacked aircraft, procedures for dealing with illegal immigrants, and a settlement of fishing rights in the Taiwan Strait.

Meanwhile, Lee Teng-hui actively pursued his policy of flexible diplomacy to secure some form of recognition for the government on Taiwan beyond the two dozen nations with whom it now has diplomatic relations. Adopting a plank from the opposition party's platform, his government also sought to return to membership in the United Nations—a position it lost in 1971, when the China seat was taken from it and given to the mainland government. Flexible diplomacy made for a busy travel schedule, as Lee paid formal visits to the nations that still recognized his government and informal visits to others and worked closely with a group of UN member states that, each year since 1993, have proposed that the issue of Taiwan's representation be added to the agenda of the General Assembly. In conducting this campaign, Lee formally abandoned his predecessors' fiction that the government on Taiwan speaks for the whole of China. Countering the "one country, two systems" formula, Lee used the phrase "one country, two governments," suggesting analogies with Germany and Korea.

Lee and the Nationalist Party for whom he spoke continued to reject independence and to support reunification, but his articulation of this position was not unequivocal. He described his position as "conditional rejection" of the opposition's pro-independence stance, but mainland authorities were skeptical of the firmness of his pro-reunification stance.

Because they have benefited so much from economic ties with Taiwan, the mainland authorities have enthusiastically supported them. And there is a group of influential individuals on Taiwan who have a vested interest in maintaining good cross-strait ties. It is even possible that the Taiwan economy could become dependent on them for its continued health and growth. Indeed, shortly after his election in 1996, President Lee called for voluntary limits on Taiwan's investments on the mainland. He suggested that no more than 30 percent of Taiwan's total overseas investment be placed in China and that investments in China amount to no more than a fifth of any Taiwan firm's domestic investments. The Chinese denounced Lee's limits as creating obstacles to the free operation of market forces.

The authorities in Beijing pushed to make the cross-strait talks between the SEF and ARATS more substantive with respect to political issues, but Beijing was unequivocal in its denunciation of the opposition DPP and its advocacy of Taiwan independence—particularly as DPP candidates began to capture major posts in the government and more seats in the legislature. A far greater threat from Beijing's perspective, however, was that the Nationalist Party, now firmly under the control of the Taiwanese majority, might pursue a policy of de facto independence. This threat elicited from the Chinese a strident response, which included conducting military exercises and weapons tests off the Taiwan coast. But Beijing's policy to intimidate Taiwanese voters backfired badly, only underscoring its naïveté in dealings with those whom it considers compatriots.

Beijing finds the policy of flexible diplomacy especially aggravating. That foreign governments should accord Taiwan or its representatives respect as anything other than a province of China is absolutely unacceptable. (The applications of Taiwan and China to join the World Trade Organization are especially contentious. Applying under the name "The Customs Territory of Taiwan, Penghu, Quemoy, and Matsu," Taiwan has pressed to be first, and of course Beijing insists on being approved first so that it can have a voice in deciding the terms under which Taiwan is admitted.) That foreign governments should sell arms to Taiwan, strengthening its ability to resist China's use of force to accomplish reunification, is equally unacceptable.

Successive American administrations since 1972 have taken the position that relations between Taiwan and the mainland can only be settled by the two sides themselves, a hands-off policy that a substantial group in the U.S. Congress has from the outset found unacceptable. With the congressional elections in 1994, Taiwan's supporters were able to muster a majority—in some cases, near unanimity—on questions affecting Taiwan, but Beijing was unsympathetic to the Clinton administration's protestations that its freedom to maneuver was severely limited by Congress.

Cross-strait relations reached a low point during the period between President Lee's visit to the United States in the summer of 1995 and his election to the presidency in March 1996. China's leaders appeared to believe that despite his statements to the contrary,

Lee was a closet advocate of independence for Taiwan, and they found the contrast between the rapid expansion of democracy on Taiwan and their own hardening resistance to political liberalization highly distasteful and potentially embarrassing. As a result, Beijing actively worked to bring about Lee's defeat in the presidential election or at least to cut the size of his majority. The official press carried blistering denunciations of him.

More alarming, the People's Liberation Army dropped hints to an American visitor to Beijing in December 1995 that, should Lee be elected, it would conduct daily missile strikes on the island for thirty days. Fueling the rumors, the PLA moved more than 150,000 troops into Fujian Province, opposite Taiwan, in late February 1996 and began a series of missile test firings into the Taiwan Strait in early March. A week later a series of war games was announced involving the use of live ammunition in a large sector of the strait northwest of the island. The sites of these exercises were chosen to cause disruption in the sea-lanes used for shipping in and out of Taiwan's major ports and to demonstrate China's capability to interrupt the island's maritime commerce. What was particularly disturbing about these measures was that the People's Liberation Army seemed to be calling the shots with very little interference from the civilian authorities.

Generally speaking, the reaction among the Taiwan population was the opposite of that anticipated by Beijing. Although Taiwan's stock market fluctuated even more wildly than usual and there were some who laid in a large supply of rice and other staples, support remained strong for Lee and even for those advocating a more extreme anti-Chinese position than he did. The U.S. government, though it did not take seriously the threat of actual attack on Taiwan, denounced the military exercises as "unnecessarily provocative and reckless," moved a carrier group into the vicinity of the island, and agreed to the sale to Taiwan of Stinger air defense missiles, advanced targeting and navigating systems for jet aircraft, and three hundred additional M60-A3 tanks.

In the event, more than three-quarters of those eligible participated in the first direct election for the chief executive, giving Lee and Lien Chan, his vice presidential running mate, 54 percent of the vote. In fact, it was the first such election in any Chinese society and was regarded by many as a major milestone in the emergence of Chinese democracy. Lee campaigned on a de facto platform of independence from the mainland. Combining his share of the vote with the 21 percent garnered by Peng Ming-min, the opposition DPP candidate who campaigned on a platform of de jure independence, one could argue that three-quarters of the voters on Taiwan expressed their opposition to reunification with the mainland—a figure borne out by subsequent public opinion polls on the subject.

Beijing's interpretation of the election results was very different. Ignoring Lee's covert support of independence and pointing to the decline in support for the DPP between the legislative elections in December 1995 (in which it received 41 percent of the vote) and the presidential elections, the Chinese press said that the election results offered irrefutable proof that the people of Taiwan had rejected independence. It advocated an early meeting between Lee Teng-hui and the Chinese president, Jiang Zemin, and the opening of direct air, shipping, and mail links across the Taiwan Strait. At his inauguration in May, President Lee, too, proposed an early meeting with President Jiang.

Among the first tasks Lee took up following the election was the reconstitution of the government. The National Development Conference held late in 1996 recommended reforms that would strengthen executive power at the expense of the legislature. Under the proposed system, the Legislative Yuan and the National Assembly would be combined into a new body of between 200 and 250 representatives. The legislature would no longer have the power to appoint the prime minister, but it could conduct a vote of no confidence in the prime minister or the president. The president, in turn, would have the power to dissolve the legislature and hold new elections. The conference also called for eliminating the provincial government on Taiwan, calling it redundant.

This latter recommendation triggered the opposition of the New Party. It also caught the attention of the authorities in Beijing. Finally, it was opposed by James Soong, the popular Nationalist Party governor of Taiwan who had recently been elected by a substantial majority. All of them argued that eliminating the provincial government appeared to be a step toward abandoning the idea that Taiwan is a province of China and treating it instead as an independent state. The New Party representatives walked out of the conference, the Chinese government issued a strong objection to the recommendations, and James Soong found himself at odds with President Lee.

The situation was complicated by the fact that the conference recommendations required the approval of the National Assembly, which was, in effect, being asked to vote itself out of office. This became especially problematic when the Assembly—in which the Nationalists held only the most tenuous of majorities—held the reforms hostage while it expressed its disapproval of a range of other government initiatives. The reform package was eventually passed by the Assembly in the summer of 1997.

Of particular concern beginning in the spring of 1997 was the public sense that crime was careening out of control and the government wasn't dealing with it. In May, the legislature, citing an 18 percent rise in the crime rate and three high-profile murder cases that remained unsolved, attempted a no-confidence vote. Meanwhile, in the streets of Taipei, fifty thousand marched in protest against the government's apparent impotence in dealing with the surge in crime. A fortnight later, New Party delegates interrupted Lee Teng-hui when he tried to address the National Assembly, demanding that he publicly apologize for the rapid decline in public order. Simultaneously, Ma Ying-jeou, the highly respected, Harvard-educated former justice minister in the national government, resigned from the Cabinet, calling for the vice president to resign from his concurrent appointment as prime minister. Lien did resign during the summer and was replaced by Vincent Siew, but few seemed satisfied that the government had effectively dealt with the breakdown of public order.

In November 1997 and again in January 1998, popular dissatisfaction with the ruling party was manifested in local elections, in which the

Nationalist Party continued to take a declining share of the vote. The stakes were much higher, however, in elections held in December 1998 for the Legislative Yuan and mayors' offices in the island's large cities. DPP candidate Chen Shui-bian, in one of his party's most important election victories, had won the Taipei slot four years earlier, as we have seen. The Nationalists found in Ma Ying-jeou a highly personable and ethical candidate who campaigned not only on issues of national policy but also on opposition to Chen's term as mayor—a term marked, Ma argued, by inefficiency and corruption.

Finding himself seriously threatened by Ma, Chen played the mainlander card during his campaign. Chen identifies himself as Taiwanese; although born in Hong Kong, Ma's family are counted among the mainlanders. With the support of President Lee, Ma claimed identity as a "New Taiwanese," observing during his campaign that after all, "I eat Taiwanese food. I drink Taiwanese water." Lee endorsed him as "the boy next door." In the end, Ma narrowly defeated Chen with 51 percent of the votes cast in an election that attracted close to 80 percent of eligible voters.

In the national legislative elections, the Nationalists took 124, or 55 percent, of the 225 contested seats, up from 52 percent in the 1995 elections. The DPP's share of votes declined to 30 percent from 33 percent in 1995; and although it gained 16 seats to hold 70 of the total 225 seats, its percentage of seats declined from 33 percent to 31 percent, because the size of the legislature had been increased. The vote was appropriately interpreted as a major victory for the Nationalists, reversing its decline; nonetheless it freed the popular Chen Shui-bian to run as a candidate for president in the national elections scheduled for 2000.

In the fall of 1998, Koo Chen-fu, chairman of the SEF, and Wang Daohan, chairman of ARATS, met in Shanghai; Koo subsequently met with Jiang Zemin in Beijing. The two sides agreed that Wang would go to Taiwan "at an appropriate time" and that cross-strait talks would resume on political and economic issues. This progress made it all the more startling when, the following year—near the end of his four-year term—Lee used the occasion of an interview recorded in early July for broadcast in Germany to assert that any further discourse across the Taiwan Strait must be conducted on a "state-to-state" basis.

This statement sharply clarified and radically altered the very ambiguous fictions that, as we have seen, had characterized the dialogue. Lee's confrontational move was initially interpreted as being motivated by an interest in bolstering the Nationalist Party's chances in the upcoming presidential election by shifting its position closer to that of the DPP. But Lee's move may have had less to do with domestic politics and more to do with the triangular relationship among Taipei, Beijing, and Washington. American policy was laid out, as we have seen, in the Shanghai Communiqué of 1972, but after the serious glitch following Lee's visit to Cornell in 1995, the 1972 policy was subtly but importantly modified. In a 1995 letter to Jiang Zemin and then in public remarks during his visit to China in 1998, President Bill Clinton claimed to "clarify our Taiwan policy, which is that we don't support independence for Taiwan, or two Chinas, or one Taiwan/one China." What was "acknowledged" in 1972 as the Chinese and Taiwanese position had, twenty-six years later, become the American position.

This Three Noes policy, as authorities on Taiwan referred to it, was followed in the spring of 1999 by Assistant Secretary of State Stanley Roth's calling for "interim agreements . . . on any number of topics" between China and Taiwan. This was interpreted in Taipei as pressure to negotiate with Beijing. The Taiwan authorities also found it disturbingly reminiscent of a proposal made in Taipei by Kenneth Lieberthal, director of East Asia policy at the National Security Council, prior to his joining the government in 1998: Lieberthal had called for an "interim arrangement" in which the governments in Taipei and Beijing would agree to the concept of "one China" but would delay actual reunification for fifty years. Taiwan authorities thought this was tantamount to an endorsement of Beijing's "one country, two systems" solution. And indeed, in June, Roth reiterated his call for "technical agreements" on "significant issues." When two weeks later Lee put forward his "state-to-state" proviso to any further cross-strait talks, he might well have been responding to what he perceived as American pressure to accept China's terms for reunification.

Whatever Taiwan's motivation, the response from China was immediate and angry. It looked and sounded as if there would be a repeat of the saber-rattling that preceded Taiwan's first presidential election in 1996. Clinton, in a half-hour telephone conversation with Jiang Zemin, dissociated himself and his government from support of Lee's formulation and reiterated American backing for "one China." Perhaps influenced by this gesture from Washington and perhaps reflecting on the fact that its earlier bellicose response had only succeeded in increasing the margin by which Lee won the 1996 election, China confined itself to a barrage of angry prose.

Meanwhile, Taiwan's friends in the U.S. Congress used the summer's events as an opportunity to fish in troubled waters. They renewed the call for a theater missile defense system in East Asia that would protect Taiwan, along with Japan and South Korea, from attack. They simultaneously put forward the "Taiwan Security Enhancement Act," which would create a relationship between American and Taiwanese military establishments tantamount to a military alliance while upgrading and expanding U.S. arms sales to Taiwan. The bill was tabled at the beginning of November under pressure from the Clinton administration, which argued that the provocative proposal would derail sensitive negotiations over China's entry into the World Trade Organization.

It was against this international backdrop that Taiwan undertook its second presidential election in March 2000. The Nationalist Party's candidate was President Lee's vice president and chosen successor, Lien Chan; Lien's rival for the candidacy would have been James Soong, the popular governor of the Taiwan provincial government until it was dissolved in 1997. Shortly after Lien's nomination and Lee's broadcast, Soong left the Nationalist Party and declared himself an independent candidate. The DPP named Chen Shuibian. The campaign among the three was hard fought and the outcome considered too close to predict. Lien proved lackluster, Soong was accused of pocketing Nationalist Party funds, and Chen took pains to dissociate himself from the DPP's independence plank. In the end, Chen won with 39 percent of the vote to Soong's 37 percent, Lien trailing behind with an embarrassing 23 percent. Angry Nationalist Party members blamed Lee for the defeat, citing his having driven Soong from the Party; under attack, Lee resigned his position as Party chair. In May, marking a second milestone for Chinese democracy, a peaceful transition from the long-ruling Nationalist Party to the opposition DPP took place when Chen was sworn in as Taiwan's second popularly elected president.

Chen inherited an economy that had ridden out the financial crisis of the late 1990s with relatively little damage. Taiwan had also survived the aftermath of a devastating earthquake (7.6 on the Richter scale) that struck in September 1999, killing twenty-one hundred, injuring eight thousand, and leaving more than a hundred thousand homeless, an earthquake estimated to have cost some $11 billion. Despite these setbacks, overall economic growth for 1999 was projected at a healthy 5.3 percent, significantly ahead of that of Hong Kong and Singapore.

Beijing remained remarkably calm through these startling events. Although Jiang Zemin, Zhu Rongji, and former foreign minister Qian Qichen vigorously reiterated China's intention to respond to any declaration of Taiwan independence with full-scale war, they adopted a "wait and see" attitude toward Chen's presidency, weighing their options for influencing a now much more unpredictable Taiwan.

The Chinese armed forces have shown that they can pressure the civilian leadership to take a strong stand with respect to Taiwan. Short of military invasion, which the PLA is ill-equipped to carry out, there are several steps the Chinese government might choose to take if negotiations were to break down. Intimidation, such as the military exercises and tests conducted during 1995 and 1996, is one. Another might well be a reversion to the economic policy of the early 1970s, when firms doing business on Taiwan were not permitted to do business in China. A third step—well within the current capability of the PLA—might be to carry out a blockade of Quemoy and Matsu Islands, very close to the mainland coast. The two islands are guarded by a garrison of some hundred thousand troops: substantial pressure could be brought to bear on the Taiwan government were these troops held hostage by mainland forces.

A fourth step—a considerable escalation—would be to blockade Taiwan itself. This would immediately and adversely affect the Taiwan economy, but it would also invite international intervention in order to keep international shipping lanes open.

A final step to wring compliance from an intransigent Taiwan would be a direct missile or amphibious attack on the island, but launching such an attack would be a high-risk maneuver. The PLA navy is ill-equipped and untrained to launch an amphibious attack, Taiwan is well defended (its military budget is somewhat in excess of $10 billion per year, or about 3 percent of GNP, a fifth of the estimated actual budget for the PLA in dollar terms and about the same proportion of GNP), and although somewhat outdated compared with the most advanced American, European, and Russian capabilities, the Taiwan air force is better equipped and better trained than the PLA air force. Though it is not clear that Taiwan would win an armed conflict with China, it would at least make it a protracted and costly war, which would seriously damage the island's economy, the strength of which is one of the most important motivations for reunification, and the economy of the coastal provinces in which it has invested most heavily.

Armed conflict between Taiwan and the mainland could also trigger international intervention, notably from two of China's major trade and investment partners that have strong economic ties to Taiwan—Japan and the United States. Many Americans would favor military action on Taiwan's behalf. Whether either Japan or the United States would go to war with China to defend Taiwan is highly questionable, but at the very least each country would feel compelled to adopt economic and military sanctions that would be certain to slow China's economic development.

Any of these steps is likely to have an undesirable effect on the Taiwan population. Threatened with blockade or outright attack, the people on Taiwan are likely to rally in support of their independence from the mainland. Even if beaten into submission, they would probably be at least as difficult to control from Beijing as were their Ming-loyalist ancestors three centuries ago.

One reason that the Taiwan issue touches such a raw nerve in Beijing is that Taiwan's democratization is a counter-model for the political repression that China's authoritarian leaders are trying to keep in place. The two governments once closely resembled each other, but now Taiwan has set aside its authoritarian practices in favor of a no-holds-barred democracy, while at the same time enjoying continued economic prosperity, and this is a thorn in Beijing's side.

The Taiwan model of political liberalization starts with an autocratic party holding a monopoly over the political system and enforcing its control by a heavy reliance on armed force. The transformation of that system occurred because of the coincidence of two key factors: the emergence of courageous individuals who, risking arrest and persecution, actively campaigned against the autocratic party; and the forward-looking decision by the autocrat Chiang Ching-kuo to permit a political evolution. But there are key differences between Taiwan and mainland China that make the new Taiwan a questionable model. First and most obvious is that of scale. The people of Taiwan, for all their diversity, are a highly integrated island population of 22 million. China's people, for all their much-vaunted ethnic unity, are a highly diverse population of 1.3 billion scattered over a very large territory. A second important difference is in the levels of economic development. Taiwan's per capita GNP was about ten times that of mainland China when its political transformation began. If it is true that economic development produces a demand for political liberalization, then we should not expect that demand to be made in China—particularly in its poorer areas—for some time to come.

A third difference is that in mainland China there is no single mobilizing issue. Gaining a political voice for the Taiwanese majority was an issue that united up to 85 percent of Taiwan's population, but, despite all the complaints that citizens of the People's Republic have about their government, no single complaint has the potential to mobilize a comparable opposition.

External pressure affected the political evolution of Taiwan, but it is not clear that it could do so in China. When the liberalization process was inaugurated, Taiwan was at its most isolated internationally, and democratization was a course of action that was certain to elicit international support, though that support has been a long time in coming. But since 1989, the Chinese government has dug in its heels and become more repressive and more defiant, apparently presuming that an economically burgeoning China cannot be ignored and will not long be isolated in the world economy.

Finally, there is a substantial difference between the senior leaders on the two sides of the Taiwan Strait. Knowing death was near, Chiang Ching-kuo had the political courage and vision to open and revivify his government. Knowing death was near, Deng Xiaoping demonstrated the limits to his political courage and vision by moving in the opposite direction.

XVII
CHINA'S FOREIGN RELATIONS

THERE WERE THOSE who said that the collapse of the Soviet Union in 1991 marked the beginning of a new world order. There is no question that the sudden demise of the second superpower rearranged the familiar landmarks of international politics in the last half of the twentieth century, but if there is a new order in the rearrangement, it has yet to become manifest. In the old order, China was equidistant from the two superpowers and, because of this position as a balancing force, could influence world politics out of all proportion to its national strength. Today, although China's national strength is growing, its strategic importance has declined. Like the United States, China has not yet defined the strategic role it hopes to play in a future world order or set the foreign policy goals that flow from that intended role.

Foreign policy questions, like domestic ones, are subject to the power grid of the Chinese political system, though this has not always been the case. The formulation of foreign policy used to be confined to a small number of people at the apex of the Party-state, and its implementation was the exclusive purview of the Foreign Ministry. But several changes during the 1980s opened the field to other players.

The first was the increasing dominance of economic issues. When China was largely cut off from the world economy, ideological and

strategic issues dominated foreign policy. With the economic reforms, these have receded to the background, and a vastly expanded
trade and investment, creating new links to the outside world, have
become central.

A second, more recent change is the emergence of the People's
Liberation Army (PLA) as a principal player. During the 1990s, as we
have seen, the PLA developed extensive international connections of
its own, many of them economic rather than military or strategic. As
a consequence, the PLA has interests that are often at variance with
the interests of China's Party-state.

Finally, as the balance of power between the central government
and the regions has shifted in the direction of the latter, they, too,
have begun to affect foreign policy. But they do not speak with a single voice.

Still, the most important player remains the Party-state, and within
it divergent views are held with respect to China's foreign policy
goals. A small number of conservatives have a kind of "fortress
China" mentality. They believe that Deng Xiaoping's open policy
has resulted in dangerous dependencies and noxious influences. In
their view, the country would be far better off if it returned to economic autarky and strategic disengagement. But the opposite point of
view is also represented within the Party-state by those who argue that
there should be no limit to China's interaction with the world economy, that new sources of investment capital and technology should
be sought, that new markets for Chinese goods should be actively
cultivated, and that market forces should be allowed to determine
foreign economic links and drive the domestic economy. Although
they might not want to say so, it is an American model of international economic policy that they have in mind for China.

A third group within the Party-state takes a cautious middle position. They share the conservative minority's concern about China's
becoming too dependent on foreign interests. But they are favorably
impressed with the results of Japan's government-managed industrial
policy and its carefully calculated penetration of foreign economics

in search of markets, raw materials, and labor. They consider this mercantilist approach to economic development to have greater potential for China than one based exclusively on free trade.

As for the armed forces, which during 1995 and 1996 began to look as though they might be the dominant voice, they speak from several different perspectives. From the perspective of its strategic concerns, the PLA aims to have enough military strength to assert China's sovereignty, to secure and defend its national borders, and to guarantee access for China to offshore energy sources and shipping lanes. From the perspective of its varied and substantial economic interests, it wants to maintain open access to foreign capital and markets. From the perspective of its institutional self-interest, it is inclined to support a foreign policy that justifies military expansion— whether in the South China Sea, in Burma, or in dealing with Taiwan—and helps it to get more and better equipment and a larger budget. Also in its self-interest, however, is access to the expertise and technology of the most advanced military establishments, particularly that of the United States, and seeking to ensure that access may dampen the PLA's expansionist tendencies.

The horizontal components in China's power grid have their own foreign policy interests, too. The southern China coast, for example, with its heavy concentration of Taiwan-invested enterprises, has its own point of view on relations with Taiwan. Similarly, Guangdong and its special economic zones, closely linked as they are to the Hong Kong economy, can be expected to advocate policies that foster the preservation of Hong Kong's economic viability. In like fashion, the southeastern macroregion has close links with Burma and the former Indochinese states, Shandong Province is closely tied to Korea, the northeastern provinces to Russia and Japan. Each regional player is likely to act as an advocate for policies that foster its external ties. Although every effort is made to ensure that the PLA speaks with a single voice and is immune to power-grid politics, regional military commanders persist in cultivating local ties against these heavy odds. The connections they make with foreign powers serve both economic and military interests. In some cases, they appear to have been cultivated without the blessing of the central command.

Taking one or two steps back from the interests of specific nodes in the power grid, it is possible to discern some broad and generally accepted priorities in Chinese foreign policy in the post–Cold War world. The first priority is clearly that of pursuing policies that promote China's economic development.

China was a late arrival in the modern global economy but in a very short period has become a highly important contestant, deeply involved in the game. On a price-parity basis, China's is the world's third largest economy after those of the United States and Japan. Were it to maintain its current rate of growth, it would surpass both Japan and the United States by 2050. Its foreign trade is growing at 12 percent per year—nearly twice the growth rate of the economy itself. Total two-way trade in 1998 was $323 billion, which amounts to 30 percent of gross domestic product (50 percent higher than the ra tio of the United States' trade to its GDP). Foreign direct investment totaled $45 billion in 1998 (but this calculation includes investment from Hong Kong). A cumulative total of foreign investment in China's economy is approximately $250 billion, coming from Hong Kong (about two-thirds of the total), Japan (somewhat less than one-fifth), Taiwan (somewhat more than one-tenth), and the United States (just behind Taiwan).

It is to help consolidate China's position in the global economy that Jiang Zemin and Zhu Rongji pushed so diligently for China's entry into the World Trade Organization (WTO), despite substantial opposition from many in China who (accurately) see their economic interests as compromised, at least in the short term, by limits WTO membership will impose.

Certain constraints could prevent the Chinese economy from realizing its potential, as we have seen, notably the parlous state of the banking system; the drain on the national budget created by the state-owned enterprises' mounting losses; the shortage of arable land,

Table 13

CHINA'S ECONOMIC INTERACTION WITH SELECTED NATIONS, 1998
(IN BILLIONS OF U.S. DOLLARS)

	Total two-way trade	China's exports	China's imports	Incoming direct investment
Japan	57.89	29.69	28.20	3.40
United States	54.93	37.97	16.96	3.89
Hong Kong	45.41	38.75	6.66	18.50
South Korea	21.26	6.26	15.00	1.80
Taiwan	20.49	3.86	16.63	2.91
Germany	14.34	7.35	6.99	0.74
Singapore	8.15	3.93	4.22	3.40
Britain	6.58	4.63	1.95	1.17
France	6.02	2.82	3.20	0.71
Russia	5.48	1.84	3.64	0.02
Malaysia	4.26	1.59	2.67	0.34
Indonesia	3.63	1.17	2.46	0.07
Philippines	1.24	1.02	0.22	0.18
Vietnam	1.05	0.72	0.33	0.01
Burma	0.58	0.51	0.07	0.00
North Korea	0.41	0.35	0.06	0.00
Total all countries (including those not listed)	323.92	183.75	140.16	45.46

(Source: *China Statistical Yearbook 1999*)

and the limits that places on China's ability to feed its population without resorting to massive grain imports; its inability to slow its population growth; the growing income inequality compounded by rampant and apparently uncontrollable corruption; and the possibility of regional fragmentation. Still, it is likely that China's foreign trade will continue to grow, albeit at a slower pace. China's trading partners are very likely to develop protectionist measures to defend their own domestic industries against competition from less expensive Chinese products. Moreover, as production costs rise at home, Chinese products will begin to lose their early competitive lead. China is likely to continue to look to foreign capital markets as a source of investment capital, particularly as a means to fund major public-works projects and to resolve the crisis in the state-owned sector of the economy.

China's economy is remarkably open in comparison with those of other Asian nations and is likely to continue to be so. Closed economies tend to restrict imports, but the Chinese import substantial quantities of goods (to the point of running up trade deficits in ten of the last twenty years), have placed few restrictions on foreign investors, and have tried to put in place regulations and incentives to encourage foreign participation in Chinese economic development. A measure of their success is the fact that exports of goods produced in foreign-invested enterprises made up two-fifths of China's total exports in 1998. Exports from foreign-invested firms are growing five times as fast as exports from domestically owned firms.

The offshore components of Greater China—Taiwan, Hong Kong, Singapore, and the overseas Chinese communities in North America and Europe—are likely to continue to be the most reliable and lucrative sources of investment capital, and this constrains Chinese policy on delicate issues of sovereignty. The Chinese authorities probably find rattling sabers in the Taiwan Strait and venting spleen against Hong Kong democrats highly gratifying in the short term, but soberer heads in Beijing are well aware that the continuing viability of the economies of Taiwan and Hong Kong is indispensable to the continuing economic growth of mainland China.

The Japanese were among the first to trade with the newly opened and reforming China, but they have been slow to invest there, though Japan is now third after Hong Kong and the United States as a source of external capital. China's economic policy with respect to Japan is to encourage additional investment while trying to balance its trade.

China's trade with South Korea has grown rapidly and now vastly outweighs its economic connections with North Korea, though because it shares a border as well as, nominally speaking, a political ideology with North Korea, China is not interested in alienating that government. Moreover, its ability to communicate with Pyongyang is a unique asset that can be used with other nations, the United States among them, as a bargaining chip. On the other hand, there are limits to China's willingness to oblige North Korea, and Beijing has made it clear that it will not take up the slack in foreign assistance that resulted from the collapse of the Soviet Union. Knowing that re-unification of North and South Korea would divert South Korea's trade and investment potential, China has not strongly advocated a settlement but instead has encouraged South Koreans to invest in China, particularly in neighboring Shandong Province, and has actively promoted Sino-Korean trade.

China's foreign economic policy often puts a damper on the natural instincts of Chinese leaders with respect to the United States. Concerns about sovereignty and face, taken alone, would surely lead them to cut themselves off from annoying American criticism, but they cannot be taken alone, and economic interests dictate caution. It would be possible but difficult for China to find better or other markets for its goods, other sources of capital and technology, and thus it is prepared to grant concessions in order to keep Sino-American links open and functioning. Some Chinese decision makers believe that, from an economic perspective, the United States needs Chinese markets, labor power, and investment opportunities more than China needs the United States. This group is more likely to bring issues of sovereignty and face to the fore and is willing to grant concessions only grudgingly and at the eleventh hour.

In Europe, China finds trading partners and potential investors who are much more relaxed about difficult questions of human rights than Americans are. And while in some fields, high technology can be found only in the United States, European substitutes for American goods are usually acceptable and often much easier to acquire.

A second goal of Chinese foreign economic policy is to develop new markets for Chinese goods in order to balance with exports the demand for costly high-tech imports. In years past, it was the Third World to which China turned: China's championing of the cause of less developed countries in Africa, Asia, and Latin America was motivated in part by its interest in finding buyers for the low-end manufactured goods it turned out in such great quantity. More recently, Russia has become an avid customer; some of this export business moves through ordinary trade channels, some of it is cross-border trade involving barter arrangements, and Chinese goods also make their way to Russian consumers via duffel bags carried on the Trans-Siberian Railroad by Russian and Chinese merchants in search of a fast profit. But Russia is likely to be only a temporary market for Chinese consumer goods, since soon the latter will be replaced by goods produced in Russian factories.

Chinese factories are now turning out more and more high-quality, sophisticated products, for which new markets must be sought, most likely in developed countries. Expanding this market will help to bring China's trade with Japan into balance but only exacerbate the already serious problem of a trade surplus with the United States. It is also likely to elicit protectionist reactions from manufacturers within the developed world.

A third goal of China's foreign economic policy, to curb its competition, is of longer-term significance. As China's economy develops, what are now complementary and symbiotic relationships are likely to become fraught. The relationship with Taiwan is an excellent example: China's need for investment capital and Taiwan's need for cheap labor and real estate for its manufacturing sector make for mutually beneficial relations. But as costs rise on the mainland, it will no longer serve Taiwan's needs to locate manufacturing operations there, and as China's products become more sophisticated, they will compete in foreign markets with goods produced on Taiwan.

China's most immediate source of competition is the newly opened economy of Vietnam. Although on a much smaller scale, Vietnam has been just as aggressive (though less successful) in pursuing foreign investors as China, and its production costs are, for the moment, considerably lower than in China's coastal provinces.

During the Cold War, the strategic triangle in East Asia was made up of the United States, the Soviet Union, and China. In economic and military terms, China was not in the same league with the other two (only much later did we learn that the Soviet Union wasn't either), but it served the interests of the two superpowers to use China as a makeweight against each other. Today, Japan has taken the place of the Soviet Union in the East Asian strategic triangle, and the gaps between the world's three largest economies are narrowing rapidly, though in strategic terms, the relationships are far from parity. Despite computer simulations that show China besting the United States in military conflicts under certain circumstances, the Chinese armed forces are far outmatched in equipment, training, and logistics by the Americans. Japan, prevented by its constitution from creating an offensive military capability, nonetheless now spends just over 1 percent of its GNP on its military establishment under the rubric of "self-defense forces." And the Chinese have long voiced concern about the revival of Japanese militarism. Having borne the brunt of that militarism through much of the first half of the twentieth century, they are not persuaded that it was ended once and for all with Japan's defeat in 1945. Until very recently, the Chinese argument seemed counterintuitive: the Japanese were prevented from rearming by their constitution; so long as the United States was prepared to serve as a shield for Japan, it would be economically foolish for the Japanese government to take over that responsibility; and Japanese public opinion has consistently opposed rearmament in any form.

But recently reasons to question all these safeguards have lent more credence to the Chinese view. There is talk in Japanese political circles of the need to reconsider the constitution. Some argue that it is time for Japan once again to become a "normal nation," by which is meant a nation with a full-scale defense establishment. The American shield was designed to protect Japan from Soviet aggression, but today a threat to Japan's national security is unlikely to come from Russia, and Japanese (and American) planners question whether American forces would leap reliably to Japan's defense in any other case. Moreover, the United States has for some years pressured the Japanese to bear a greater share of the cost of their defense, and recent public opinion polls show that a majority of Japanese citizens agree that it is time for their country to have a full-scale military force.

Toward this end, the United States and Japan completed a joint review of the U.S.-Japan Defense Cooperation Guidelines in 1998, clarifying the noncombat support roles Japan would carry out in the event of the outbreak of hostilities in its region. Of significant concern to the Chinese are discussions between Tokyo and Washington on the subject of a proposed "theater missile defense" system to defend the United States, Japan, Taiwan, and South Korea. The Japanese government has earmarked $8 million for theater missile defense research and development.

Deployment of such a system requires modification of the United States' antiballistic missile treaty with Russia, to which the Russian government is strongly opposed. Beijing argues that the system would seriously shift the balance of power in East Asia, but its particular concern is the latitude Taiwan would enjoy if defended by a missile shield.

Japan's potential military expansion serves as a rationale for the expansion of the People's Liberation Army. The growth of Chinese military capability, in turn, serves as an argument for those in Japan favoring its becoming a normal nation. The Sino-Japanese relationship, focused on economic issues almost exclusively since 1972, must at some point in the near term concentrate on strategic concerns as well.

If China's goal is to reduce the possibility of the reemergence of Japanese militarism, two steps are called for that the Chinese may find difficult to take. First, a continued U.S. presence in East Asia must be actively encouraged. Unfortunately, the Chinese have persuaded themselves that American policy makers are trying once again to encircle China and thwart its emergence as a world power. Given this mind-set, Chinese strategic planners find it hard to separate what they believe are the baneful effects on China of the American presence in East Asia from its beneficial effects on Japan.

Second, China should not do anything that can be construed as military expansionism, since Japan would use this as a pretext for its own military buildup. But the PLA's institutional self-interest, which is so influential in policy making, leads it to seek out external situations that will justify a larger, technologically more sophisticated military establishment.

Sovereignty and national security also figure importantly in China's relations with Russia and the other former Soviet republics. Sino-Soviet hostility reached the point of armed conflict in 1969, and the two sides did not begin the long process of reconstructing their relationship until the early 1980s. Mikhail Gorbachev's visit to China, which unexpectedly coincided with and was engulfed by the Tiananmen demonstrations in 1989, marked the culmination of that process of rapprochement. With the collapse of the Soviet Union and its Communist Party two years later, however, Russia again became an unpredictable and potentially dangerous neighbor. Once, the Soviet Union was a strong and heavily armed source of Communist heterodoxy; today, Russia is a weak and heavily armed source of democratic heterodoxy. In particular, the border area remains heavily armed. Although the two sides negotiated an agreement to demilitarize their borders, Russia has been unable to carry it out for lack of resources to cover the cost of troop relocation.

During his term of office as Russia's president, Boris Yeltsin met with Jiang Zemin on eight occasions, the last one in 1999 just prior to his resignation. Both sides appear eager to expand their trade relations. The Russians have offered technical assistance for the Three Gorges Dam project, and the Chinese have been ready buyers of excess Russian military equipment. As for the Mongol, Kazakh, and Kirghiz ethnic minorities who live in China's far west, adjacent to their ethnic cousins in Mongolia, Russia, and the central Asian republics, the Chinese are interested in avoiding at all costs collaboration among ethnic separatists arguing for national self-determination. Indeed, as we have seen, an August 1999 summit was held in Bishkek, Kyrgyzstan, during which Yeltsin and Jiang Zemin, together with representatives from Kazakhstan, Kyrgyzstan, and Tajikistan, signed agreements that resolved long-standing differences over their common borders and called for a peace zone in the area.

Meanwhile the Russians are worried about the two-million-odd Chinese entrepreneurs living and working in Siberia. Although it is likely that they only mean to make money and go back to the somewhat more hospitable clime of their homes, their presence seems to resurrect Russian fears of a "yellow horde" engulfing Mother Russia.

With Russia no longer a viable candidate for superpower status, Beijing has come to view with grave concern the lack of constraint on American power in the world arena. China raised strenuous objections to American action against Iraq in defense of the interests of the government of Kuwait, and American participation in NATO attacks against Serbian forces in Kosovo (particularly, in the latter case, after bombs from American aircraft damaged the Chinese embassy in Belgrade, killing two staff members and injuring others). In search of partners that might provide makeweights to what they call the "hegemonic" behavior of the United States, Chinese policy makers have considered the possibility of reviving a Sino-Russian alliance and of adding India as a third partner. But China remains concerned that the government in Moscow will either lose control or be taken over by Russian nationalists who would profit from reviving the conflict with China. And China's relations with India, while significantly improved in recent years, have never fully recovered from the border disputes that erupted into armed conflict in 1962.

China's actions in the South China Sea continue to be a serious concern for its neighbors in East and Southeast Asia. The Chinese claim that the Spratly Island chain, which lies in the South China Sea between Vietnam, the Philippines, and the island of Borneo, is Chinese territory, while the Philippines, Vietnam, Malaysia, Brunei, and Taiwan make rival claims to sovereignty over it. By its very liberal reading of the Law of the Sea Convention of 1982 (which it signed but has not ratified), China not only owns the islands but controls the twelve-mile contiguous zone and the two-hundred-mile "exclusive economic zone" around each island. Laws passed by the National People's Congress in 1992 refer to the area as China's "territorial sea" and claim the right to "take all necessary measures" to assert and protect its sovereignty.

It has long been assumed that the principal reason for interest in the islands is the possibility that they have substantial offshore oil deposits; control over fishing rights is also at issue, though the sea has been heavily overfished. Finally, the South China Sea is regarded by other countries as a critical international maritime passage, open access to which they would be prepared to defend.

China began to enforce its claim to the islands in 1988, when it captured six atolls from the Vietnamese in the Johnson Reef area. Since then, it has established outposts on a number of the islands, and Chinese naval vessels have had frequent encounters with those of the other claimants. Pressed by Vietnam to state its intentions, China proposed that the two sides pursue a policy of "joint exploitation first" and leave awkward questions of sovereignty to be resolved later. But these intentions were called abruptly into question in the spring of 1995, when it was discovered that China had built an outpost on one island—appropriately named Mischief Reef—located only 135 miles off the Philippines coast. The boldness of this move, in the context of a substantial increase in military spending and the acquisition of much new equipment designed to strengthen the Chinese navy, raised many questions about China's intentions in the area. The initial American reaction was to say that the question must be settled between the Chinese and Philippine governments, but then Washington said it was prepared to intervene if the international right of free passage was interrupted. The issue remains unresolved between Beijing and Manila, and in 1999 the Chinese rejected a code of conduct for the island chain drafted by the Association of Southeast Asian Nations (ASEAN), arguing that it was preparing a code of its own.

China's actions in the South China Sea are on the face expansionist. There was no Chinese presence in the area in the past and now there is. Is this a harbinger of a broader expansionist policy? Is this a policy on which there is general agreement in Beijing, or is it an initiative undertaken by the Chinese navy to strengthen its claim on scarce budget dollars?

As we have seen, China's foreign policy decisions are driven by a desire to enhance the respect that other nations show for China—to gain face—and by an equally strong desire to avoid situations in which the strength and competence of China and its political leaders are publicly called into question.

It took the government of the People's Republic three decades to obtain the recognition of other governments. Securing representation in the United Nations was a particularly important goal, and China has taken its participation in that organization very seriously. Although it resists the incursions on its sovereignty that such participation might entail and consistently favors backstairs negotiations over public sanctions as a means of resolving international disputes, it nonetheless savors the status that derives from permanent membership on the Security Council. A measure of the importance it still accords to UN membership is the vigor with which it opposes Taiwan's participation.

Securing membership in the World Trade Organization (WTO) was a high priority on the Chinese foreign policy agenda. China had expected to be offered membership in the General Agreement on Tariffs and Trade (GATT) before that organization became the WTO in January 1995, since it was one of the original contracting parties to GATT in 1948, though the Nationalist government withdrew its membership four years later. Beijing began applying for membership in 1988. The United States took the lead in making the case that China should have no special treatment, and the other leading members of GATT supported this position, but China saw it as one more indication of a concerted anti-China policy. At issue were China's policies protecting state-owned enterprises and its lack of transparency in trade and investment regulations. China sought membership as a developing country; the United States and others responded that the Chinese economy was already too large and well developed for that category to be appropriate. The question of China's membership in WTO was complicated by the fact that Taiwan's application was being considered simultaneously.

Late in 1999, a crucial hurdle was crossed when, after thirteen years of negotiations and a cliff-hanging finish, China and the United States signed a trade agreement. A similar agreement with the European Union was signed the following spring, clearing the way for China's entry into the WTO. A provision of the Sino-American agreement called for extending to China permanent normal trade relations, thereby eliminating Congress's annual review under the Jackson-Vanik amendment to the trade act of 1974 (a provision originally written to permit the free emigration of Russian Jews) of China's eligibility for what was formerly referred to as "most favored nation" trade status. Although U.S. trade unions made defeat of this initiative a high priority, business and farming organizations favored it. The initiative was carried in the House by a vote of 237 to 197—nineteen more yeas than needed to pass—and was passed by the Senate in September 2000.

China takes its role as a regional power seriously and actively participates in several new international groupings, such as the ASEAN Regional Forum on Security, which includes the ASEAN states (Brunei, Indonesia, Malaysia, the Philippines, Singapore, Thailand, and, as of 1995, Vietnam) plus Australia, Cambodia, Canada, the European Union, Japan, Laos, New Zealand, Papua New Guinea, Russia, South Korea, and the United States. At the meeting of the Regional Forum in August 1995, the issue of China's actions in the South China Sea was taken up. It was a measure of Chinese respect for the forum and for its membership in it that China came to the table with a conciliatory approach, agreeing to multilateral negotiations.

A slightly different configuration of members makes up the Asian Pacific Economic Cooperation (APEC) Forum, which excludes Cambodia, Laos, the European Union, Papua New Guinea, and Russia but includes Taiwan and Hong Kong. Although the agenda of

APEC Forum meetings is intended to focus on Pacific Rim economic issues, its meetings ordinarily include a session of its Eminent
Persons Group, the agenda for which is more far-ranging.

China is also involved in a proposal to set up an Asian common
market, the European Union being the model. The proposed membership for the Community of Asian Nations (CAN), much more extensive than any existing economic and security organizations in the
region, is to include all the APEC states (excluding the United States
and Canada), as well as Mongolia, North Korea, Laos, Cambodia,
Burma, India, Afghanistan, Bhutan, Nepal, Sri Lanka, Bangladesh,
Pakistan, and the Maldives.

As the new century begins, the key strategic relationship in East Asia—
among China, Japan, and the United States—should be the central focus of American foreign policy toward China. China needs concrete
reassurances that isolating it is not the goal of American foreign policy.
China and Japan need to come to a long-term strategic understanding,
which the United States is in a good position to facilitate.

To be able to reassure China, the United States needs, in the first
instance, a clear and consistent policy, and Congress needs to take a
calmer view. Currently, when Congress is not agitated about China's
human-rights record or treatment of Taiwan, it is agitated over
China's rapidly developing trade surplus, which threatens to become
a perennial sore point, as Japan's trade surplus is in our relations with
that country. In the early 1980s, the United States enjoyed a modest
annual trade surplus with China. The situation was reversed in 1983,
when China realized a $68 million surplus in total two-way trade of
just over $4 billion. According to American figures, the surplus had
grown to $60 billion by 1999, nearly equaling the size of Japan's sur-
plus. China and the United States differ in their methods of calculating trade figures: the United States counts goods from China
transshipped through Hong Kong as imports from China; China
counts them as exports to Hong Kong. Although other factors are also
involved, the result is that U.S. trade data show a surplus in China's

favor more than double the size of that surplus shown in Chinese trade data.

Another factor needs to be taken into account: as Taiwan and Hong Kong manufacturers have relocated their production facilities to mainland China, goods produced in those facilities and exported to the United States count in American trade statistics as exports from China, not from Taiwan or Hong Kong, and our trade deficits with Taiwan and Hong Kong show a decrease as the one with China increases. Our trade deficit with China increased by a factor of more than six between 1987 and 1992, but if one adds in Taiwan and Hong Kong, the growth in the deficit drops to just under 10 percent.

A second step toward improving Sino-American relations would be to use multilateral forums rather than bilateral negotiations to influence Chinese behavior whenever feasible. Although most nations do not share the intense American feeling about human-rights abuses in China, they do share America's concern over nuclear proliferation and weapons sales; American concerns about these issues should be voiced through regional and international forums where pressure brought to bear on China is not unilateral.

Finally, we should actively pursue contact at all levels of the Chinese government—particularly with the People's Liberation Army. Contacts with the Chinese developed rapidly after normalization of relations in 1979, but virtually all these were interrupted after the Tiananmen massacre. Contacts with the PLA, which were renewed in the early 1990s, were severed once again following China's military action in the Taiwan Strait in 1996. As we have seen, contacts were renewed, severed, and renewed for a third time in the ensuing three years. Although the expressions of American—and international—outrage were appropriate at the time, our being out of contact is counterproductive, especially when China's armed forces exert such a strong influence on the political system and may be nursing dreams of military expansion.

There are lessons to be learned from our century and a half of dealing with China, lest we repeat our past mistakes. First, despite the increasing veneer of Westernization, China's culture is still based on premises very different from our own. Second, we should bear in mind that although we have tried hard over the years to change China after our image, we have never succeeded in doing so. In the nineteenth century, we tried to Christianize China; in the twentieth century, we tried to democratize China; currently we are eager to transform China after American economic and technological models. We are very likely to be unsuccessful once again.

It seems paradoxical that there are more active Chinese Christians today than there were when the American missionary movement was at its height early in the twentieth century. Although no one would mistake China for a fully functioning democracy, there are more elements of grassroots democracy in the political system today than there were when American political influence was at its height in the 1930s and 1940s. And economic, scientific, and technological progress is occurring at a startlingly rapid rate. All of these changes, however, have come about as a result of Chinese decisions to change, not because of American pressure on China to change.

A final point: we need to be less passionate and more neutral about the American relationship with China, however special it is. China is neither the utopia we thought it was when we "rediscovered" it in the 1970s, nor is it the unmitigatedly evil place we sometimes think of its being today. If we can be more realistic about our expectations for China, we are likely to be less frequently disappointed.

CONCLUSION:
CHINA IN THE TWENTY-FIRST CENTURY

THIS BOOK SET OUT to consider three questions: What are the principal problems confronting China today? What is the capacity of the Chinese political system to address these problems successfully? And, given the problems and the government's capacity, what is the outcome likely to be?

Preceding chapters have described the formidable challenges to which the Chinese Party-state must respond in order to restore its authority, maintain public order, and create the conditions under which continued economic development can occur. I have also tried to show how that Party-state is seriously weakened by a lack of public confidence, a habit of corruption, and a rigidity in the face of change. Now we must ask, What is China's near-term future likely to be?

It may be useful to begin by offering some scenarios that are *not* likely and then to consider more probable ones. Least likely of all, I believe, is more of the same.

Deng Xiaoping adopted a unique method of overseeing China's entry into the modern world. Nearly seventy-five years old when he returned to power and launched the economic reforms, Deng had succession on his mind from the outset. It was his plan to avoid assuming the most senior positions in the Party-state himself and to appoint individuals to them whom he thought he could trust to carry on his reform program. If the process had worked as planned, he would gradually have retired and vanished like Lewis Carroll's cat, "quite slowly, beginning with the end of the tail, and ending with the grin, which remained some time after the rest of it had gone." But the process did not work as he planned: he did retire from office and become an éminence grise, whispering into his successors' ears from behind the curtain, but all too quickly, he lost confidence in the men he had appointed and intervened either to replace them or to reverse what he believed was their incorrect course. This continued until the eve of his ninety-first birthday, when, emerging from a coma and stepping back from the brink of death, he is alleged to have called Jiang Zemin to his bedside for a heart-to-heart talk about Taiwan and the United States.

With his vision, his revolutionary credentials, and his clout, Deng was an indispensable element of the political machine he put in place to change China. He was also irreplaceable. None of his contemporaries possessed his special combination of qualities, all but a very few of them have followed him on his journey "to see Marx," and China's political system cannot function in the same way following their death that it did while they were still alive.

I include here as equally implausible the option of "muddling through"—making incremental changes here and there to cope with the many problems confronting the Chinese political system in the new millennium. As I hope I have made clear in the preceding pages, the state of the regime and the magnitude of the problems it faces render muddling a hopelessly inadequate response.

Equally unlikely, in my view, is a reversal of course and the reestablishment of a centrally planned economy built around a strong state-owned sector cut off from the outside world. First, no one in China of any consequence advocates such a reversal. Second, decades of reform have created far too many interests vested in the growth of the Chinese economy—its collective and private sectors—and in linking it to the world economy. It would take a massive turn in China's economic fortunes or in the world economy as a whole to make rebuilding a Soviet-style socialist economy seem sensible, and it would take a political revolution to implement that.

Taiwanization is a third scenario, very unlikely in the near term, but it is my hope that it might be realized over the longer term. By "Taiwanization" I mean the duplication on mainland China of the political transformation that occurred on Taiwan: a relaxation of political repression, the emergence of a viable political opposition, and the reconstitution of the government so that a number of different parties might become the ruling one. Indispensable to this transformation are, as we have seen, a forward-looking leader with the political power to carry out his plans, courageous politicians willing to take risks to express opposition, and an electorate interested in and enthusiastic about democracy. A fledgling democracy is often somewhat chaotic and occasionally ineffective. One needs economic prosperity and the absence of serious political challenges to allow for tranquillity while a new system tries its wings.

At the moment, there are no signs in China of a visionary and powerful leader ready to launch a move toward democratization. Nor are there bold politicians prepared to form an opposition movement. Most of them have been imprisoned, placed under house arrest, or thoroughly intimidated. Also lacking is a strong commitment to democracy on the part of a politically aware and active public. In fact, among the politically conscious citizenry there is widespread skepticism about democracy. Many of them argue that democracy is ill-suited to China, either because of its history and culture or because of its size and ungovernability. Others believe that democracy may be appropriate for China at some future date but not now, when China needs honest authoritarianism. Therefore, a political liberalization of the Chinese government similar to Taiwan's seems a highly unlikely scenario in the near term.

Somewhat more likely, I think, is an abrupt collapse of the Party-state, similar to what happened in the Soviet Union in the summer of 1991. There are ample reasons in China today for popular dissatisfaction with the Party-state. Of the problems that brought people into the streets in 1989—inflation and corruption—one, inflation, has abated. The other, corruption, is mounting rapidly. To these problems have been added widespread unemployment brought on by reform of the ailing state sector and serious unrest in China's ethnic minority areas. Moreover, unlike in 1989, there is reason to believe that the level of anger among the rural population is even higher than among the urban population. Country people are showing no hesitation in taking their grievances to the village streets, even in today's repressive political atmosphere.

What is the spark that might set off a conflagration that brings down the government? Students might act as a vanguard, as they did in the late 1980s, though the reservoir of idealism and political activism in the student community seems well below the high-water mark then. Or rural protests over excess taxes, a shortage of cash to pay for harvested crops, or egregious examples of corruption might become more numerous and less isolated and spread from the hinterlands to the cities. More likely, I think, is urban workers being the first to rise. Laid off or furloughed in the state sector and unable to find jobs in the collective or private sector, workers may take to the streets, and if they do, their protests will quickly be echoed in the surrounding countryside. Controlling a nation in the streets is surely beyond the weakened Party-state's capability. A rapid meltdown of the Chinese Communist Party and the government it controls is plausible under these circumstances.

Or the process may be slower, triggered not by aggrieved citizens but by dissident regions. Assuming that simultaneous weakening of central authority and strengthening of local authority continues, interregional and interethnic conflicts are sure to arise, and the central government will no longer be in a position to mediate or end those conflicts. Some observers have called this situation "economic warlordism," using a term meant to remind us of the period between the collapse of dynastic authority and the reassertion of a strong central authority under the Chinese Communist Party in 1949. During this period, whichever warlord controlled Beijing and its environs claimed that he spoke for the government of China, but, apart from receiving foreign envoys, he had no effective national power. If one wanted to do business in Shanghai or settle a claim in Guangzhou, one addressed oneself to the local warlord, not to Beijing. Disputes between warlords were settled by armed conflict between the troops loyal to each. A repeat of this collapse of civil order and central control is certainly a possibility in the near term.

Were either of these last two sets of circumstances to come about, there is no question that the People's Liberation Army would intervene, but in neither instance to prop up the incumbents of the weakened Party-state. Rather, I believe, it would intervene in the name of Chinese patriotism and in defense of the Chinese national entity, resulting in a de facto military caretaker government. Given the strengths and weaknesses of the PLA as potential praetorians, such a government is more likely to be successful in the first set of circumstances—citizens on the streets—than with regional dissidence. It could very likely gain substantial popular support if it refused to endorse a discredited civilian leadership and set itself apart as an alternative to weakened and corrupted institutions. A promise to restore order to city streets and village roads would appeal to the people's natural distaste for anarchy and chaos.

An optimistic conclusion assumes that the PLA succeeds in restoring order, finds new and uncorrupted civilian leaders, rebuilds the power of the central government, and begins to address the nation's agenda of problems. It also assumes that military professionalism is stronger than the pleasures of politics and that the Army returns to its barracks at an early date. A pessimistic conclusion assumes that the PLA, like the Party, cannot restore the credibility of central authority and that personal and institutional self-interest preclude a successful political reconstitution.

Ending civil war among competing economic warlords would be a substantially more formidable challenge. The PLA would be stretched very thin, and even if some of its units were not actually involved as combatants, its own regional interests would not be easy to separate from patriotism. Chiang Kai-shek spent twenty years trying to create a national entity out of a patchwork of regional fiefdoms. In the end, he created a web of tenuous alliances among warlords, not a strong central state, which came only as a result of a revolution that won popular support by its appeal to nationalism and its promise to run an honest government and improve living standards. That process can hardly be accomplished by the PLA acting on its own.

In sum, regardless of which of these or other circumstances comes to pass, China has a protracted and problematical time ahead, in which the Army is likely to be heavily involved in the political process. The extraordinary growth of its economy will continue, but at a slower pace, during this transitional period, and China's best-endowed regions will weather this more successfully than the others. Because perceived threats from outside are always effective in creating national unity, we can expect China's national ego to be especially sensitive.

Understanding China is a necessity if we hope to be able to deal effectively with it during this sensitive period. To do so requires that we keep in the closest possible touch with a broad spectrum of Chinese people and institutions, for that is the only way to keep ourselves as well informed as we can be about the changes taking place there. It also requires sensitivity and flexibility in responding to the changes we observe. It requires that we bear in mind our past experience. We have, over the years, exerted a great deal of influence on China indirectly, rather than directly, and we have been most successful in doing so when we have taught by example, least successful when we have tried to teach through sanctions.

To understand China is not to hold it to a standard of its own and to exempt it from the standards to which we hold ourselves and other nations. It is to suggest that since it had very little to do with setting those standards in the past, it may have difficulty in living up to them in the present. To understand China is not necessarily to love it, but understanding China is a prerequisite of dealing with it effectively in the years ahead. And, given its size and its potential, and the degree to which the rest of the world has become linked with it both economically and politically, there is no avoiding the necessity of dealing with China in the years ahead.

APPENDIX

COMPARATIVE OUTPUT, GROWTH, AND INVESTMENT BY REGION AND PROVINCE, 1952–1998

	Index of 1952 per capita output* (national average=100)	Rank	Index of 1979 per capita output (national average=100)	Rank	Index of 1998 per capita GDP* (national average=100)	Rank	Growth 1997–1998 (%)	Rank	1998 Foreign direct investment (billion $)	Rank
Coastal China	1	1	1	1	1	1	1	1	1	1
Beijing	187	5	232	3	233	2	10	10	2.16	7
Fujian	72	21	46	23	146	6	11	1	4.21	3
Guangdong	89	16	57	18	160	5	10	6	12.01	1
Hainan	NA	NA	NA	NA	84	15	8	26	0.71	14
Hebei	95	13	68	9	93	11	11	4	1.10	10
Heilongjiang	238	3	103	4	108	10	8	27	0.52	16
Jiangsu	95	14	89	5	145	7	11	2	6.63	2
Jilin	164	6	84	6	85	14	9	18	0.40	19
Liaoning	222	4	79	7	135	8	8	28	2.19	6
Shandong	72	20	68	10	117	9	11	3	2.20	5
Shanghai	771	1	510	1	363	1	10	8	3.60	4
Tianjin	479	2	241	2	201	3	9	12	2.11	8
Zhejiang	98	12	63	12	161	4	10	9	1.31	9
Average	215		137		156		9.69		3.01	

Central China	3	3		2		2		2	2	2
Anhui	56	29	43	26	65	21	9	22	0.27	22
Chongqing	NA	NA	NA	NA	67	20	8	25	0.43	18
Henan	65	24	62	15	67	19	9	21	0.61	15
Hubei	101	11	64	11	90	13	10	5	0.97	11
Hunan	76	18	53	20	71	18	9	14	0.81	13
Jiangxi	93	15	45	24	64	22	8	29	0.46	17
Shaanxi	75	19	56	19	55	27	9	15	0.30	21
Shanxi	81	17	69	8	72	17	9	19	0.24	23
Sichuan	65	25	45	25	61	25	9	16	0.37	20
Average	77		55		68	20	9.07		0.50	

Western China	2	2		3		3		3	3	3
Gansu	65	26	63	13	50	29	9	13	0.04	27
Guangxi	69	22	41	27	59	26	9	17	0.88	12
Guizhou	66	23	31	29	33	31	9	23	0.04	26
Inner Mongolia	126	7	53	21	73	16	10	11	0.09	25
Ningxia	109	10	60	17	61	24	9	24	0.02	23
Qinghai	109	9	63	14	63	25	9	20	NA	NA
Tibet	67	27	62	16	52	23	10	7	NA	NA
Xinjiang	110	8	52	22	92	12	7	31	0.02	28
Yunnan	60	28	41	28	36	30	8	30	0.15	24
Average	87		52		58	24	8.82		0.18	

(Sources: *China Statistical Yearbook* 1985 and 1999)

*Figures for 1952 show industrial and agricultural output. Figures for 1998 show gross domestic product, which, in addition to industrial and agricultural output, includes output of the commercial and service sectors.

BIBLIOGRAPHY

INTRODUCTION

Kristof, Nicholas D., and Sheryl Wudunn. *China Wakes: The Struggle for the Soul of a Rising Power.* New York: New York Times Books, 1994.

Schell, Orville, and David Shambaugh, eds. *The China Reader: The Reform Era.* New York: Vintage, 1999.

Tyson, James, and Ann Tyson. *Chinese Awakenings: Life Stories from the Unofficial China.* Boulder, Colo.: Westview, 1995.

I. GEOGRAPHICAL INEQUALITIES

Blunden, Caroline, and Mark Elvin. *Cultural Atlas of China.* London: Phaidon, 1983.

Cannon, Terry, and Alan Jenkins, eds. *The Geography of Contemporary China: The Impact of Deng Xiaoping's Decade.* London: Routledge, 1990.

Gedlan, P. J., and D. C. Twitchett, eds. *The Times Atlas of China.* London: Times Books, 1974.

Linge, Godfrey, ed. *China's New Spatial Economy: Heading toward 2020.* Hong Kong: Oxford University Press, 1997.

Skinner, G. William. "Marketing and Social Structure in Rural China." *Journal of Asian Studies* 24 (1965), pp. 1–3.

Smil, Vaclav. *Energy in China's Modernization: Advances and Limitations.* Armonk, N.Y.: M. E. Sharpe, 1988.

Smith, Christopher J. *China: People and Places in the Land of One Billion.* Boulder, Colo.: Westview, 1990.

Van Slyke, Lyman P. *Yangtze: Nature, History, and the River.* New York: Addison-Wesley, 1988.

II. PATTERNS FROM THE PAST

Chang Jung. *Wild Swans: Three Daughters of China.* New York: Simon & Schuster, 1991.

Cheng, Nien. *Life and Death in Shanghai.* New York: Grove Press, 1986.

Fairbank, John K., and Albert Feuerwerker, eds. *Cambridge History of China.* Vol. 13: *Republican China, 1912–49.* Cambridge, U.K.: Cambridge University Press, 1984.

Fairbank, John K., and Merle Goldman. *China: A New History.* Enlarged ed. Cambridge, Mass.: Harvard University Press, 1998.

Fairbank, John K., and Roderick MacFarquhar, eds. *Cambridge History of China.* Vols. 14–15: *The People's Republic of China, 1949–79.* Cambridge, U.K.: Cambridge University Press, 1985.

Huters, Ted, R. Bin Wong, and Pauline Yu, eds. *Culture and State in Chinese History: Conventions, Accommodations, and Critiques.* Stanford, Calif.: Stanford University Press, 1997.

Jenner, W.J.F. *The Tyranny of History: The Roots of China's Crisis.* New York: Penguin, 1992.

Spence, Jonathan D. *The Search for Modern China.* New York: W. W. Norton, 1990.

Su Xiaokang, Wang Luxiang, and Xia Jun. *Deathsong of the River: A Reader's Guide to the Chinese TV Series "He Shang."* Ithaca, N.Y.: Cornell University East Asia Program, 1991.

III. CHINA'S POLITICAL SYSTEM

Brook, Timothy, and B. Michael Frolic, eds. *Civil Society in China.* Armonk, N.Y.: M. E. Sharpe, 1997.

Goldman, Merle. *Sowing the Seeds of Democracy in China: Political Reform in the Deng Xiaoping Era.* Cambridge, Mass.: Harvard University Press, 1994.

Gong Ting. *The Politics of Corruption in Contemporary China: An Analysis of Policy Outcomes.* Westport, Conn.: Praeger, 1994.

Jia Hao and Lin Zhimin, eds. *Changing Central-Local Relations in China: Reform and State Capacity.* Boulder, Colo.: Westview, 1994.

Levy, Richard. "Corruption, Economic Crime, and the Social Transformation since the Reforms." *Australian Journal of Chinese Affairs* 33 (1995), pp. 183–216.

Li Cheng. "Jiang Zemin's Successors: The Rise of the Fourth Generation of Leaders in the PRC." *China Quarterly* 161 (2000), pp. 1–40.

Lieberthal, Kenneth. *Governing China: From Revolution through Reform.* New York: W. W. Norton, 1995.

Lieberthal, Kenneth, and David M. Lampton, eds. *Bureaucracy, Politics, and Decision Making in Post-Mao China.* Berkeley and Los Angeles: University of California Press, 1992.

Lieberthal, Kenneth, and Michel Oksenberg, eds. *Policy Making in China: Leaders, Structures, and Processes.* Princeton, N.J.: Princeton University Press, 1990.

MacFarquhar, Roderick, ed. *The Politics of China, 1949–1989.* New York and Cambridge, U.K.: Cambridge University Press, 1993.

Nathan, Andrew J. *Chinese Democracy.* New York: Alfred A. Knopf, 1985.

O'Brien, Kevin J. *Reform without Liberalization: China's National People's Congress and the Politics of Institutional Change.* New York and Cambridge, U.K.: Cambridge University Press, 1990.

Shambaugh, David L. "Losing Control: The Erosion of State Authority in China." *Current History* 93 (1993), pp. 253–59.

Shue, Vivienne. *The Reach of the State: Sketches of the Chinese Body Politic.* Stanford, Calif.: Stanford University Press, 1988.

Tian Hung-Mao and Chu Yun-han, eds. *China under Jiang Zemin.* Boulder, Colo.: Lynne Rienner, 2000.

White, Gordon, ed. *The Chinese State in the Era of Economic Reform. The Road to Crisis.* Armonk, N.Y.: M. E. Sharpe, 1991.

Yang, Mayfair Mei-hui. *Gifts, Favors, and Banquets: The Art of Social*

Relationships in China. Ithaca, N.Y.: Cornell University Press, 1994.

IV. CHINA'S ECONOMY

Cheng Tiejun and Mark Selden. "The Origins and Social Consequences of China's *hukou* System." *China Quarterly* 139 (1994), pp. 644–68.

Cheng Yuk-shing and Tsang Shu-ki. "The Changing Grain Marketing System in China." *China Quarterly* 140 (1994), pp. 1080–104.

Findlay, Christopher, Andrew Watson, and Harry X. Wu, eds. *Rural Enterprises in China.* New York: St. Martin's Press, 1994.

Kelliher, Daniel. *Peasant Power in China: The Era of Rural Reform, 1979–89.* New Haven: Yale University Press, 1992.

Kueh, Y. Y., and Robert Ash, eds. *Economic Trends in Chinese Agriculture: The Impact of the Post-Mao Reforms.* Oxford: Clarendon Press, 1993.

Lardy, Nicholas. *China's Unfinished Economic Revolution.* Washington, D.C.: Brookings Institution, 1998.

McKinley, Terry. *The Distribution of Wealth in Rural China.* Armonk, N.Y.: M. E. Sharpe, 1995.

Naughton, Barry. "China's Macroeconomy in Transition." *China Quarterly* 144 (1995), pp. 1083–104.

———. *Growing Out of the Plan: Chinese Economic Reform, 1978–1993.* New York and Cambridge, U.K.: Cambridge University Press, 1995.

Putterman, Louis. "The Role of Ownership and Property Rights in China's Economic Transition." *China Quarterly* 144 (1995), pp. 1047–64.

Shirk, Susan L. *The Political Logic of Economic Reform in China.* Berkeley and Los Angeles: University of California Press, 1993.

Sicular, Terry. "Redefining State, Plan, and Market: China's Reforms in Agricultural Commerce." *China Quarterly* 144 (1995), pp. 1020–46.

Steinfeld, Edward S. *Forging Reform in China: The Fate of State-Owned Industry.* New York: Cambridge University Press, 1998.

Walder, Andrew G. "China's Transitional Economy: Interpreting Its Significance." *China Quarterly* 144 (1995), pp. 963–79.

White, Lynn T., III. *Unstately Power.* Vol. 1: *Local Causes of China's Economic Reforms.* Vol. 2: *Local Causes of China's Intellectual, Legal, and Governmental Reforms.* Armonk, N.Y.: M. E. Sharpe, 1998.

World Bank. *China: Internal Market Development and Regulation.* Washington, D.C.: The World Bank, 1994.

V. THE CHINESE ARMED FORCES

Bernstein, Richard, and Ross H. Munro. *The Coming Conflict with China.* New York: Knopf, 1997.

Bickford, Thomas J. "The Chinese Military and Its Business Operations: The People's Liberation Army as Entrepreneur." *Asian Survey* 34.5 (1994), pp. 460–74.

Bitzinger, Richard A. "Arms to Go: Chinese Arms Sales to the Third World." *International Security* (Fall 1992), pp. 84–111.

Cheung Tai Ming. "The People's Armed Police: First Line of Defense." *China Quarterly* 146 (1996), pp. 525–47.

Gurtov, Mel, and Hwang Byong-Moo. *China's Security: The New Roles of the Military.* Boulder, Colo.: Lynne Rienner, 1998.

Lewis, John Wilson, and Xue Litai. *China's Strategic Seapower: The Politics of Force Modernization in the Nuclear Age.* Stanford, Calif.: Stanford University Press, 1994.

McNamara, Robert S., David E. Jeremiah, James P. McCarthy, William R. Richardson, Jimmy D. Ross, David M. Lampton, and June Mei. *Sino-American Military Relations: Mutual Responsibilities in the Post-Cold War Era.* New York: National Committee on U.S.-China Relations, 1994.

Nathan, Andrew J., and Robert J. Ross. *The Great Wall and the Empty Fortress: China's Search for Security.* New York: W. W. Norton, 1997.

Nelsen, Harvey W. *The Chinese Military System: An Organizational Study of the Chinese People's Liberation Army.* 2nd ed. Boulder, Colo.: Westview, 1981.

Segal, Gerald. *Defending China.* New York and Oxford: Oxford University Press, 1985.

Swaine, Michael D. *The Military and Political Succession in China: Leadership, Institutions, and Beliefs.* Los Angeles: Rand Corporation, 1992.

Wang Shaoguang. "Estimating China's Defense Expenditure: Some Evidence from Chinese Sources." *China Quarterly* 147 (1996), pp. 889–911.

Yang, Richard H., ed. *China's Military: The PLA in 1992–93.* Boulder, Colo.: Westview, 1993.

VI. SOURCES OF RURAL DISCONTENT

Burns, John P. *Political Participation in Rural China.* Berkeley and Los Angeles: University of California Press, 1988.

Carter, Colin A., and Zhong Fu-ning. *China's Grain Production and Trade: An Economic Analysis.* Boulder, Colo.: Westview, 1988.

Howard, Pat. *Breaking the Iron Ricebowl: Prospects for Socialism in China's Countryside.* Armonk, N.Y.: M. E. Sharpe, 1988.

Jacka, Tamara. *Women's Work in Rural China: Change and Continuity in an Era of Reform.* New York and Cambridge, U.K.: Cambridge University Press, 1997.

Kelliher, Daniel. "The Chinese Debate over Village Self-Government." *China Journal* 37 (1997), pp. 63–90.

Knapp, Ronald G. *China's Traditional Rural Architecture: A Cultural Geography of the Common House.* Honolulu: University of Hawaii Press, 1987.

Oi, Jean C. *Rural China Takes Off: The Institutional Foundation of Economic Reform.* Berkeley: University of California Press, 1999.

———. *State and Peasant in Contemporary China: The Political Economy of Village Government.* Berkeley and Los Angeles: University of California Press, 1989.

Parish, William L., ed. *Chinese Rural Development.* Armonk, N.Y.: M. E. Sharpe, 1985.

Parish, William L., Zhe Xiaoye, and Li Fang. "Nonfarm Work and

Marketization of the Chinese Countryside." *China Quarterly* 143 (1995), pp. 697–730.

Putterman, Louis. *Continuity and Change in China's Rural Development: The Collective and Reform Eras in Perspective.* New York and Oxford: Oxford University Press, 1992.

Rozelle, Scott, Li Guo, Shen Minggao, Amelia Hugart, and John Giles. "Leaving China's Farms: Survey Results of New Paths and Remaining Hurdles to Rural Migration." *China Quarterly* 158 (1999), pp. 367–93.

Siu, Helen, ed. *Furrows: Peasants, Intellectuals, and the State.* Stanford, Calif.: Stanford University Press, 1990.

Vermeer, Eduard B., Frank N. Pieke, and Woei Lien Chong. *Cooperative and Collective in China's Rural Development: Between State and Private Interests.* Armonk, N.Y.: M. E. Sharpe, 1998.

Yan Yunxiang. *The Flow of Gifts: Reciprocity and Social Networks in a Chinese Village.* Stanford, Calif.: Stanford University Press, 1996.

Zweig, David. *Freeing China's Farmers: Rural Restructuring in the Reform Era.* Armonk, N.Y.: M. E. Sharpe, 1997.

VII. CHINA'S CITIES

Bian Yanjie. *Work and Inequality in Urban China.* New York: State University of New York Press, 1994.

Davis, Deborah, and Ezra Vogel, eds. *Chinese Society on the Eve of Tiananmen: The Impact of Reform.* Cambridge, Mass.: Harvard University Press, 1990.

Davis, Deborah, Richard Kraus, Barry Naughton, and Elizabeth Perry, eds. *Urban Spaces in Contemporary China: The Potential for Autonomy and Community in Post-Mao China.* New York and Cambridge, U.K.: Cambridge University Press, 1995.

Davis, Deborah, and Stevan Harrell, eds. *Chinese Families in the Post-Mao Era.* Berkeley and Los Angeles: University of California Press, 1993.

Day, Lincoln H., ed. *Migration and Urbanization in China.* Armonk, N.Y.: M. E. Sharpe, 1994.

Dutton, Michael, ed. *Streetlife China.* New York: Cambridge University Press, 1998.

Ikels, Charlotte. *The Return of the God of Wealth: The Transition to a Market Economy in Urban China.* Stanford, Calif.: Stanford University Press, 1996.

Kirkby, R.J.R. *Urbanization in China: Town and Country in a Developing Economy, 1949–2000* A.D. New York: Columbia University Press, 1985.

Kwok, R. Yin-wang, William L. Parish, et al., eds. *Chinese Urban Reform: What Model Now?* Armonk, N.Y.: M. E. Sharpe, 1990.

Lewis, John W., ed. *The City in Communist China.* Stanford, Calif.: Stanford University Press, 1971.

Sit, Victor F.S., ed. *Chinese Cities: The Growth of the Metropolis since 1949.* New York and Oxford: Oxford University Press, 1988.

Solinger, Dorothy J. *Contesting Citizenship in Urban China: Peasant Migrants, the State, and the Logic of the Market.* Berkeley: University of California Press, 1999.

Yang Zhong, Chen Jie, and John Scheb. "Mass Political Culture in Beijing: Findings from Two Surveys." *Asian Survey* 38:8 (1998), pp. 763–83.

Zhao Shukai. "Criminality and the Policing of Migrant Workers." *China Journal* 43 (2000), pp. 101–10.

VIII. THE CENTRIFUGAL FORCES OF REGIONALISM

Ash, Robert, and Y. Y. Kueh. "Economic Integration within Greater China: Trade and Investment Flows between China, Hong Kong, and Taiwan." *China Quarterly* 136 (1993), pp. 711–45.

Cheung, Peter T. Y., Chung Jae Ho, and Lin Zhimin. *Provincial Strategies of Economic Reform in Post-Mao China: Leadership, Politics, and Implementation.* Armonk, N.Y.: M. E. Sharpe, 1998.

Davin, Delia. *Internal Migration in Contemporary China.* New York: St. Martin's, 1999.

Goodman, David S.G., ed. *China's Provinces in Reform: Class, Community, and Political Culture.* New York: Routledge, 1997.

———. *China's Regional Development*. London: Routledge, 1989.

———. *The Evolution of Greater China and What It Means for America*. New York: National Committee for United States–China Relations, 1994.

Hendrischke, Hans, and Feng Chongyi, eds. *The Political Economy of China's Provinces: Comparative and Competitive Advantage*. New York: Routledge, 1999.

Segal, Gerald. *China Changes Shape: Regionalism and Foreign Policy*. London: International Institute for Strategic Studies, Adelphi Papers, 1994.

Shambaugh, David L., ed. *Greater China: The Next Superpower*. New York and Oxford: Oxford University Press, 1995.

Skinner, G. William, ed. *The City in Late Imperial China*. Stanford, Calif.: Stanford University Press, 1977.

Wong, Christine, ed. *Financing Local Government in the People's Republic of China*. Hong Kong: Oxford University Press, 1997.

Yahuda, Michael. "The Foreign Relations of Greater China." *China Quarterly* 136 (1993), pp. 687–710.

Yang Dali. *Beyond Beijing: Liberalization and the Regions in China*. New York: Routledge, 1997.

Yeung Yue-man and Hu Xu-wei. *China's Coastal Cities: Catalysts for Modernization*. Honolulu: University of Hawaii Press, 1992.

Zhang Le-Yin. "Chinese Central-Provincial Fiscal Relationships." *China Quarterly* 157 (1999), pp. 115–41.

IX. HAN AND NON-HAN

Barnett, A. Doak. *China's Far West: Four Decades of Change*. Boulder, Colo.: Westview, 1993.

Benson, Linda, and Ingvar Svanberg. *China's Last Nomads: The History and Culture of China's Kazaks*. Armonk, N.Y.: M. E. Sharpe, 1998.

Cao Changching and James D. Seymour, eds. *Tibet through Dissident Chinese Eyes: Essays on Self-Determination*. Armonk, N.Y.: M. E. Sharpe, 1998.

Christoffersen, Gaye. "Xinjiang and the Great Islamic Circle: Impact on Chinese Regional Economic Planning." *China Quarterly* 133 (1993), pp. 130–51.

Dikotter, Frank. *The Discourse of Race in Modern China*. Stanford, Calif.: Stanford University Press, 1992.

Dreyer, June Teufel. *China's Forty Millions: Minority Nationalities and National Integration in the People's Republic of China*. Cambridge, Mass.: Harvard University Press, 1976.

———. "The Xinjiang Uygur Autonomous Region at Thirty: A Report Card." *Asian Survey* 26:7 (1986), pp. 721–44.

Gladney, Dru C. *Muslim Chinese: Ethnic Nationalism in the People's Republic*. Cambridge, Mass.: Council on East Asian Studies, Harvard University, 1996.

Goldstein, Melvyn C. *The Snow Lion and the Dragon: China, Tibet, and the Dalai Lama*. Berkeley: University of California Press, 1997.

Goldstein, Melvyn C., and Matthew Kapstein. *Buddhism in Contemporary Tibet: Religious Revival and Cultural Identity*. Berkeley: University of California Press, 1998.

Grunfeld, A. Tom. *The Making of Modern Tibet*. Rev. ed. Armonk, N.Y.: M. E. Sharpe, 1996.

Gyatso, Tenzin Dalai Lama XIV. *My Tibet*. Berkeley: University of California Press, 1990.

Hansen, Mette Halskov. "The Call of Mao or Money? Han Settlers on China's Southwestern Borders." *China Quarterly* 158 (1999), pp. 394–413.

Harrell, Stevan, ed. *Cultural Encounters on China's Ethnic Frontiers*. Seattle: University of Washington Press, 1995.

Heberer, Thomas. *China and Its National Minorities: Autonomy of Assimilation*. Armonk, N.Y.: M. E. Sharpe, 1989.

Mackerras, Colin. *China's Minority Cultures: Identities and Integration since 1912*. New York: St. Martin's, 1995.

Shakya, Tsering. *The Dragon in the Land of the Snows: A History of Modern Tibet since 1947*. New York: Columbia University Press, 1999.

Xu Guangqiu. "The United States and the Tibet Issue." *Asian Survey* 37:11 (1997), pp. 1062–77.

X. THE CHALLENGE OF ENVIRONMENTAL DEGRADATION

Banister, Judith. "Population, Public Health, and the Environment in China." *China Quarterly* 156 (1998), pp. 986–1015.

China's Environment. Special issue of *China Quarterly* 156 (1998).

Dai Qing. *The River Dragon Has Come! The Three Gorges Dam and the Fate of China's Yangtze River and Its People.* Armonk, N.Y.: M. E. Sharpe, 1997.

Edmonds, Richard Louis. *Patterns of China's Lost Harmony: A Survey of Environmental Degradation and Protection.* London: Routledge, 1994.

Elvin, Mark, and Liu Ts'ui-jung, eds. *Sediments of Time: Environment and Society in Chinese History.* New York: Cambridge University Press, 1997.

Jahiel, Abigail R. "The Contradictory Impact of Reform on Environmental Protection in China." *China Quarterly* 149 (1997), pp. 80–103.

Jing Jun. "Rural Resettlement: Past Lessons for the Three Gorges Project." *China Journal* 38 (1997), pp. 65–94.

Luk Shui-hung and Joseph Whitney, eds. *Megaproject: A Case Study of China's Three Gorges Project.* Armonk, N.Y.: M. E. Sharpe, 1993.

McElroy, Michael B., Chris P. Nielsen, and Peter Lydon, eds. *Energizing China: Reconciling Environmental Protection and Economic Growth.* Cambridge, Mass.: Harvard University Press, 1998.

Qu Geping and Li Jinchang. *Population and the Environment in China.* Boulder, Colo.: Lynne Rienner, 1994.

Robinson, Thomas W., ed. *The Foreign Relations of China's Environment Policy.* Washington, D.C.: American Enterprise Institute, 1992.

Smil, Vaclav. *The Bad Earth: Environmental Degradation in China.* Armonk, N.Y.: M. E. Sharpe, 1984.

———. *China's Environmental Crisis: An Inquiry into the Limits of National Development.* Armonk, N.Y.: M. E. Sharpe, 1993.

XI. ONE BILLION PLUS

Aird, John S. *Slaughter of the Innocents: Coercive Birth Control in China*. Lanham, Md.: University Press of America, 1990.

Brown, Lester, and H. Kane. *Full House*. New York: W. W. Norton, 1994.

Harrell, Stevan. *Chinese Historical Microdemography*. Berkeley and Los Angeles: University of California Press, 1995.

Merli, M. Giavanna. "Underreporting of Births and Infant Deaths in Rural China: Evidence from Field Research in One County in Northern China." *China Quarterly* 155 (1998), pp. 637–55.

Peng Xizhe. *Demographic Transition in China: Fertility Trends since the 1950s*. Oxford: Clarendon Press, 1991.

Smil, Vaclav. "Who Will Feed China?" *China Quarterly* 143 (1995), pp. 801–13.

Tien, H. Yuan. *China's Strategic Demographic Initiative*. Westport, Conn.: Praeger, 1991.

XII. HUMAN RIGHTS AND THE RULE OF LAW

Alford, William P. "Tasseled Loafers for Barefoot Lawyers: Transformation and Tension in Chinese Legal Work." *China Quarterly* 141 (1995), pp. 22–38.

———. *To Steal a Book Is an Elegant Offense: Intellectual Property Rights in Chinese Civilization*. Stanford, Calif.: Stanford University Press, 1995.

Barmé, Geremie, and John Minford. *Seeds of Fire: Chinese Voices of Conscience*. New York: Hill and Wang, 1989.

Brook, Timothy. *Quelling the People: The Military Suppression of the Beijing Democracy Movement*. New York and London: Oxford University Press, 1992.

Chiu Hungdah and Leng Shao-chuan. *Criminal Justice in Post-Mao China*. New York: State University of New York Press, 1985.

Clarke, Donald C., and James V. Feinerman. "Antagonistic Contradictions: Criminal Law and Human Rights in China." *China Quarterly* 141 (1995), pp. 135–54.

Copper, John Franklin, and Lee Ta-ling. *Tiananmen Aftermath: Hu-*

man Rights in the People's Republic of China, 1990. College Park: University of Maryland Press, 1992.

Davis, Michael C., ed. *Human Rights and Chinese Values: Legal, Philosophical, and Political Perspectives.* Hong Kong: Oxford University Press, 1995.

de Bary, William Theodore. *Asian Values and Human Rights: A Confucian Communitarian Perspective.* Cambridge, Mass.: Harvard University Press, 1998.

Gilmartin, Christina K., Gail Hershatter, Lisa Rofel, and Tyrene White, eds. *Engendering China: Women, Culture, and the State.* Cambridge, Mass.: Harvard University Press, 1994.

Jones, William C., ed. *Basic Principles of Civil Law in China.* Armonk, N.Y.: M. E. Sharpe, 1989.

Kent, Ann. *Between Freedom and Subsistence: China and Human Rights.* Hong Kong: Oxford University Press, 1993.

Lubman, Stanley B. "The Future of Chinese Law." *China Quarterly* 141 (1995), pp. 1–21.

Nathan, Andrew J. "Human Rights in Chinese Foreign Policy." *China Quarterly* 139 (1994), pp. 622–43.

Potter, Pitman B. *The Economic Contract Law of China: Legitimation and Contract Antonomy in the PRC.* Seattle: University of Washington Press, 1992.

———, ed. *Domestic Law Reforms in Post-Mao China.* Armonk, N.Y.: M. E. Sharpe, 1994.

Tanner, Murray Scot. "The Erosion of Communist Party Control over Lawmaking in China." *China Quarterly* 138 (1994), pp. 344–72.

Wei Jingsheng. *The Courage to Stand Alone: Letters from Prison and Other Writings.* New York: Viking, 1997.

XIII. INTELLECTUAL FREEDOM AND CHINESE EDUCATION

Angelasto, Michael, and Bob Adamson, eds. *Higher Education in Post-Mao China.* Hong Kong: Hong Kong University Press, 1998.

Deng Peng. *Private Education in Modern China.* Westport, Conn.: Praeger, 1997.

Fang Lizhi. *Bringing Down the Great Wall: Writings on Science, Culture, and Democracy in China.* New York: W. W. Norton, 1992.

Hayhoe, Ruth, ed. *Education and Modernization: The Chinese Experience.* New York: Pergamon, 1992.

Lin Jing. *Education in Post-Mao China.* Westport, Conn.: Praeger, 1993.

Link, Perry. *Evening Chats in Beijing.* New York: W. W. Norton, 1992.

Liu Binyan. *China's Crisis, China's Hope.* Cambridge, Mass.: Harvard University Press, 1990.

Ogden, Suzanne, Kathleen Hartford, and Lawrence Sullivan. *China's Search for Democracy: The Student and Mass Movement of 1989.* Armonk, N.Y.: M. E. Sharpe, 1992.

Pepper, Suzanne. *China's Education Reform in the 1980's: Policies, Issues, and Historical Perspectives.* Berkeley and Los Angeles: University of California Press, 1990.

——. *Radicalism and Education Reform in 20th Century China.* Hong Kong: Cambridge University Press, 1996.

Schoenhals, Martin. *The Paradox of Power in a PRC Middle School.* Armonk, N.Y.: M. E. Sharpe, 1993.

Yan Jiaqi. *Toward a Democratic China: The Intellectual Autobiography of Yan Jiaqi.* Trans. by David S.K. Hong and Denis C. Mair, Honolulu: University of Hawaii Press, 1992.

XIV. Artistic Freedom and China's Contemporary Culture

Andrews, Julia. *Painters and Politics in the People's Republic of China, 1949–79.* Berkeley and Los Angeles: University of California Press, 1994.

Barlow, Tani E., ed. *Gender Politics in Modern China: Writing and Feminism.* Durham, N.C.: Duke University Press, 1993.

Barmé, Geremie R. *In the Red: On Contemporary Chinese Culture.* New York: Columbia University Press, 1999.

Browne, Nick, Paul G. Pickowicz, Vivian Sobchack, and Esther Yau, eds. *New Chinese Cinemas: Forms, Identities, Politics.* New York and Cambridge, U.K.: Cambridge University Press, 1994.

Chang Tsong-zung, Valerie C. Doran, et al. *China's New Art Post 1989*. Seattle: University of Washington Press, 1994.

Chow, Rey. *Primitive Passions: Visuality, Sexuality, Ethnography, and Contemporary Chinese Cinema*. New York: Columbia University Press, 1995.

Cohen, Joan Lebold. *The New Chinese Painting, 1949–86*. New York: Harry N. Abrams, 1987.

Donald, Stephanie. *Public Secrets, Public Spaces: Cinema and Civility in China*. Lanham, Md.: Rowman & Littlefield, 2000.

Duke, Michael S., ed. *Modern Chinese Women Writers*. Armonk, N.Y.: M. E. Sharpe, 1990.

Gao Minglu, ed. *Inside Out: New Chinese Art*. Berkeley: University of California Press, 1998.

Gold, Thomas B. "Go With Your Feelings: Hong Kong and Taiwan Popular Culture in Greater China." *China Quarterly* 136 (1993), pp. 907–25.

Goldblatt, Howard, ed. *Chairman Mao Would Not Be Amused: Fiction from Today's China*. New York: Grove/Atlantic, 1996.

Holm, David. *Art and Ideology in Revolutionary China*. Hong Kong: Oxford University Press, 1991.

Jones, Andrew F. *Like a Knife: Ideology and Genre in Contemporary Chinese Popular Music*. Ithaca, N.Y.: Cornell University Press, 1992.

Kolatch, Jonathan. *Is the Moon in China Just as Round? Sporting Life and Sundry Scenes*. London: Jonathan David, 1992.

Kraus, Richard Curt. *Brushes with Power: Modern Politics and the Chinese Art of Calligraphy*. Berkeley and Los Angeles: University of California Press, 1991.

Larson, Wendy. *Women and Writing in Modern China*. Stanford, Calif.: Stanford University Press, 1998.

Leung Laifong. *Morning Sun: Interviews with Post-Mao Chinese Writers*. Armonk, N.Y.: M. E. Sharpe, 1993.

Lu, Sheldon Hsiao-peng, ed. *Transnational Chinese Cinemas: Identity, Nationhood, Gender*. Honolulu: University of Hawaii Press, 1997.

McDougall, Bonnie S., and Kam Louie. *The Literature of China in the Twentieth Century.* New York: Columbia University Press, 1997.

Riley, Jo. *Chinese Theatre and the Actor in Performance.* New York and Cambridge, U.K.: Cambridge University Press, 1997.

Semsel, George S., Hou Jianping, and Xia Hong, eds. *Chinese Film Theory: A Guide to the New Era.* Westport, Conn.: Praeger, 1990.

Sullivan, Michael. *Art and Artists of Twentieth-Century China.* Berkeley and Los Angeles: University of California Press, 1997.

Wang, David Der-Wei, and Jeanne Tai, eds. *Running Wild: New Chinese Writers.* New York: Columbia University Press, 1994.

Wang Jing. *High Culture Fever: Politics, Aesthetics, and Ideology in Deng's China.* Berkeley and Los Angeles: University of California Press, 1997.

Widmer, Ellen, and David Der-Wei Wang, eds. *From May Fourth to June Fourth: Fiction and Film in Twentieth Century China.* Cambridge, Mass.: Harvard University Press, 1993.

Zha Jianying. *China Pop: How Soap Operas, Tabloids, and Bestsellers Are Transforming a Culture.* New York: The New Press, 1995.

Zhang Xudong. *Chinese Modernism in the Era of Reforms: Cultural Fever, Avant-Garde Fiction, and the New Chinese Cinema.* Durham, N.C.: Duke University Press, 1997.

Zhao, Henry Y.H. *The Uneasy Narrator: Chinese Fiction from the Traditional to the Modern.* New York and Oxford: Oxford University Press, 1995.

XV. HONG KONG AND MACAO

Cameron, Nigel. *An Illustrated History of Hong Kong.* Hong Kong: Oxford University Press, 1991.

Chan, Ming K., and Gerard Postiglione, eds. *The Hong Kong Reader: Passage to Chinese Sovereignty.* Armonk, N.Y.: M. E. Sharpe, 1996.

Chang, David Wen-wei, and Richard Y. Chuang. *The Politics of Hong Kong's Reversion to China.* New York: St. Martin's, 1998.

Cheng, Joseph Y S., and Beatrice Leung, eds. *Hong Kong Special Administrative Region: In Pursuit of Domestic and International Order*. New York: Cambridge University Press, 1998.

Chiu Hungdah. *Hong Kong's Transition to 1997: Background, Problems, and Prospects*. College Park: University of Maryland School of Law, 1993.

Edmonds, Richard Louis, and Herbert S. Yee. "Macau: From Portuguese Autonomous Territory to Chinese Special Administrative Region." *China Quarterly* 160 (1999), pp. 801–17.

Gunn, Geoffrey C. *Encountering Macau: A Portuguese City on the Periphery of China, 1557–1999*. Boulder, Colo.: Westview, 1996.

Ho Yin-ping. *Trade, Industrial Restructuring, and Development in Hong Kong*. Honolulu: University of Hawaii Press, 1992.

Hsu, Berry Fong-chung. *The Common Law System in Chinese Context: Hong Kong in Transition*. Armonk, N.Y.: M. E. Sharpe, 1992.

Lane, Kevin P. *Sovereignty and the Status Quo: The Historical Roots of China's Hong Kong Policy*. Boulder, Colo.: Westview, 1990.

Leung, Benjamin K.P. *Perspectives on Hong Kong Society*. Hong Kong: Oxford University Press, 1996.

McMillen, Donald H., and Michael E. DeGolyer, eds. *One Culture, Many Systems: Politics in the Reunification of China*. Hong Kong: Chinese University of Hong Kong Press, 1993.

Postiglione, Gerard A., ed. *Education and Society in Hong Kong: Toward One Country and Two Systems*. Armonk, N.Y.: M. E. Sharpe, 1991.

Scott, Ian. "The Disarticulation of Hong Kong's Post-handover Political System." *China Journal* 43 (2000), pp. 29–54.

———. *Institutional Change and the Political Transition in Hong Kong*. New York: St. Martin's, 1998.

Segal, Gerald. *The Fate of Hong Kong*. London: St. Martin's Press, 1993.

Wang Enbao. *Hong Kong, 1997: The Politics of Transition*. Boulder, Colo.: Lynne Rienner, 1995.

Welsh, Frank. *A Borrowed Place: A History of Hong Kong*. New York: Hill and Wang, 1994.

Yahuda, Michael. *Hong Kong: China's Challenge*. London: Routledge, 1996.

XVI. TAIWAN: MODEL OR RIVAL?

Aberbach, Joel D., David Dollar, and Kenneth J. Sokoloff. *The Role of the State in Taiwan's Development*. Armonk, N.Y.: M. E. Sharpe, 1994.

Chang, Parris H., and Martin L. Lasater. *If the People's Republic of China Crosses the Taiwan Strait: An International Response*. Lanham, Md.: University Press of America, 1993.

Chao, Linda, and Ramon H. Myers. *The First Chinese Democracy: Political Life in the Republic of China on Taiwan*. Baltimore, Md.: Johns Hopkins University Press, 1998.

Cheng Tun-jen, Chi Huang, and Samuel S.G. Wu. *Inherited Rivalry: Conflict across the Taiwan Straits*. Boulder, Colo.: Lynne Rienner, 1995.

Cheng Tun-jen and Stephan Haggard, eds. *Political Change in Taiwan*. Boulder, Colo.: Lynne Rienner, 1992.

Clough, Ralph N. *Cooperation or Conflict in the Taiwan Strait?* Lanham, Md.: Rowman & Littlefield, 1998.

Harrell, Stevan, and Huang Chun-chieh, eds. *Cultural Change in Postwar Taiwan*. Boulder, Colo.: Westview, 1994.

Hickey, Dennis Van Vranken. *Taiwan's Security in the Changing International System*. Boulder, Colo.: Lynne Rienner, 1997.

Hughes, Christopher. *Taiwan and Chinese Nationalism: National Identity and Status in International Society*. London: Routledge, 1997.

Lasater, Martin L. *U.S. Interests in the New Taiwan*. Boulder, Colo.: Westview, 1993.

Leng Shao-chuan and Lin Cheng-yi. "Political Change on Taiwan: Transition to Democracy?" *China Quarterly* 136 (1993), pp. 805–39.

Moody, Peter R., Jr. *Political Change on Taiwan: A Study of Ruling Party Adaptability*. Westport, Conn.: Praeger, 1991.

Myers, Ramon H. *Two Societies in Opposition: The Republic of*

China and the People's Republic of China after Forty Years. Stanford, Calif.: Hoover Institution, 1991.

Qi Luo and Christopher Howe. "Direct Investment and Economic Integration in the Asia Pacific: The Case of Taiwan Investment in Xiamen." *China Quarterly* 136 (1993), pp. 746–69.

Rubenstein, Murray A. *Taiwan: A New History.* Armonk, N.Y.: M. E. Sharpe, 1999.

Shambaugh, David, ed. *Contemporary Taiwan.* Oxford, U.K.: Clarendon Press, 1998.

Simon, Denis Fred, and Michael Ying-mao Kau, eds. *Taiwan: Beyond the Economic Miracle.* Armonk, N.Y.: M. E. Sharpe, 1992.

Sutter, Robert G., and William R. Johnson, eds, *Taiwan in World Affairs.* Boulder, Colo.: Westview, 1994.

Thornton, Arland, and Lin Hui-sheng. *Social Change and the Family in Taiwan.* Chicago: University of Chicago Press, 1994.

Tien Hung-mao and Cheng Tun-jen. "Crafting Democratic Institutions in Taiwan." *China Journal* 37 (1997), pp. 1–30.

Tsang, Steve, ed. *In the Shadow of China: Political Developments in Taiwan since 1949.* Honolulu: University of Hawaii Press, 1994.

Tsang, Steve, and Tien Hung-mao. *Democratization in Taiwan.* New York: St. Martin's, 1999.

Tucker, Nancy Bernkopf. *Taiwan, Hong Kong, and the U.S., 1945–92: Uncertain Friendships.* London and New York: Twayne, 1994.

Wachman, Alan M. *Taiwan: National Identity and Democratization.* Armonk, N.Y.: M. E. Sharpe, 1994.

Wang, N. T., ed. *Taiwan Enterprises in Global Perspective.* Armonk, N.Y.: M. E. Sharpe, 1992.

Wu Hsin-hsing. *Bridging the Strait: Taiwan, China, and the Prospects for Reunification.* Hong Kong: Oxford University Press, 1994.

Wu, Jaushieh Joseph. *Taiwan's Democratization: Forces behind the New Momentum.* New York and Oxford: Oxford University Press, 1995.

XVII. CHINA'S FOREIGN RELATIONS

Cohen, Warren I., and Akira Iriye, eds. *The Great Powers in East Asia.* New York: Columbia University Press, 1990.

Copper, John Franklin. *China Diplomacy: The Washington-Taipei-Beijing Triangle.* Boulder, Colo.: Westview, 1992.

Dittmer, Lowell, and Samuel S. Kim, eds. *China's Quest for National Identity.* Ithaca, N.Y.: Cornell University Press, 1993.

Economy, Elizabeth, and Michel Oksenberg. *China Joins the World: Progress and Prospects.* New York: Council on Foreign Relations, 1999.

Faust, John R., and Judith F. Kornberg. *China in World Politics.* Boulder, Colo.: Lynne Rienner, 1995.

Foot, Rosemary. *The Practice of Power: U.S. Relations with China since 1949.* Hong Kong: Oxford University Press, 1995.

Garver, John W. *Foreign Relations of the People's Republic of China.* Englewood Cliffs, N.J.: Prentice-Hall, 1993.

Goodman, David S.G., and Gerald Segal, eds. *China Rising: Nationalism and Interdependence.* London: Routledge, 1997.

Greenfield, Jeanette. *China's Practice in the Law of the Sea.* Oxford: Clarendon Press, 1992.

Harding, Harry. *A Fragile Relationship: The United States and China since 1972.* Washington, D.C.: Brookings Institution, 1992.

Hartland-Thunberg, Penelope. *China, Hong Kong, Taiwan, and the World Trading System.* London: Macmillan, 1990.

Kim, Samuel S. *China and the World: Chinese Foreign Policy in the Post-Mao Era.* 3rd ed. Boulder, Colo.: Westview, 1994.

Lampton, David M., and Alfred D. Wilhelm, Jr., eds. *United States and China Relations at a Crossroads.* Lanham, Md.: University Press of America, 1995.

Lardy, Nicholas R. *China in the World Economy.* Washington, D.C.: Institute for International Economics, 1994.

Madsen, Richard. *China and the American Dream: A Moral Inquiry.* Berkeley and Los Angeles: University of California Press, 1995.

Robinson, Thomas W., and David Shambaugh, eds. *Chinese Foreign Policy: Theory and Practice.* Oxford and New York: Oxford University Press, 1994.

Ross, Robert S. *Negotiating Cooperation: The U.S. and China, 1969–1989.* Stanford, Calif.: Stanford University Press, 1995.

Sutter, Robert G. *Chinese Policy Priorities and Their Implications for the United States.* Lanham, Md.: Rowman & Littlefield, 1999.

Sutter, Robert G., and Shirley Kan. *China as a Security Concern in Asia: Perceptions, Assessment, and U.S. Options.* Washington, D.C.: Congressional Research Service, 1994.

Tan Qingshan. *The Making of U.S. China Policy: From Normalization to the Post–Cold War Era.* Boulder, Colo.: Lynne Rienner, 1992.

Taylor, Robert. *Greater China and Japan: Prospects for Economic Partnership in East Asia.* New York: Routledge, 1996.

Tyler, Patrick. *A Great Wall: Six Presidents and China: An Investigative History.* New York: Century Foundation, 1999.

Unger, Jonathan, ed. *Chinese Nationalism.* Armonk, N.Y.: M. E. Sharpe, 1996.

Whiting, Allen S. "Chinese Nationalism and Foreign Policy after Deng." *China Quarterly* 142 (1995), pp. 295–316.

Zhang Ming. *Major Powers at a Crossroads: Economic Interdependence and an Asian Pacific Security Community.* Boulder, Colo.: Lynne Rienner, 1995.

Zhang Ming and Ronald N. Montaperto. *A Triad of Another Kind: The United States, China, and Japan.* New York: St. Martin's, 1999.

Zheng Yongnian. *Discovering Chinese Nationalism in China: Modernization, Identity, and International Relations.* New York: Cambridge University Press, 1999.

INDEX